Displacement, Asyl

CH00957350

Kate E. Tunstall is Fellow a
at Worcester Colle_, _...._

The Oxford Amnesty Lectures is a registered charity. Its purpose is to raise funds to increase awareness of Amnesty International in the academic and wider communities. It is otherwise independent of Amnesty International. It began as a fund-raising project for the local Amnesty group in Oxford, and is now one of the world's leading name-lecture series. To date, Oxford Amnesty Lectures has raised over £100,000 for Amnesty International.

Displacement, Asylum, Migration

The Oxford Amnesty Lectures 2004

Edited by

Kate E. Tunstall

OXFORD
UNIVERSITY PRESS

OXFORD

UNIVERSITY PRESS

Great Clarendon Street, Oxford OX2 6DP

Oxford University Press is a department of the University of Oxford.
It furthers the University's objective of excellence in research, scholarship,
and education by publishing worldwide in

Oxford New York

Auckland   Cape Town Dar es Salaam   Hong Kong   Karachi
Kuala Lumpur Madrid Melbourne Mexico City   Nairobi
New Delhi Shanghai Taipei Toronto
With offices in
Argentina Austria Brazil Chile Czech Republic France Greece
Guatemala Hungary Italy Japan South Korea Poland Portugal
Singapore Switzerland Thailand Turkey Ukraine Vietnam

ISBN 978-0-19-280724-3

Printed in the United Kingdom by
Lightning Source UK Ltd., Milton Keynes

Preface

The lectures on which this book is based were originally given in the Sheldonian Theatre in Oxford in January and February 2004. I should like to express my gratitude to all the lecturers—Slavoj Zizek, Bhikhu Parekh, Caryl Phillips, Saskia Sassen, Harold Hongju Koh, Jacqueline Rose, and Ali Mazrui—for coming to speak in Oxford and for giving us permission to publish their lectures in aid of Amnesty International. I am grateful to Matthew Gibney for writing a piece for this volume, though he did not lecture in the series. I should like also to thank the respondents—Michael Ignatieff, Seyla Benhabib, Elleke Boehmer, Christian Joppke, Rey Koslowski, Ali Abunimah, Iftikhar Malik, and Melissa Lane—for their contributions to this book.

Thanks are also due, as ever, to the other members of the Oxford Amnesty Lectures Committee without whose hard work there would be no lectures and no book. They are Tim Chesters, Melissa McCarthy, Chris Miller, Nick Owen, Fabienne Pagnier, Deana Rankin, Richard Scholar, Stephen Shute, and Wes Williams.

K. E. T.

Contents

Contributors

ALI ABUNIMAH is a writer and commentator on the Middle East and Arab–American affairs. He is Researcher in Social Policy at the University of Chicago and Co-Founder of the Electronic Intifada.

SEYLA BENHABIB is Eugene Meyer Professor of Political Science and Philosophy at Yale. Her books include *The Reluctant Modernism of Hannah Arendt* (1996), *The Claims of Culture: Equality and Diversity in the Global Era* (2003), and The John Seeley Memorial Lectures, *The Rights of Others: Aliens, Residents and Citizens* (2004).

ELLEKE BOEHMER is the Hildred Carlile Professor in Literatures in English at Royal Holloway, University of London, and author of *Colonial and Postcolonial Literature: Migrant Metaphors* (1995) and *Empire, the National and the Postcolonial: 1890–1920: Resistance in Interaction* (2002). Her fictional writing includes *Bloodlines* (2000), and she recently edited Robert Baden-Powell, *Scouting for Boys: A Handbook for Instruction in Good Citizenship* (2004).

MATTHEW J. GIBNEY is Elizabeth Colson Lecturer in Forced Migration at Oxford University, and author of *The Ethics and Politics of Asylum: Liberal Democracy and the Response to Refugees* (2004).

MICHAEL IGNATIEFF is Director of the Carr Centre for Human Rights Policy, John F. Kennedy School of Government, at Harvard University. His books include *The Needs of Strangers:*

An Essay on the Philosophy of Human Needs (1984), *Blood and Belonging: Journeys into the New Nationalism* (1993), *The Warrior's Honour: Ethnic War and the Modern Conscience* (1998), *Virtual War: Kosovo and Beyond* (2000), *The Rights Revolution* (2001), and *The Lesser Evil: Political Ethics in an Age of Terror* (2005).

CHRISTIAN JOPPKE is Professor of Sociology at the University of Bremen, and author of *Immigration and the Nation-State: The United States, Germany and Great Britain* (1999) and *Selecting by Origin: Ethnic Migration in the Liberal State* (2005).

HAROLD HONGJU KOH is Dean of the Law School at Yale University. When he was Assistant Secretary of State for Human Rights, Democracy and Labour in the Clinton administration, he brought cases against the US government for its repatriation of refugees from Haiti and Cuba.

REY KOSLOWSKI is Associate Professor of Political Science at the University at Albany, SUNY, and author of *Migrants and Citizens: Demographic Change in the European States System* (2000) and *Global Human Smuggling: Comparative Perspectives* (2001).

MELISSA LANE is Lecturer in History at King's College, Cambridge, and author of *Method and Politics in Plato's States-man* (1998) and *Plato's Progeny: How Socrates and Plato Still Captivate the Modern Mind* (2001).

IFTIKHAR H. MALIK is Senior Lecturer in History, Bath Spa University. His publications include *Islam, Nationalism and the West: Issues of Identity in Pakistan* (1999) and *Islam and Modernity: Muslims in Europe and the United States* (2003). His latest book is *Crescent between Cross and Star: Muslims after 9/11* (2006).

ALI A. MAZRUI holds, among many other titles, that of Albert Schweizer Professor in the Humanities and Director of the Institute of Global Cultural Studies at Binghamton, State University of New York, and of Albert Luthuli Professor-at-Large in the Humanities and Development Studies at the University of Jos in Nigeria. His recent books include *Black Reparations in the Era of Globalisation* (2002) and *The African Predicament and the American Experience: A Tale of Two Edens* (2004). He authored and narrated the BBC series 'Africans: A Triple Heritage' (1986).

BHIKHU PAREKH is former Deputy Chair of the Commission for Racial Equality, and Chair of the Runnymede Commission on the Future of Multi-Ethnic Britain. He holds professorships at both Hull University and the London School of Economics, and is a working Labour peer. His books include *Rethinking Multiculturalism: Cultural Diversity and Political Theory* (2000) and *Gandhi: A Very Short Introduction* (2001).

CARYL PHILLIPS is a writer and Professor of English at Yale University. His fiction includes *Cambridge* (1991), *Crossing the River* (1993), *The Nature of Blood* (1997), and *A Distant Shore* (2001). Among his works of non-fiction are *The Atlantic Sound* (2000), *The New World Order* (2001), and the anthology *Extravagant Strangers: A Literature of Belonging* (1997). His latest novel is *Dancing in the Dark* (2005).

JACQUELINE ROSE is Professor of English at Queen Mary, University of London. She works on modern literature, psychoanalysis, and the political imagination. She is the author of

The Case of Peter Pan, or the Impossibility of Children's Fiction (1984), *Sexuality in the Field of Vision* (1986), the Oxford Clarendon Lectures, *States of Fantasy* (1996), the novel, *Albertine* (2001), *On Not Being Able to Sleep: Psychoanalysis and the Modern World* (2003), and *The Question of Zion* (2005).

SASKIA SASSEN is Ralph Lewis Professor of Sociology at the University of Chicago and Centennial Visiting Professor at the London School of Economics. Her publications include *The Global City* (1991, new edn 2001), *Guests and Aliens* (1999). Her latest book is *Territory, Authority and Rights: From Medieval to Global Assemblages* (2006).

KATE E. TUNSTALL is Fellow and Tutor in French at Worcester College, Oxford.

SLAVOJ ZIZEK is Professor of Philosophy at the University of Ljubljana. His publications include *The Ticklish Subject: The Absent Centre of Political Ontology* (1999), *Did Somebody Say Totalitarianism? Five Interventions on the (Mis)Use of a Notion* (2001), and *Welcome to the Desert of the Real: Five Essays on September 11th* (2002).

Epigraph

LINCOLN *(to the prentices)* Peace, hear me! He that will not see a red herring at a Harry groat, butter at eleven pence a pound, meal at nine shillings a bushel, and beef at four nobles a stone, listen to me.

OTHER It will come to pass if strangers be suffered. Mark him.

LINCOLN Our country is a great eating country; argo, they eat more in our country than they do in their own.

OTHER By a halfpenny loaf a day, troy weight.

LINCOLN They bring in strange roots, which is merely to the undoing of poor prentices, for what's a sorry parsnip to a good heart?

OTHER Trash, trash. They breed sore eyes, and 'tis enough to infect the city with the palsy.

LINCOLN Nay, it has infected it with the palsy, for these bastards of dung—as you know, they grow in dung—have infected us, and it is our infection will make the city shake, which partly comes from the eating of parsnips.

OTHER True, and pumpions together.

SERJEANT *(coming forward)* What say you to the mercy of the King? Do you refuse it?

LINCOLN You would have us upon th' hip, would you? No, marry, we do not. We accept of the King's mercy; but we will show no mercy upon the strangers.

[. . .]

MORE Grant them removed, and grant that this your noise
    Hath chid down all the majesty of England.
    Imagine that you see the wretched strangers,

Their babies at their backs and their poor luggage,
Plodding to th' ports and coasts for transportation,
And that you sit as kings in your desires,
Authority quite silent by your brawl,
And you in ruff of your opinions clothed:
What had you got? I'll tell you. You had taught
How insolence and strong hand should prevail,
How order should be quelled—and by this pattern
Not one of you should live an aged man,
For other ruffians as their fancies wrought,
With selfsame hand, self reasons, and self right,
Would shark on you, and men like ravenous fishes
Would feed on one another.
[. . .] You'll put down strangers,
Kill them, cut their throats, possess their houses,
And lead the majesty of law in lyam,
To slip him like a hound—alas alas!
Say now the King,
As he is clement if th' offender mourn,
Should so much come too short of your great trespass
As but to banish you: whither would you go?
What country, by the nature of your error,
Should give you harbour? Go you to France or Flanders,
To any German province, Spain or Portugal,
Nay, anywhere that not adheres to England—
Why, you must needs be strangers. Would you be pleased
To find a nation of such barbarous temper,
That breaking out in hideous violence,
Would not afford you an abode on earth,
Whet their detested knives against your throats,
Spurn you like dogs, and like as if that God
Owed not nor made not you, nor that the elements

Were not all appropriate to your comforts,
But chartered unto them, what would you think
To be thus used? This is the strangers' case;
And this your mountainish inhumanity.

    Sir Thomas More, attributed to William Shakespeare[1]

Introduction

Kate E. Tunstall

There can be few issues in the United Kingdom and else-where that are in greater need of intelligent and humane analysis than those relating to the 'strangers' case'. The quota-tion from *Sir Thomas More*, which serves as an epigraph to this book, has particularly powerful resonances today. Set on May Day 1517, when London witnessed anti-immigrant riots, we hear the broker, Lincoln, and an unnamed apprentice protest-ing that the King of England has been too merciful to the strangers. Their words bring to mind the complaints con-stantly voiced by the British tabloid press and by increasingly large numbers of politicians that the UK is a 'soft touch' for asylum-seekers and economic migrants. And as Lincoln and the prentice complain about the threat to England posed by the strangers—how much they will push up prices, what they eat (the choice of root vegetables—parsnips and pumpions!— allowing for a pun on the immigrants' own 'strange roots') and the diseases they carry (palsy, sore eyes)—we cannot help but recall the contemporary media's claims that asylum-seekers are all infested with HIV-Aids and that they ate the Queen's swans (a fantastical tale of *lèse-majesté*).[1] In this cli-mate, voices like that of More (presented here as a tolerant man and not the persecutor of Protestants that he really was) are essential.

There can be little doubt that the most significant phe-nomenon of the last thirty years has been the vast human migration across the globe as a result of war, persecution, regime change, ethnic cleansing, religious or tribal conflict, ecological devastation, persistent poverty, unemployment, and hunger. The response of the West to this unprecedented movement of people when they arrive at its borders has been anxious, to say the least. An example, particularly pertinent in the context of this book of Oxford Amnesty Lectures, is Campsfield House, a detention centre located six miles outside the centre of Oxford, in which are detained at any one time approximately 200 men who have fled one or more of the phenomena just listed, to seek refuge in the UK. Some will also have fled the threat of unexplained imprisonment and detention without charge, only to find themselves precisely detained without charge, imprisoned without explanation.[2]

The United Nations Convention on the Status of Refugees signed in 1951 in Geneva defines a refugee as 'an individual with a well-founded fear of persecution on the grounds of nationality, race, political opinion, religion, or membership of a political social group'.[3] This definition requires some revision. Persecution may occur on grounds other than those listed; it has been evident since antiquity that gender can be grounds for persecution—in his play, *The Suppliants*, Euripides portrays women fleeing forced marriage and seeking asylum at Argos. In addition, people may be forced to leave their homes owing to conditions such as chronic poverty, malnutrition, and hunger, which put their lives in threat. Yet any attempt today to modify the Convention is risky since many nations now consider its terms generous. (In the recent British election campaigns, the right-wing Conservative Party stated that if elected, the UK would withdraw from the Convention.)

Oxford's mini Guantanamo is representative of the West's response to the displaced, signalling a kind of blind spot within globalization and its logic of 'flow'. According to this logic, everything—goods, capital, information—must flow freely, cross national borders unhindered. Everything that is, except people. For the system to function properly, people must not circulate freely because they embody a commodity—labour—which must be kept in place. The new transnational corporations rely for their competitive edge on the cheap labour of the developing world, and the system would collapse if the low-paid workers in Indonesia, Bangladesh, Guatemala, and the Democratic Republic of Congo were free to 'flow', to move into the high-wage labour market of the West. And yet, against the logic of the system, people are moving, and in unprecedented numbers. As Stuart Hall observed in his lecture in the previous series of the Oxford Amnesty Lectures (2003):

Migration is increasingly the joker in the globalisation pack, the subterranean circuit connecting the crisis of one part of the global system with the growth rates and living standards of the other. [. . .] Seeking by whatever means they can—legal or illegal—to escape the consequences of globalisation and the new world order, [those stigmatized as economic migrants, refugees, and asylum-seekers] move along uncharted routes, secrete themselves in the most inhospitable interstices, mortgage their worldly goods to the human traffickers, seal life-threatening contracts with gang-masters and pimps, and exploit their lateral family connections in order to subvert the physical barriers, legal constraints and immigration regimes which metropolitan powers are vigorously putting in place.[4]

This is not flow, but flight, and many Western states are seeking to stem it as much as possible.

What is the impact of this displacement on the countries

they arrive in, on the countries they leave behind, and on the displaced themselves? In 2004, the Oxford Amnesty Lectures invited major international figures from a range of disciplines—philosophy, political science, sociology, literature, and law—to consider the challenges that these questions pose to our notions of human rights and to our pursuit of equality and social justice. The series of lectures was entitled 'Displacement, Asylum, Migration', and this book is based on them.

The book is in two sections. The first section, containing three lectures and their accompanying responses, offers a set of debates about human rights, their ideology and application, both in general terms and with reference to the specific challenges of asylum and migration. The second section explores particular issues related to the problem of displacement—the legal and administrative procedures regulating asylum in Europe and the US; legal and philosophical conceptions of citizenship and alienage; slavery, both nineteenth- and twenty-first-century; Israel-Palestine. Each of the lectures may be read on its own, but frameworks and themes are echoed from one section and from one lecture to the next. There is much discussion of the nation state and of the Geneva Convention, its definitions and principles, and the themes of multiculturalism, identity, and memory resonate throughout the book as a whole. Each lecture is accompanied by a critical response from another leading thinker in the field who appraises, develops, and/or mounts challenges to the positions adopted by the lecturer. This structure is intended to give the reader an insight into the live nature of the debates sparked off by the Oxford Amnesty Lectures and to indicate the lectures' inspirational qualities.

Bhikhu Parekh begins with a wide-ranging presentation of human rights, their history, language and current place within the British and European judicial systems. Multiculturalist and (among other things) Chair of the Runnymede Commission on the Future of Multi-Ethnic Britain, Parekh presents the idea of human rights as a great historical achievement. Unlike constitutional rights which belong only to the citizens of a state, human rights belong to all humans, protecting citizens and *sans-papiers* alike. Because this universally accessible moral and political language is a significant achievement, Parekh expresses serious concern that overuse of it may lead to its being compromised. Moreover, human rights do not, he argues, cover the full range, depth, and complexity of moral life, and so it follows that if we allow them to become hegemonic, we risk undermining the integrity of many valuable forms of moral and political sensibility. In particular, Parekh is sceptical that an appeal to human rights is the best way of requiring a state to provide asylum to refugees and other displaced persons. Kant's 'cosmopolitan right to hospitality' has been much discussed recently, in particular by Continental philosophers,[5] but for Parekh, such a discourse of rights is less persuasive than the language of duties and obligations.

Seyla Benhabib disagrees. In her view, one cannot, under the conditions of democratic equality, immunize the private sphere from the ideals of the public sphere, and as a vigorous defender of a rights-based approach to asylum, she focuses in particular on the cosmopolitan right to hospitality. Offering a more detailed reading of Kant than the scope of Parekh's lecture could afford, she suggests that what Kant calls the 'right to associate, which all men have' is philosophically more promising than duties and obligations as a way forward in dealing with the challenges posed by asylum.

At one moment in his lecture, Parekh quotes with appreciation Milan Kundera's novel *Immortality* (2000), in which he observes:

because people in the West are not threatened by concentration camps and are free to say and write what they want, the more the fight for human rights gains in popularity, the more it loses any concrete content, becoming a kind of universal stance of everyone towards everything, a kind of energy that turns all human desires into rights. The world has become man's rights and everything in it has become a right; the desire for love the right to love; the desire for rest the right to rest; the desire for friendship the right to friendship; the desire to exceed the speed limit the right to exceed the speed limit; the desire for happiness the right to happiness.

Such a view is doubtless shared by Slavoj Zizek, the left-wing philosopher and controversial contributor to political debates, who mounts in his lecture a spirited opposition to the ideology of human rights. Unlike Parekh, however, his is also an opposition to the values of liberal multiculturalism. For Zizek, not only are human rights the most obvious sign of the pernicious effects of late capitalist society in which individuals relate to themselves as though they were contingent embodiments of abstract universals, but they are fundamentally patronizing and hypocritical in the sense that they pretend to be universal while in fact privileging a Western set of values. It is this latter point that he develops in most detail here, arguing that liberal, tolerant multiculturalism is flawed: it is tolerant only up to a point, and that point is precisely where real Otherness begins. Moreover, in his view, advocating respect for the Other's belief is an inadequate ethical project. He draws here on Kant, Wittgenstein and Lenin in order to advocate a politics, less of rights, than of truth.

6

Michael Ignatieff takes a diametrically opposing view, arguing here for the importance of human rights to those for whom the threat of the concentration camps or similar is real and to those, even within the West, whose freedoms are limited. His focus is the invasion of Iraq and the human rights' abuses committed under Saddam Hussein's regime. Such abuses, which led to many Iraqis becoming refugees, victims of persecution on political or ethnic grounds, provide Ignatieff with justification for the invasion.

The broad range of Parekh's lecture with its focus on cultural diversity finds echoes in Ali A. Mazrui's lecture which seeks ethical commonalities between different cultures. Mazrui, Director of the Institute of Global Cultural Studies at Binghamton, describes the history of empire and colonialism in the Arab world and Africa since the end of the First World War, and charts the rise of the American empire since the end of the Cold War. Observing that the greatest military casualties of this new empire are Muslims and the greatest economic casualties, Africans, Mazrui urges the West to be attentive to both these ethnic and religious groups which make up an increasingly important sector of Western society, but whose voices are infrequently heard. Comparing, for example, the place of women and of religion in politics in Islam, Africa, and the West, Mazrui offers what he calls a global ethic, one which is inclusive of the wisdom and values of the 'strangers in our midst'.

The idea that the West might learn from strangers is optimistic, to say the least, argues Iftikhar Malik, when those strangers are Muslims. In his response to Mazrui, Malik gives a searing exposé of the manifold ways in which the United States and its allies, following the events of September 11th 2001, are distorting and silencing Muslim voices. This is a topic to which the Oxford Amnesty Lectures will return: the 2005 lecture series is entitled 'The War on Terror'.

The second part of the book focuses on questions that are more closely related to particular aspects of displacement, asylum, and migration. Where in Part One, Parekh and Benhabib debate the relationship between human rights and asylum, Part Two begins with Matthew J. Gibney's consideration of the rights of refugees as they are laid down in the Geneva Convention. In addition to defining a refugee, this document accords him or her a set of rights, which include those to work and to travel freely. And yet, not only are many states currently violating those rights by denying people access to work and by detaining them, but they are also preventing them from claiming the rights in the first place. Gibney, an expert in the study of forced migration, explores the 'non-arrival measures' taken by Western states to prevent asylum-seekers from reaching their borders where they would be entitled to claim protection. Such measures involve shifting entrance decisions away from state borders to a range of new places (the high seas, consular offices, and foreign airports) and empowering new and sometimes unaccountable actors (airline officials, coastguards, smugglers and traffickers), with the effect that the paradoxical and hypocritical nature of state practices has been conveniently located out of sight. Gibney's powerful exposé brings this hypocrisy back into view, evaluates recent justifications for the measures, and proposes ways in which they might be implemented such that they conflict less radically than at present with refugees' rights.

Melissa Lane develops Gibney's analysis of non-arrival measures to show that it has implications for the principle of 'non-refoulement', also established in the Geneva Convention and according to which a state must not send a refugee back—'refouler'—to a country in which he or she would face persecution. She argues that even a state which prevents refugees from arriving at its borders remains bound by the principle of non-refoulement; indeed, in her view, preventing refugees from arriving is tantamount precisely to returning them to the place where they are in danger. Lane offers then another way in which the non-arrival measures described by Gibney constitute violations of the Geneva Convention.

Many refugees do, of course, arrive, and the manifold ways in which the displaced make do in their new surroundings is part of the material explored by Saskia Sassen, the groundbreaking analyst of globalization and its effects on the lives of ordinary people. Here she argues that the two traditional modes of membership of the modern nation-state—the citizen and the alien—are undergoing profound changes today. They are becoming blurred, and although this blur is not formally recognized, it is nonetheless visible, in particular in what she terms 'the global city'. Sassen delineates two new kinds of informal membership: the 'authorized yet unrecognized' subject and the 'unauthorized yet recognized' subject. As an example of the former, she offers the 'housewife'—though a citizen, her political and social agency is not often recognized; the latter is exemplified, according to Sassen, by the undocumented immigrant, whose informal daily practices make them recognizable as social and political actors, though formal status and legislation continue to evade them. Sassen finds inspiration in these informal patterns of membership; she discovers in them the possibility of a new politics, one that is localized but, crucially, not defined by the national.

Sassen's recognition of political possibilities in the informal practices of the excluded prompts a strong challenge from

KATE E. TUNSTALL

Christian Joppke. While both agree on the changes that have recently occurred at a judicial level, they disagree fundamentally as to who or what has brought such changes about. In contrast to Sassen, Joppke sees the more traditional, formal mode of political engagement—legal systems and civic pressure from liberal media, academics, and intellectuals—as the channel for change and reform.

The writer Caryl Phillips takes a different approach, a personal one, to the theme of displacement. In his lecture, he tells of voluntary migrations, notably his own from the UK to the US in 1990 and that of his parents with him as a baby from St Kitts to the UK in 1958, and he connects and contrasts these with another migration, this one involuntary: that of his ancestors from Africa to the Caribbean, as slaves. The distinction between voluntary and forced migration is absolute for Phillips here, and it is to be felt in the toll it takes on the human heart. The desire to cross a border is, in his view, simply a human instinct connected to the desire to better oneself, and although first- and second-generation immigrants may experience bewilderment (and in the case of his parents in the UK, anger, hurt, and betrayal), such pain is of a fundamentally different order, in his view, to that inflicted by forced migration. In his powerful lecture, Phillips writes: 'Our displacement on arrival in the Americas was profound and caused a psychic wound which, for millions of people of African origin, continues to fester.'

Elleke Boehmer responds by situating Phillips's lecture in the context of his œuvre to date in which displacement has been his abiding concern. She observes that his distinction between forced and voluntary migration is more trenchantly made here than elsewhere in his writing, and that such a binary structure is in fact rare in his fiction, which more usually exhibits patterns of three. Reading what he has to say elsewhere about the displaced, she suggests that the journeys made today by economic migrants, refugees, and asylum-seekers, although not forced in the same way that slavery was, can be seen to inflict psychic damage of the same order as that inflicted by the Atlantic Slave Trade.

If Phillips makes it plain that the effects of slavery are still being felt, the actual institution of slavery is a thing of the past, or so conventional wisdom would have it. Harold Hongju Koh challenges that wisdom in his lecture. An internationally known human rights lawyer, notable for his campaigning against the US government's repatriation of refugees from Cuba and Haiti when he was himself Assistant Secretary of State in the Clinton administration, Koh exposes here what he calls 'the new global slave trade'. Every year, between 800,000 and 900,000 people are trafficked, generating $7–10 million a year. In contrast to the policymakers who tend to view this as a faceless criminal problem, or an economic, immigration, or public health problem, Koh makes here a persuasive case for viewing it as a human rights problem, describing the vicious cycle of interconnected human rights violations that human trafficking commits and then proposing ways in which such a cycle might be broken. If trafficking is the underside of globalization, globalization also provides the tools—money, the Internet, and human rights—with which to combat it. Koh urges us to make use of the means many of us have at our disposal to outlaw this new form of slavery.

Responding to Koh, Rey Koslowski places human trafficking within the broader context of human smuggling. Where the former is easily thought of as criminal, the latter is often the means of escape for refugees. Though broadly supportive of Koh's call for prevention, protection, and prosecution,

Koslowski sounds a note of caution: since the smuggler and the trafficker are often one and the same, the prevention that Koh advocates may be risky. Echoing Gibney's description of the barriers that face refugees, Koslowski observes that prevention runs the risk of producing an unintended outcome, that of closing down one of the few means of escape left open to refugees.

The volume ends with a lecture by Jacqueline Rose, literary critic and novelist, with whom we turn to the exceedingly fraught displacements in Israel–Palestine. She observes that while we are often attentive to the modern paradox according to which boundaries have become both increasingly mobile or porous with more people on the move, and at the same time increasingly entrenched, policed ever more tightly, we pay very little attention to the mobility and immobility of the mind. Hers is a psychoanalytical approach to the traumas of displacement as experienced by Palestinians and Jews. Probing what she calls 'the peculiar relationship between the shifting sands of migration and the fortress of the soul', she asks: 'In a teeming world of diasporas, how, or perhaps we should be asking why, do identities—against the surface drift, as it were—so fiercely entrench themselves?' Her answer is formulated through readings of Freud, to whose thinking the term 'displacement' is so central, and of the novelists, David Grossman and W. G. Sebald. She finds in them the possibility of non-defensive forms of memory and identity, both personal and national.

Rose's psychoanalytic conception of displacement proves fruitful to Ali Abunimah. In his response, he quotes at length from an interview he conducted with an Israeli peace campaigner and reveals the extent to which his interviewee is unable to accept a one-state solution. His interviewee would rather reorder the physical landscape, move tens of thousands of Israeli settlers and leave millions of Palestinians in exile, than reorder his mental landscape so as to accept a single political entity which would offer full citizenship to both Israelis and Palestinians.

This volume offers then a wide range of responses to the issues of displacement, asylum, and migration, as well as to the language and ideology of human rights. Among the common themes running through the book, a particular insight, shared by all the lectures, is discernible, one perhaps best encapsulated in Jacqueline Rose's idea of 'mental baggage'. There is, she says, a 'baggage of the mind', which people carry with them when they are 'on the move'. The phrase is striking, and contains an insight pertinent not only into the condition of the displaced, but also of those of us who live in the countries in which the displaced arrive. Weighed down by feelings, concepts, and traditions, such as national identity, which can so easily solidify into myth and prejudice, we too must 'unpack' our mental baggage, develop greater intellectual agility and overcome the 'mountainish inhumanity' with which our governments and media so often greet the displaced. These lectures and their responses offer numerous ways for us to set in motion a dynamics of political, social, and cultural change.

Part One
Human Rights

1

Finding a Proper Place for Human Rights

Bhikhu Parekh

The language of human rights is increasingly acquiring the status of a universally understood and accepted mode of moral communication. Violations of human rights in any part of the world are widely denounced, vigorously investigated by journalists, and used to embarrass and shame governments including those that systematically ignore them in practice and sometimes do not even see their point. Oppressed and marginalized groups turn to them in the firm belief that this is the most effective way to draw attention to their grievances and seek their redress. Even in the democratic West, where human rights are securely established, individuals and groups are discovering their new dimensions and uses, and invoke them to demand new protections, opportunities, and services not only from their governments but also from other public institutions and private organizations. Even Britain, which had long preferred the language of liberty to the continental European language of rights, has now opted for the latter, and made the creation of the culture of human rights a national goal.[1]

The idea of human rights represents a great historical achievement. For the first time in history it provides a universally accessible moral and political language in which to articulate our shared concerns and differences. In so doing it builds moral bonds between human beings in different parts of the world and helps create an awareness of our shared humanity. Unlike constitutional rights which are given only to the citizens, human rights belong to all human beings and protect non-citizens including refugees and asylum-seekers. They affirm that human beings are more than the sum of their social positions and share a common identity that transcends their differences. Since human rights lay down the moral minimum to which all human beings are deemed to be entitled in reasonably clear terms, they give our moral and political life a clear focus. And since the moral minimum that it prescribes reflects our deeply held beliefs concerning what it is to be human, it has a great evocative and inspirational power. The language of human rights also has a considerable moral depth in the sense that it allows us to expand and adopt them to changing circumstances by either adding new rights or suitably reinterpreting and broadening the scope of the existing ones.[2]

Since the doctrine of human rights is a precious and fragile achievement, we need to protect it against its overzealous advocates and cynical detractors lest they should in their own different ways discredit, weaken, or undermine it. While its enemies are easy to identify and the harm they do is obvious, the unwitting damage done by its overenthusiastic devotees is often too subtle to detect, and hence more worrying. In this chapter I concentrate on the latter and offer a sympathetic critique of the current approach to human rights. My criticism is threefold. I begin by arguing that the term 'human rights' is used so indiscriminately that it is losing its specificity and focus, and that human rights risk being brought into ridicule by being extended to areas where they make little if any sense. I then go on to argue that although the doctrine of human rights contains valuable insights, it does not cover the full range, depth, and complexity of moral life, and that when it becomes hegemonic, it risks delegitimizing and even undermining the integrity of many valuable forms of moral and political sensibility. I end by suggesting that although human rights have a cross-cultural validity, their meanings and implications are culturally mediated and that their universality is appropriated and realized in culturally distinct forms.

I. What Are Human Rights?

The term 'human rights' is ambiguous because of the ambiguity of the term 'human'. It could be used in a descriptive sense to refer to the bearers of rights, namely human beings as opposed to the animals, or in a normative sense to refer to the kinds of rights they should enjoy. In the ordinary discourse, the normative usage is the most common. It too contains an ambiguity. Human rights in the normative sense could refer to all the rights human beings should enjoy or only to those that are central or fundamental to their humanity. The UN Declaration, the first widely known public document to popularize the term 'human rights', reflects this ambiguity. Sometimes it talks of 'human rights', at other times of 'fundamental human rights'. This ambiguity is also evident in many a subsequent statement of human rights including the two International Covenants on civil and political as well as economic, social, and cultural rights. When they talk of human rights, they generally mean rights of human beings; when they talk of fundamental human rights they mean those rights that are of utmost moral importance and deserve to be given the greatest moral weight. In recent years the term 'human rights' has come to be used synonymously with fundamental human rights, and that is how I shall use it.

Human beings have certain unique capacities, which mark them out from the rest of the natural world and give them a privileged ontological status. They include rational, moral, aesthetic, and other capacities which enable them to understand, control, and humanize their natural environment, rise above the automatic processes of nature, lead the life of freedom and self-determination, create a rich world of scientific, aesthetic, literary, moral, and other achievements, and introduce a novel form of existence in the world based on such great values as truth, goodness, love, and beauty. As beings capable of creating a world of meaning and values, they deserve to be valued themselves and have an intrinsic worth or dignity.[3] Human beings should therefore be treated in a manner that is consistent with their dignity and should have access to those conditions and opportunities that are essential to a life of dignity. Since we consider these forms of treatment and conditions of life central to their humanity, we believe that human beings should enjoy them as of right and not as an expression of the contingent goodwill of others.

Human rights are socially defined and validated. They are normative statements about what human beings require to lead a life of dignity and what is therefore due to them. They are not natural or inherent in human nature but social in origin in the sense that we decide what is essential to their dignity and that they should receive this as of right. It is, of course, true that we take this view because human beings possess certain unique rational, moral, and other capacities. However these capacities do not by themselves 'demand' or 'entail' these rights. It is because we value these capacities, make them the basis of human dignity, and respect and cherish the latter that we endow human beings with certain rights.[4] Human rights are not self-evident either, but arrived at by a slow process of collective deliberation and negotiation. Alisdair MacIntyre is therefore wrong to dismiss them on the ground that the 'belief in them is one with the belief in witches and in unicorns'.[5] He assumes that human rights are empirical assertions like those about witches and unicorns, and that is not the case. MacIntyre makes the same mistake when he says in defence of his view that every attempt to give good reasons for believing in human rights such as self-evidence and intuition has failed. Human rights are not out there staring us in the face or waiting to be intuited; rather we establish them because we believe that human beings have intrinsic worth and may rightfully claim certain forms of treatment and conditions of life. Human rights are not natural or objective attributes of human beings but norms of conduct, a moral practice, which we think we have good reasons to adopt.

I have argued that human rights refer to those conditions and forms of treatment that human beings require to lead a life of dignity and which they may demand as of right. Although these two are linked in the current view of human rights, they are separable. We endow human beings with the right to demand these conditions and forms of treatment to ensure, first, that they receive these not as a matter of charity but in recognition of their dignity, and second, that their access to them is guaranteed and not dependent on the pre-carious goodwill of others. Can these two purposes be real-ized by other means than making them a matter of right? The old natural law tradition thought so. According to it, justice required that certain things were due to all human beings and should be given to them as a matter of duty. Doing one's duty was morally imperative and not a matter of contingent good-will, and one did it not as an act of charity but because that was the right thing to do. In this view, justice led to duty without being mediated by a right. The ultimate outcome is the same, though the moral mechanism involved is different. Like the doctrine of human rights, the old natural law tradition insisted that human beings should receive the conditions and treatment they require to lead a life of dignity. Although it avoided the *language* of human rights, it respected the basic *principle* or the underlying concern of human rights. For all kinds of historical reasons we have opted for the language of human rights, but it would be wrong to conclude that premodern societies were innocent of or indifferent to the demands of human dignity simply because they used a different language and relied on different moral and social mechanisms.[6]

Plato, Aristotle, and others had argued that since human beings possessed their uniquely human capacities in unequal degrees, some were more human than others and enjoyed greater rights. Defenders of European colonialism took a broadly similar view. For them only those who had developed rational and moral powers and led 'civilized' lives were fully human and were entitled to the full complement of human rights. The rest were not fully human and had only a limited set of rights, such as the rights to life and some measure of personal liberty. The doctrine of human rights rightly rejects this hierarchical view of humanity and the consequent gradation of human beings. Whatever their differences, all human beings possess the basic capacities that are needed to participate in the human world and that constitute and define the human identity. They all belong to the same species or human community, possess equal dignity and worth, and need the same basic rights to lead worthy and fulfilling lives. Their other rights might be unequal, but not their human rights.[7]

The doctrine of human rights presupposes that there is a global consensus on what forms of treatment and conditions of life are consistent with human dignity and are due to all human beings. Since different cultures and societies conceptualize human beings differently and entertain different ideals of human excellence, such a consensus is not easy to arrive at. However it is not impossible. Since human beings share certain common features and require common conditions for leading worthwhile lives, there is a considerable moral convergence among them. They agree, for example, that human beings are different from the animals and deserve better treatment, that human life should be respected, that promises should be kept, that no one should be punished unless he or she is guilty of wrongdoing, that murder, rape, and gratuitous inflictions of physical harm are all bad, and so on. When disagreements remain, at least some of them can be resolved by discussion and dialogue, increased contacts, greater uniformity of the economic, social, and other conditions of life, and better mutual understanding. And some of what cannot be resolved in this way may nevertheless be settled by negotiations and compromise. The various international declarations show how a global consensus can be reached.

Since different societies arrive at human rights by different routes, their reasons for accepting them vary greatly and are sometimes likely to lead to differences of interpretation and application. However that does not matter as long as they are broadly agreed on the contents of these rights. Buddhism, for example, values human life just as much as and in some respects even more than the Western liberal tradition, but its rationale is quite different. It rejects the humanist or the Christian idea of man being the crown of the creation and does not much like the Western language of human dignity, which it seeks to replace with such analogous notions as the sacredness of the human person or reverence for human life. It starts with a commitment to the unity of life, from which it derives the ethic of non-injury, and from this, the duty to protect human life, respect personal autonomy, cultivate humility and the spirit of tolerance. While disagreeing with the liberals and others on its reasons, it nevertheless agrees with them on the need to respect and protect human life, liberty, and dignity.[8]

Different societies might also take different views on the institutional structure needed to realize human rights in practice. Those who prefer the language of duties might rely on moral education, cultivation of character, and social pressure backed up by suitable legal sanctions rather than the familiar legal and political institutions on which the conventional doctrine of human rights relies. Even those who opt for the latter might prefer different types of institution either because they make different assumptions about the nature of the law, the role of the state, the limits of coercion, etc., or because they believe that these institutions must fit in with the unique histories and traditions of the societies concerned. On the basis of our own experience and our reading of human history, we might feel that what is due to human beings is best secured by making it a matter of right rather than duty or by adopting a particular set of institutions. However it is wrong to be dogmatic about this and limit the scope for human ingenuity and experiments. As long as a society adequately ensures its members the forms of treatment and the conditions of life that human dignity requires, it respects human rights and its autonomy should be respected.

Human rights properly so called should satisfy three conditions. First, they should be integrally related to and indispensable for a life of dignity. This distinguishes them from ordinary rights and explains why they deserve to be privileged over the latter. Secondly, they should be universal or rather universalizable in the dual sense that all human beings are entitled to claim them and that this claim extends to all societies. A right is not a human right if some groups of human beings are in principle excluded from it or if its moral validity is limited to certain societies. Thirdly, human rights should be widely accepted as such by a cross-cultural consensus or we should offer good reasons why they should be. This is important for several related reasons. The cross-cultural consensus ensures that the rights are not culturally parochial or peculiarly liberal or Western. It also ensures that the agreement on human rights is not arrived at by imposing our views on others but either by spontaneous convergence or by rational discussion and persuasion, and that we may therefore legitimately expect all societies to respect them. Individuals and societies cannot be required to respect human rights unless they see the point of them and give them their broad approval.

It is sometimes argued, mistakenly in my view, that human rights should also be unconditional in the sense that their enjoyment should not be made dependent on their bearers meeting certain conditions. A society may rightly require that participation in the conduct of its collective affairs should be limited to those who have a stake in it or have demonstrated their commitment to and familiarity with it. It may therefore require that newcomers may not own property or vote in elections unless they have lived in it for a certain period of time, or that they may not claim welfare benefits unless they are willing to work when offered a job. It is important that these conditions should be justifiable in terms of and proportionate to legitimate objectives. If they were unduly stringent or imposed in bad faith, and virtually ruled out the enjoyment of the relevant rights, the society concerned could rightly be accused of violating the human rights of those involved.

I have argued that human rights should be essential to the life of dignity and universal in their validity. Although the two generally go together, they sometimes do not. In some African societies, the right to a decent burial, or burial next to one's ancestors or on a sacred communal land is regarded as central to the individual's dignity and considered as important as the right to life. In some East Asian societies the right to be maintained by one's children in one's old age and to be cared for by them at home rather than be sent off to a nursing home is widely seen as a matter of one's dignity and an integral part of what it is to lead a good life. As different from the ordinary rights, these rights are seen by the societies concerned as central to their conceptions of a dignified life, and are as important to them as the rights to life, liberty, and property are in the West.

This raises the question whether they should be called human rights. At one level they should be, because they are central to a life of dignity as understood in the society concerned. At another level they should not be because other societies neither share their views nor can be persuaded by rational arguments to see them as such. Members of the society concerned cannot therefore demand that these rights should be made available to them when they travel or settle abroad. These rights are human rights for them but not for others and lack universalizability. Since they are not human rights in the full sense of the term, we cannot call them human rights *sans phrase*. We might either say that they are human rights *for* or *in* a particular society, or more properly, give them some other name.[9]

Not all desirable rights are human rights unless they meet the three criteria mentioned above. Human rights are a subset of and do not exhaust or encompass all valuable rights. Given their importance, they should be enshrined in the constitution of the country and given a privileged and protected status. We may also do the same with other valuable rights. The fact that they too are given a constitutional status does not by itself make them human rights. And in order to show that some rights should be constitutionally protected, we do not need to show that they are or can be derived from human rights.

Views as to what rights qualify as human rights have varied over the centuries. The seventeenth-century theorists of natural rights, the intellectual godfathers of the contemporary discourse on human rights, were content to stress three natural rights, namely life, liberty, and property, to which the United States later added the pursuit of happiness. The ambiguously entitled French Declaration of the Rights of Man and Citizen added about a dozen civil and political rights, seeing the latter sometimes as rights of citizens and at other times as rights of man and even as natural rights. The UN Declaration over a century and a half later replaced the philosophically freighted language of 'natural' rights with a less problematic language of human rights and introduced an even larger list of over twenty human rights. Subsequent declarations and international covenants have added economic, social, and cultural rights and, more recently, environmental and developmental rights.[10]

In recent years there has been a tendency to extend the term 'human rights' yet further to cover all kinds of desirable rights. The European Court has interpreted the European Convention on Human Rights and Fundamental Freedoms to generate a litany of rights, all of which are called human rights. These include freedom of competition and trade, free movement of goods, the right to confidentiality of business information, and the rights of the elderly, the disabled, the mentally ill, adolescents in remand homes, prisoners, and others to be treated in decent ways and to receive certain kinds of services. The Court has also ruled that detaining a person before a court hearing for more than four days, denying transsexuals the right to acquire a new civic identity, and corporal punishment in schools that exceeds strict limits are all violations of the human rights of those involved. Not only has the list of human rights expanded to cover all desirable rights, their scope too has increased. They are extended to public and private organizations including business corporations, schools, hospitals, and universities, and used to demand certain kinds of service and forms of relationship. They are even extended to interpersonal relations, including those between married couples and parents and their children.

Such an indiscriminate expansion of human rights deprives them of their moral force and focus. Human rights have the power to evoke strong moral feelings, and to mobilize our moral energies for and against certain kinds of actions, because we consider them crucial to our humanity, and believe that to deny or violate them is to treat the relevant individuals and groups as if they belonged to an inferior species. We assign different moral status to different rights depending on their moral importance, which we in turn determine on the basis of their relation to our conception of human beings and their fundamental interests. This is why we identify some rights as human rights, and make a further distinction between fundamental rights, which are given a constitutional status and placed beyond day-to-day politics, and ordinary rights which can be altered with relative ease.

When all or almost all rights become human rights, we lose this sense of moral discrimination. Human rights properly so called lose their unique moral authority, and other rights acquire exaggerated importance. The right not to be enslaved, tortured, or disposed of by murder squads is morally quite different from the right not to be detained without a trial for more than four days or to receive prompt and adequate medical attention. And at a different level a prisoner's or a patient's right not to be subjected to degrading treatment is quite different from their right to hot meals and comfortable beds. Human rights require countless specific rights either as a means to their realization or as conditions of their exercise. Since the latter are derivative and instrumental in nature, contingent in the sense that human rights can be realized through other rights as well, specific to particular societies and cultures, and dependent on the availability of resources, they are not and should not be called human rights. They are valuable and ought to be guaranteed, but they should not be confused with human rights.

John Rawls has argued that only the rights mentioned in Articles 3 to 18 of the UN Declaration are 'human rights proper', and that the rest are either statements of 'liberal aspirations' (Art. 2) or presuppose specific kinds of institutions, such as the right to social security in Art. 22 and to equal pay for equal work in Art. 23.[11] Rawls's reasons are inconsistent and do not rest on clear criteria. It is not clear why the rights to education (Art. 26), to participate freely in the cultural life of the community (Art. 27), to vote in an election (Art. 21), and to work and to have a free choice of employment (Art. 23), do not qualify as human rights, whereas the freedom of movement and residence within the state (Art. 13), the right to leave the country (Art. 13), to enjoy asylum (Art. 14), etc.

do. However Rawls is right to suggest that the language of human rights badly needs a conceptual quality control.

As I argued earlier, human rights should be limited to those that are cross-culturally agreed to be essential to a life of dignity, can be claimed by all human beings, and are binding on all societies. Rights to life, liberty, basic necessities of life, freedom from slavery and degrading treatment, freedom of conscience, fair trial, freedom of expression, equality of treatment, personal property, etc. eminently qualify as human rights. Rights to freedom of trade and competition, business confidentiality, to stand for elected offices, to set up and own business, etc. do not. This does not mean that human rights are fixed forever and may not be tampered with. As our insights deepen into how human dignity is sustained, as new threats to it emerge, as unexpected historical experiences such as the Holocaust highlight the need to stress certain rights, or as we feel the need to break up general rights into clusters of specific rights, we may rightly expand and even occasionally contract the list of human rights. However we should not do so indiscriminately, inadvertently, lazily, or for political convenience. We should have compelling reasons, and any right we classify as a human right should satisfy the three basic criteria mentioned earlier.

II. Moral Pluralism

The inflationary spiral of human rights has gone hand in hand with and been in part propelled by the increasing tendency to conceptualize almost all moral relations in terms of human rights. Human beings are seen exclusively or primarily as bearers of rights, and moral conduct is taken to consist in scrupulous respect for others' rights. Parents are expected to love their children because the latter have a human right to their love, spouses are to cherish and be faithful to each other because each has a right to expect this from the other, doctors are to be meticulous in their treatment of patients because the latter have a right to proper care and would otherwise sue them for negligence, and professors and teachers are to take their classes regularly and prepare their lectures conscientiously because their students have a right to be taught properly and receive their money's worth.[12] In all these cases it is easy to see the point of what is being said. Children, parents, patients, and pupils have certain interests and needs, and make claims on those charged with the relevant responsibility. If the latter ignore their responsibility, they should certainly be compelled by law to discharge it.

There are, however, serious limitations to this way of thinking. Many worthwhile things in life are not a matter of right but a freely given gift, for example, love and friendship. Some of these can be made a matter of right, but they lose part of their value and even get corrupted when demanded as of right or given as an anticipated response to it. Parents bring their children into the world because they want to. They are bonded to them, care for them, raise them with love and tenderness, worry about their well-being, and make countless small and large sacrifices for them. They do all this out of love for their children. In the absence of love and the general sense of parental duty, many of the things they do simply would not be possible. Children do, of course, have a right to be cared for, but this is not the reason why parents care or should care for them. We invoke the right only in relation to those who show a complete lack of parental concern and duty, and who therefore have to be morally and even legally coerced into doing what they ought to do. The appeal to rights is an indispensable safety-net for situations where the normally constitutive motivations of parent–child relationship have dried up, but it cannot be its basis. This is just as true of the relations between spouses, friends, close relations, colleagues, and so on. The only sensible long-term answer in each case is not to tighten the regime of rights but rather to trace and address the deeper causes of the absence of appropriate motivations.

Moral life involves duties, responsibilities, character, and virtues, which cannot all be reduced to rights. While some duties are entailed by others' rights, many are not, such as the duties to tell truth, keep promises, relieve human suffering, help a person in distress, report a crime, and vote in an election. Some moral actions, again, do not involve either rights or duties. We stand up against injustices, challenge the ugly customs and practices of our society, seek ways of improving the quality of our public life, highlight atrocities in other countries, protect the environment, protest against cruelty to animals, etc., not because we have a duty to do so, for often there is none, but because we have a strong sense of public responsibility, have cultivated and delight in exercising relevant virtues, love our fellow men, animals, or nature, or because we have developed a certain type of character and cannot act otherwise. If moral life were to be limited to rights and duties, most of these actions would never get done.

We then speak in several moral languages, that of human rights being one of them. In different areas of life, different languages make sense, and moral literacy consists in knowing when to speak which. We also act out of a wide range of motives, of which respect for the rights of others is but one. Since moral life is inherently and irreducibly plural, it cannot be reduced to the one-dimensional vocabulary of human rights without suffering serious distortion. When we therefore talk of cultivating the culture of human rights, we need to be careful as to what we mean by it. We could mean either a culture that respects human rights and assigns them their due place in moral life along with duties, responsibilities, virtues, compassion, love, etc., or one that is wholly defined and structured in terms of human rights. The former respects the plurality of moral life and has much to be said for it; the latter is reductionist and highly impoverished and must be avoided at all cost. It distorts not only the other moral languages but also that of the human rights itself, because we have to keep multiplying human rights until they cover every form of human relationship, and then they lose their moral force and meaning.

In a society with a rights-based approach to life, we find it difficult to cope with situations unless an actual or a potential right is at play. We therefore keep inventing all kinds of rights, and worry deeply about how to justify them. The question as to how best to respond to asylum-seekers and the displaced persons in general is a good example of this. We, at any rate many of us, wish to help these unfortunate people in all ways we can, and predictably endow them with an appropriate right, which in such cases has to be a human right. Much debate has taken place on how this right is derived. Calling it a cosmopolitan right to hospitality, Kant, for example, argued that since the earth was originally a common possession, and since the national boundaries were contingent and arbitrary, every human being retained the right to move freely to other parts of the world, especially in times of need. This is a weak argument because the idea of the earth ever being a common possession in either a negative or a positive sense is incoherent. And although initially arbitrary, the boundaries of a country over time become an integral part of its history, identity, and self-understanding and cease to be arbitrary, giving it a moral right to its territorial and cultural integrity including the right to limit the entry of outsiders.[13]

Although a good case can perhaps be made for the cosmopolitan right to hospitality on other grounds, a better or at least an equally strong case can be made in the language of duties and obligations. As moral beings, we have a duty to alleviate human suffering and help those in need within the limits of our abilities. The greater their suffering and need, the stronger is our duty to help them, and the duty becomes compelling if we have the necessary resources. Those fleeing persecution and death are a desperate people, and we, especially the citizens of the affluent and politically stable Western societies, have a duty to offer them a home and treat them with respect. This duty is reinforced if we happen to have signed relevant international treaties such as the Geneva Convention, or if we happen to have historical ties with the countries involved. Our duty is grounded in justice, altruism, human solidarity, and even an enlightened self-interest, and tells us what we owe to others without at any stage introducing the language of rights. As the Greeks and the old natural law theorists maintained, the idea of justice does not have to be articulated in the language of rights. It is enough to say that certain forms of behaviour are a matter of justice or *humanitas*, and hence required of us.

When the language of human rights becomes the only or even the dominant language in a society, there is a grave danger that valuable forms of moral sensibility and motivations might suffer a decline. This can happen for several related reasons. We are encouraged to think that as long as we respect others' human rights we owe them nothing more, that whatever cannot be reduced to someone's right has no moral significance for us, or that the absence of an identifiable human right signals a morality-free zone where we may act as we please. Furthermore, in a rights-based society the moral and political weight of its major institutions is bound to be thrown behind cultivating those qualities of character that are needed to sustain the culture of rights. Since other moral motivations and virtues are treated as a dispensable luxury, they are devalued, neither cultivated nor activated, and are likely to atrophy for lack of encouragement and exercise.

The rights-based society is anxious to respect the rights of its members both because this is how it morally defines and judges itself and because it would otherwise invite expensive litigation and claims for compensation. As we have seen in the UK and elsewhere, such a society would therefore seek to work out detailed charters of services that its members have a right to demand of public institutions such as hospitals, schools, universities, the police, and various government departments. And it would want to ensure their delivery by preparing checklists of who should do what, devising systems of monitoring, audit, strict accountability, etc., and training the relevant groups of professionals accordingly. While there is much to be said for a guaranteed level of public services and bureaucratic accountability, it is not obvious that this is the best way to go about it. It relies on fear rather than professional pride, bureaucratizes the relations between the parties involved, gives greater power to and places greater trust in the administrators than the frontline professionals, and encourages litigiousness. Since it has no role for them, it also discourages a whole host of moral dispositions such as the sense of professional honour, collective pride, and the willingness to take risks and go beyond what is required lest one should fall foul of the procedures, disturb the bureaucratic rhythm, fail to meet official targets, or appear unduly enthusiastic and awkward.[14] These and other dangers are not inherent in the language of human rights, rather they arise when it becomes the only or the dominant moral language and is not checked by others.

Although human rights are an integral part of moral and political life, they are only a part and exclude several worthwhile ideals. Take, for example, the principle of equality. Although they are closely related, the ideas of human rights and equality belong to different historical traditions, rest on different presuppositions, and have different moral implications.[15] To be sure, human rights include the right to equality, including equality of consideration, respect, treatment, rights, and opportunities. However equality encompasses much more than this. We rightly feel disturbed by the vast inequalities of income, wealth, and economic and political power, but cannot adequately articulate our unease in the language of human rights. We might appeal to the principle of equal human worth and dignity, but it is difficult to see how such inequalities violate it as long as they do not stand in the way of everyone's equal right to enjoy the conditions of the good life. Inequalities damage human lives but do not seem to violate human rights. We object to them because they break up society into two relatively self-contained groups leading parallel lives, discourage common experiences and interests and frustrate a sense of community, enable some to set the moral tone of society and distort its values, foster arrogance among some and a sense of marginality and even inferiority among the rest, and so on. In making these arguments, we appeal to the great harm inequalities do to moral character, the quality of social relations, the moral culture of society, its collective ethos and valuable collective goods, all of which the language of human rights ignores.

The tension between human rights and equality arises at other levels as well. Human rights presuppose a homogeneous moral subject and are the same for all human beings. Unlike them equality takes account of relevant differences, and seeks to ensure that our treatment of others is discriminating without becoming discriminatory, suitably different yet also equal. Again, human rights concentrate on individuals; equality does that too but also has a collective dimension. When individuals are discriminated against or subjected to demeaning stereotypes on grounds of colour, ethnicity, race, or gender, they are treated unequally by virtue of their membership of the relevant group. Their discrimination and the disadvantages cannot be tackled at the individual level alone and require actions directed at them collectively. This is why we turn to such devices as group representation in positions of power, parity of esteem, targets, monitoring, and so on. In all these cases individual-based human rights prove inadequate, and we are led to introduce some notion of collective rights. We do the same when we advocate a programme of affirmative action to tackle the historically inherited deep disadvantages of certain groups. The language of human rights and the individualist theory of justice that it generates is at best of limited help and at worst a hindrance, as the controversy surrounding affirmative action demonstrates.

As we saw, human rights are predicated upon a belief in the fundamental identity of all human beings and presuppose a homogeneous subject. Human beings, however, are never like that. They are men, women, neither or both, they are adults or children or somewhere in between, and so on. Since all statements of universal human rights have until recently concentrated on a homogeneous human subject, they have predictably ignored the rights of women and children *qua* women and children. In recent years the abstract universality of human rights has rightly been questioned. While claiming the rights that all human beings should enjoy, feminists have rightly asked for rights that relate to women's specific circumstances and needs. Their gender informs and shapes their humanity, makes them a particular kind of human being with their own needs and vulnerabilities, and calls for a distinct set of rights. Feminists have rightly insisted that these rights are not inferior in status or an add-on to their human rights, but rather their human rights *as women*. The same is the case with children who are not just potential adults but human beings in their own right, and needing a distinct body of human rights. The rights of women and children are universal in the sense that they are claimed on behalf of all women and children, but they are not universal in the sense of being extended to all human beings, the point we capture by talking of *human rights of women* or *of children*.

Some of the worst forms of suffering that human beings inflict on others represent another area where the language of human rights, although relevant, seems highly inadequate. To say that Hitler violated the human rights of the millions of Jews whom he sent to the gas chambers is to fail to capture the enormity of his deed. Many despotic governments too violate the human rights of their subjects. Hitler's actions were quite different not merely in their scale and degree of brutality but their basic character. He did nothing less than deny the humanity of Jews, rejected them as members of the human community, and treated them as a subhuman species which he could crush at will. At a different level, what is deeply disturbing about ethnically organized acts of mass rape is not just that they violate the human rights of the women involved but rather that they show utter contempt for the women, deny their basic humanity and self-respect, humiliate their men, and treat both as helpless objects of fun. This is also why racial discrimination, which denies equal rights to the relevant racial groups, is different from racism, which rejects them, refuses to share a common world with them, and places little value on their lives and liberties.

Such actions, which are qualitatively different from the ordinary violations of human rights, arouse distinct moral emotions and require a different moral vocabulary. We rightly call them inhuman, monstrous, evil. Simone Weil captures part of this point well by giving an illuminating example.[16] If I browbeat a farmer to sell his eggs at a lower price, he will rightly rejoin that he has a right to set the price of his eggs and not to sell them if he does not get that price. If a young girl is being forced into a brothel, she will not say that she has a right to liberty or bodily integrity and will not allow it to be violated. 'In such a situation the word [right] would sound ludicrously inadequate.' This is so because not just her rights but her person or the very core of her being is violated. If the farmer were to be compelled to sell his eggs at a lower price, he and we would say that an injustice was done to him. In the case of the girl, she and we would find that language shallow because the evil inflicted on her is of a very different nature.

III. Cultural Mediation

Societies differ in how they interpret and relate human rights. They might all cherish the right to life, but disagree on when life begins and ends and whether the human foetus has such a right. Germany and Ireland extend the right to life to unborn children; Austria limits it to those already born; Spain shares Austria's view but gives the unborn children a 'legal interest' in constitutional protection, which allows the state to regulate the use of the cells, tissues, and organs of embryos and foetuses. Again, while deeply valuing free speech, different societies take different views on its limits and whether it includes commercial advertisements, hard pornography, and the right to burn a copy of the country's constitution. The US Supreme Court gives equal protection to all forms of expression, whereas the European Court privileges political speech and subjects it to fewer restrictions than other forms of expression. Even when societies agree on the meaning and scope of a human right, they might disagree about how to realize it. They might, for example, value the right to a free and fair trial, but reject the view that it requires a jury trial, which is a human right in some legal systems. Although formally universal, human rights are inevitably mediated by a society's traditions and cultures, and are enjoyed by individuals in varied forms. *Jus commune* needs to find space for and respect *jus proprium*.

Human rights are not all of equal status. Some are absolute and may never be restricted. Others may be restricted if the objectives are justified and the restrictions are proportionate and do not altogether frustrate the rights involved. And even here, some rights are subjected to fewer restrictions than others. The European Convention on Human Rights allows derogations from certain rights during war and public emergency but not from others which it regards as more or less absolute, such as the right to life, prohibition of inhuman and degrading treatment, retroactive criminal penalties, protection from forced labour and slavery, and the right to a fair trial. Both the USA and the European Union regard freedom of speech as a human right, but the latter subjects it to greater restrictions. The situation in unstable, developing, or deeply divided societies is even more complex. The culture of civility and self-restraint is often absent; some groups have the monopoly of the media and others lack the opportunities for public self-expression; and ethnic and religious hatred are easily aroused. Such societies may rightly limit free speech to a greater degree than others.

Human rights also conflict. They do so either inherently or in specific contexts or because we have limited resources and need to decide which rights deserve greater allocation. The right to property may lead to the concentration of the media in a few hands, and threaten the freedom of expression. Or the latter might be used to lampoon or attack a religion or an ethnic group, and lead to public disorder and a possible loss of life. Universal declarations list human rights but do not provide either the rules of priority or some other mechanism for resolving their conflicts. They either make the naive assumption that all human rights fit in nicely and form a harmonious whole, or assume rightly that such conflicts are best resolved in the light of the traditions, history, values, etc. of different societies. These traditions and values in turn are themselves subject to the test of human rights and cannot be accepted as the final authority. We criticize them on the basis of human rights, and in turn use them to interpret and balance the conflicting rights. The resulting dialectic is messy but it is the only one available. Since human rights are limited by other human rights and the demands of public interest, and since their balancing occurs within the constraints of a particular cultural community, it is deeply misleading to see them as trumps with the implied suggestions of absolute superiority, finality, and closure. While one right might trump another in

41

one context, it might itself be trumped by it in a different context. And the trade-off of human rights that finds favour in one society might not be acceptable to another.

Although cultural mediation of human rights is unavoidable, it has its obvious dangers. It might be used to emasculate and frustrate human rights or to strike morally unacceptable trade-offs, as is the case with several Muslim and East Asian societies. Although the grounds are different, the ease with which the American public opinion has been persuaded to accept torture, inhuman punishment, and drastic violations of individual liberties after the terrorist attacks of 2001 shows that the danger is not absent even in societies with a robust culture of human rights. There is no foolproof way of guarding against these dangers. One way is for international declarations to be far more specific than they have been so far, and to lay down what human rights are absolute and may never be violated and which ones may be restricted in what circumstances and on what basis. The European Convention on Human Rights is a good example of this. It would also help to ask appropriate international bodies to adjudicate on contentious issues. Above all, it is vital to build up a vigilant national and international public opinion to challenge, expose, and put pressure on governments that use the legitimate cultural defence to serve illegitimate objectives.

IV. Conclusion

As the language of human rights is increasingly becoming an intellectual and moral orthodoxy, there is a strong philosophical reason to interrogate it lest it should cripple our imagination and undermine or weaken alternative traditions. And since it is sometimes invoked to justify questionable external interventions into the affairs of other societies and even wars, there is also a strong moral reason to do so. We need to preserve its many valuable insights, such as that human beings have intrinsic worth, that a certain moral minimum in the form of modes of treatment and conditions of life should be guaranteed to them, and that the states that fail to do so are what Rawls calls 'outlaw states' and deserve the strongest condemnation. Like any valuable doctrine, however, that of human rights is open to its characteristic exaggerations, distortions, excesses, blind spots, and fanaticism, which must be exposed both in its own interest and that of other equally valuable moral perspectives.

Since the doctrine of human rights rests on certain assumptions about human beings and has a particular moral orientation and thrust, it is bound sometimes to come into conflict with other forms of human self-understanding, such as the religious, the romantic, the communitarian, and the utilitarian, that rest on different visions of the human condition and structure moral life on different principles. Each of them sees certain areas of moral life better than others, nurtures aspirations and sensibilities that are ignored or marginalized by others, and has its own evocative vocabulary. Since they are all valuable and regulate each other's biases and excesses, none including the language of human rights can be given a hegemonic status. Their ongoing dialogue, both friendly and adversarial, is the only way we can learn from their complementary insights and safeguard the inherent plurality of moral life. This means that the doctrine of human rights cannot stand on its own either logically or morally. It needs to be located in a wider pluralist moral theory that determines and assigns it its proper place in human life.

Response to Bhikhu Parekh, 'Finding a Proper Place for Human Rights'

Seyla Benhabib

There is much that I agree with and admire in Bhikhu Parekh's lucid and measured essay, 'Finding a Proper Place for Human Rights'. Yet I fear that Parekh's views vacillate between a 'weak' and a 'strong' critique of the discourse of human rights. While the weak view enables us to situate human rights more adequately within the universe of moral discourse and practice, the strong view undermines the legitimacy of this discourse in the name of a language of duties and virtues. I am particularly disturbed by the suggestion that there is no 'right to asylum'. Rather, argues Parekh, we should view the obligation we owe asylum-seekers and refugees as springing from the moral duties of benevolence as well as prudential grounds of self-interest. I consider that proposal not only philosophically wrong but politically dangerous as well.

I

It is surely one of the puzzles of post-World War II moral discourse and practice that while the philosophical quandaries surrounding the concept of 'human rights' have hardly been resolved, the vocabulary of human rights has become an almost universally accepted mode of moral communication. It is notoriously difficult to reach agreement around the normative constituents of the term 'human'. This is particularly the case in an age when the moral vision of the human embedded in religious and cosmological traditions has been cognitively challenged and no longer garners widespread assent and when all attempts to define human nature, beyond the bare minimums, have been eviscerated by postmodernist scepticism.

Accompanying these philosophical difficulties, and closely related to them, is the question of what exactly is the scope of human rights: which rights are 'basic' or 'fundamental'? Which are variable, negotiable, or contingent?

Parekh does not propose a normative strategy to address these questions. While it would be foolhardy to try to do so within the context of this exchange, I would like to propose that the most convincing strategies in contemporary philosophical ethics in justifying human rights are various forms of 'moral constructivism'. Moral constructivisms proceed from the analysis of human practices of judgement, evaluation, and justification in order to elucidate those presuppositions without which the practice in question could not be what it is. Whereas at one time Immanuel Kant named such analysis of presuppositions 'transcendental', the contemporary approach is more fallibilist. Human moral practices are considered to be either constituents of 'reflexive equilibrium' (Rawls) or the 'universal pragmatic presuppositions of speech and action' (Habermas). In very broad terms, such analyses establish the view that human beings are capable of formulating and pursuing a sense of the good and acting on principles; furthermore, that they are capable of cooperating with one another around social practices of justice. At a minimum, we must treat each other as beings with whom we can engage in moral justification: I respect your moral dignity and you respect mine when we seek to justify to one another the terms of our public cooperation, as opposed to imposing them on each other violently, through force and coercion, deceit and fraud, cruelty and manipulation. A philosophical theory of this sort provides us with an account of 'the principle of right'. It serves to justify the language of human rights.

To be distinguished from the 'principle of right' is the 'scope of rights'. While there may be some agreement around the principle of rights, there is usually widespread disagreement around the scope of rights. This distinction is important because, unlike relativists, sceptics, and postmodernists, Parekh does not deny that some principle of rights ought to be formulated and that some philosophical justification of the moral vocabulary of human rights is possible. Rather, he is concerned with the 'scope' of rights, and this in a twofold sense: first he is concerned that the vocabulary of rights and the moral perspectives inspired by them should not overstep their boundaries and distort the true quality of the moral relations involved. 'Many worthwhile things in life', he notes, 'are not a matter of right but a freely given gift, for example, love and friendship'. Parenting, he argues, is not a matter of the right of the child but rather, the duty of the parent. Furthermore, if a society increasingly views such human relationships in terms of rights claims, it becomes impoverished, cannot nurture forms of human excellence, and may not even last long.

While at some level it is hard to disagree with this observation, at another level I feel that Parekh overlooks what may be remiss in such relationships of love, friendship, and parenting. Like all human relationships, they involve a mixture of justifiable and unjustifiable dimensions of hierarchy and inequality, affection as well as resentment. It was not that long ago that corporal punishment in the family as well as in the school was considered an acceptable component of disciplining a child; it was not that long ago that erotic true love was said to be possible only among adult, heterosexual couples (the rest being deemed perversions). Lastly, although since Aristotle true friendship has been said to exist only among equals, we know that this as well is an elusive value. I do not want to be misunderstood. I wholly share Parekh's sense that our moral life would be deeply impoverished if we had never experienced some or all of these relationships. We were all children once, but we need not all become parents; a life without love and friends is conceivable although neither desirable nor exemplary.

Yet when the vocabulary of human rights starts colouring these fragile and valuable human relationships, this is not on account of the bad example set by the litigious USA or by deductively minded continental jurists, as Parekh at times suggests. Rather, the spread of ideals of democratic equality inevitably carries them from the public into the private and interpersonal spheres. When partners in love are each independent wage-earners, the language of rights, from property ownership to household chores, makes its way into everyday relations; when children learn in school and in the society around them, as well they should, that child-molesting is wrong, that corporal punishment is cruel and unjust, then they will stand up against their parents and challenge their authority. Under conditions of democratic equality one cannot immunize the private sphere from the ideals of the public. However, balancing such claims and vocabularies as between claims of equality and the special bonds and duties deriving from love, friendship, and parenting, is essential and desirable for a fulfilled moral life.

Parekh is concerned about the scope of rights in another sense as well. Here, the issue is not the distorting effects which rights language may have in the domain of human relationships but rather the justifiable scope of rights in political institutions and legal contexts. 'Rights to life, liberty, basic necessities of life, freedom from slavery and degrading treatment, freedom of conscience, fair trial, freedom of expression, equality of treatment, personal property, etc. eminently qualify as human rights,' writes Parekh. He is sceptical, though, that 'detaining a person before a court hearing for more than four days, denying transsexuals the ability to achieve a new civic identity, and corporal punishment in schools that exceeds strict limits, are all violations of the human rights of those involved'. Parekh suggests that the European Court of Human Rights may have exceeded its legitimate mandate here.

Perhaps. But Parekh's critique of the overreach of the European Court does not heed the distinction between the principle of rights and the scope of rights. Any democratic sovereign, or any public institutional body entrusted by one or more democratic sovereigns with the legitimacy to promulgate law, will exercise discretion in the interpretation of the scope of rights. It is essential for the democratic ideal of self-governance that there be a robust public debate about the scope of rights. Certain principles of rights such as the absolute prohibition of slavery, torture, mutilation, and genocide are considered incontrovertible and 'off the agenda' of public debate in most liberal democracies. A wide-ranging and contentious debate nevertheless can exist about the interpretation of these rights claims in concrete instances: is consensual prostitution of immigrant women in the hands of smugglers a form of slavery? Is torture permitted in the handling of terrorists and what counts as torture? Are the events occurring in the Darfur region of the Sudan to be deemed 'genocide' or ethnic warfare? The essentially contested nature of these and many public debates strikes me not as being an instance of the overreach of the language of rights, but rather, an aspect of the democratic hermeneutic of legal and political claim-making. Parekh writes as if such contentious debate could be brought to an end if people came to share the same moral sense of the limits of rights. This would only mean, however, stopping the democratic conversation.

II

While a defender of a strong deontological and rights-based approach such as myself can find common ground with many of Parekh's observations on the moral limits of the language of human rights, that is not the case with his comments on the right of asylum. 'Although a good case can perhaps be made for the cosmopolitan right to hospitality,' writes Parekh, 'a better or at least an equally strong case can be made in the language of duties and obligations.' Parekh believes that such a duty is grounded in the injunction to alleviate human suffering and to help those in need. Thus, in Kantian language, Parekh wishes to reframe cosmopolitan right as an instance of philanthropy and benevolence. I think that Kant was right and that Parekh is wrong on this score.

Kant introduces the right of hospitality in the Third Article of his 'Perpetual Peace' essay.[1] The German reads: 'Das Weltbuergerrecht soll auf Bedingungen der allgemeinen Hospitalitaet eingeschraenkt sein.'[2] This is usually rendered as, 'The Law of World Citizenship Shall be Limited to Conditions of Universal Hospitality.' Kant himself notes the oddity of the locution of 'hospitality' in this context, and therefore remarks that 'it is not a question of philanthropy but of right'. In other words, hospitality is not to be understood as a virtue of

49

sociability, as the kindness and generosity one may show to strangers who come to one's land or who become dependent upon one's act of kindness through circumstances of nature or history; hospitality is a 'right' which belongs to all human beings in so far as we view them as potential participants in a world republic. But the 'right' of hospitality is odd in that it does not regulate relationships among individuals who are members of a particular civil entity and under whose jurisdiction they stand; this 'right' regulates the interactions of individuals who belong to different civic entities yet who encounter one another at the margins of bounded communities. The right of hospitality is situated at the boundaries of the polity; it delimits civic space by regulating relations among members and strangers. Hence the right of hospitality occupies that space between human rights and civil rights, between the right of humanity in our person and the rights which accrue to us in so far as we are members of specific republics. Kant writes:

Hospitality [*Wirtbarkeit*] means the right of a stranger not to be treated as an enemy when he arrives in the land of another. One may refuse to receive him when this can be done without causing his destruction; but, so long as he peacefully occupies his place, one may not treat him with hostility. It is not the right to be a permanent visitor [*Gastrecht*] that one may demand. A special beneficent agreement [*ein* [. . .] *wohltaetiger Vertrag*] would be needed in order to give an outsider a right to become a fellow inhabitant (*Hausgenossen*) for a certain length of time. It is only a right of temporary sojourn [*ein Besuchsrecht*], a right to associate, which all men have. They have it by virtue of their common possession [*das Recht des gemeinschaftlichen Besitzes*] of the surface of the earth, where, as a globe, they cannot infinitely disperse and hence must finally tolerate the presence of each other.[3]

I see this argument as containing the kernel of a cosmopolitan vision, according to which all human beings everywhere would be accorded a legal personality and treated with the respect and dignity commensurate with their legal and moral status. Kant's formulations are also far-reaching in that they aim at formulating 'transborder' justice claims.

Kant, like many before and after him, however, founders at the limits of the Westphalian conception of the state. The political sovereign disposes over all objects and subjects within its territory, no longer through absolute might, but in accordance with the republican constitution. But the republican constitution, although legally and morally obliged to grant refugees and asylum-seekers first rights of admittance, is under no obligation to extend this temporary right of sojourn into a permanent right of refuge. Kant opens a hiatus between hospitality and sovereignty; a hiatus which characterizes our institutional practices of refuge, asylum, and immigration to this day.

The Universal Declaration of Human Rights of 1948 recognizes the right to freedom of movement across boundaries—a right to emigrate—that is, to leave a country, but not a right to immigrate, a right to enter a country (Art. 13). Article 14 anchors the right to enjoy asylum under certain circumstances, while Article 15 of the Declaration proclaims that everyone has a 'the right to a nationality'. The second half of Article 15 stipulates that 'No one shall be arbitrarily deprived of his nationality nor denied the right to change his nationality.'[4]

The Universal Declaration is silent on states' obligations to grant entry to immigrants, to uphold the right of asylum, and to permit citizenship to alien residents and denizens. These rights have no specific addressees and they do not appear to anchor specific obligations on the part of second and third parties to comply with them. Despite the cross-border character of these rights, the Declaration upholds the sovereignty of individual states. Thus a series of internal contradictions between universal human rights and territorial sovereignty is built right into the logic of the most comprehensive international law documents in our world.

The Geneva Convention of 1951 relating to the Status of Refugees and its Protocol added in 1967 are the second most important international legal documents governing cross-border movements. Nevertheless, neither the existence of these documents nor the creation of the United Nations High Commissioner on Refugees have altered the fact that this Convention and its Protocol are binding on signatory states alone and can be disregarded by non-signatories, and at times, even by signatory states themselves.

Parekh's suggestion that we consider the rights of refugees and asylees not as rights at all but rather as a duty of benevolence we owe to another, would only strengthen the resolve of nation-states to exempt themselves from receiving refugees and asylum-seekers when they see fit. This proposal would only expedite the implosion of an international refugee regime which is considerably burdened under its own internal contradictions.

Would this help refugees and asylum-seekers? Hardly. We would simply return to the status quo ante of the years between the two World Wars, when states resorted to denaturalization to get rid of unwanted groups of citizens, closed their doors to others, and rendered millions of human beings stateless—and, some would argue, facilitated their extermination by advancing totalitarian terror. The Geneva Convention was formulated as a consequence of the lessons learned through these horrors. They are a brilliant example of moral constructivism at work: when states voluntarily agree to bind their own political and legal wills in accordance with general principles. The duties of benevolence, which always permit situational interpretations, are hardly equivalent to the internationally guaranteed rights of asylum and refuge.

Was Kant successful in justifying the right of hospitality? Are his references to the 'common possession of the earth's surface' sufficient for this task? When reflecting on the 'temporary right of sojourn' (*Besuchsrecht*) Kant uses two different premises. The one premise justifies the right of temporary sojourn on the basis of the capacity of all human beings (*allen Menschen*) to associate—the German reads 'sich zur Gesellschaft anzubieten'.[5] The other premise resorts to the juridical construct of a 'common possession of the surface of the earth' (*gemeinschaftliches Besitzes der Oberflaeche der Erde* Ibid.). With respect to the second principle, Kant suggests that to deny the foreigner and the stranger the claim to enjoy the land and its resources, when this claim can be made peacefully and without endangering the life and welfare of original inhabitants, would be unjust.

The juridical construct of a purported common possession of the earth, which has a long and honourable antecedent in old European jurisprudence, functions as a double-edged sword in this context. On the one hand, Kant wants to avoid the justificatory use of this construct to legitimize Western colonialist expansion; on the other hand, he wants to base the right of human beings to enter into civil association with one another upon the claim that, since the surface of the earth is limited, at some point or another we must learn to enjoy its resources in common with others.

To understand the first of Kant's worries, recall here John

Locke's argument in *The Second Treatise of Civil Government*. 'In the beginning God gave the earth to men in common to enjoy.'[6] The earth is a 'res nullius', belonging to all and none until it is appropriated, but to argue that the earth is a common possession of all human beings is, in effect, to disregard property relations historically existing among communities which have already settled on the land. The justification of the claim to property thus shifts from the historical title which legitimizes it to the modes of appropriation whereby what commonly belongs to a community can then be appropriated as 'mine' or 'thine'.

In the context of European expansion to the Americas in the seventeenth century, Locke's argument served to justify the colonial appropriation of the land, precisely with the claim that the earth, being given to all 'in common', could then be justifiably appropriated by the industrious and the thrifty, without harming existing inhabitants and in fact, for the benefit of all. Kant explicitly rejects the *res nullius* thesis in its Lockean form, seeing in it a thinly disguised formula for expropriating non-European peoples who did not have the capacity to resist imperialist onslaughts.[7] He supports the Chinese and the Japanese in their attempt to keep European traders at a distance.

Despite its powerful anti-imperialist implications, the premise of the 'common possession of the earth' does not suffice to justify the right of hospitality. In my view, it is the 'right of all men to associate', to seek each other's company, and to enter into transactions with one another, that is more promising philosophically. In accordance with a constructivist strategy, I have argued elsewhere that among the terms of our association is the requirement that I be able to justify to you with good grounds the basis upon which I could exclude you from first access to the earth and its resources when you have nowhere else to go.[8] Such a justification cannot be rationally grounded; therefore, the right to first admittance for refugees and asylees holds. This right of first admittance, however, is not an automatic right to membership or citizenship. Although the spread of cosmopolitan rights is increasingly lessening the gap between hospitality and sovereignty, between the right to first admittance and the right to full membership, the regulatory privilege of existing polities is not eliminated. How and when to exercise these regulatory privileges over access to one's borders and resources is one of the most contentious issues facing contemporary state-regimes. That this debate is taking place within the framework of universal human rights is, in my opinion, to be cherished rather than lamented.

2

Against an Ideology of Human Rights

Slavoj Zizek

The critique of the notion of universal human rights usually invokes two arguments. The first is based on the well-known Marxist symptomal reading which endeavours to render visible the particular content which gives the specific 'bourgeois' ideological spin to the notion of human rights: 'universal human rights are effectively the right of the white male private owners to exchange freely on the market, exploit workers and women, as well as exert political domination . . .' Tendentially, at least, this approach considers the hidden 'pathological' spin as constitutive of the very form of the Universal. However, against this quick dismissal of the very universal form as ideological (concealing an unacknowledged particular content), post-Marxists such as Ernesto Laclau insist on the gap between the empty universality and its determinate content: the link between the empty universal notion of 'human rights' and its original particular content is contingent, i.e. the moment they were formulated, 'human rights' started to function as an empty signifier whose concrete content can be contested and widened—what about the human rights of women, children, members of non-white races, criminals, madmen . . .? Each of these supplementary gestures does not simply apply the notion of human rights to ever new domains (women, blacks . . . can also vote, own property, actively participate in public life, etc.), but retroactively redefines the very notion of human rights. Far from being in themselves a tool of ideological mystification, 'human rights' are thus a 'floating signifier', to use a once-famous term—a site of ideological struggle with no predetermined outcome.

The most succinct counter-argument against this Marxist insistence on the gap between the ideological appearance of the universal legal form and the particular interests that effectively sustain it was proposed by Claude Lefort and Jacques Rancière: the form, in other words, is never a 'mere' form; it involves a dynamics of its own, leaves its traces in the materiality of social life and is only then fully valid (the bourgeois 'formal freedom' set in motion the process of very 'material' political demands and practices, from trade unions to feminism). Rancière's basic emphasis is on the radical ambiguity of the Marxist notion of the 'gap' between formal democracy (the rights of man, political freedom, etc.) and the economic reality of exploitation and domination. One can read this gap between the 'appearance' of equality-freedom and the social reality of economic, cultural, etc. differences, either in the standard 'symptomatic' way (the form of universal rights, equality, freedom, and democracy is just a necessary, but illusory form of expression of its concrete social content, the universe of exploitation and class domination), or in the much more subversive sense of a tension in which the 'appearance' of what Etienne Balibar called 'egaliberté', precisely, is *not* a 'mere appearance', but evinces an effectivity of its own, which allows it to set in motion the process of the rearticulation of actual socio-economic relations by way of their progressive 'politicization'. (Why shouldn't women also vote? Why shouldn't conditions in the workplace also be of public political concern? etc.) One is tempted to use here the old Levi-Straussian term of 'symbolic efficiency': the appearance of 'egaliberté' is a symbolic fiction which, as such, possesses actual efficiency of its own—one should resist the properly cynical temptation of reducing it to a mere illusion that conceals a different actuality.

This identification of the particular content that hegemonizes the universal form is, however, only half the story of the Marxist critique. Its other, crucial half consists in asking a much more difficult supplementary question, that of the emergence of the very form of universality: how, in what specific historical conditions, does the abstract Universality itself become a 'fact of (social) life'? In what conditions do individuals experience themselves as subjects of universal human rights? Therein resides the point of Marx's analysis of 'commodity fetishism': in a society in which commodity exchange predominates, individuals themselves, in their daily lives, relate to themselves, as well as to the objects they encounter, as to contingent embodiments of abstract-universal notions. What I am, my concrete social or cultural background, is experienced as contingent, since what ultimately defines me is the 'abstract' universal capacity to think and/or to work. Or, any object that can satisfy my desire is experienced as contingent, since my desire is conceived as an 'abstract' formal capacity, indifferent towards the multitude of particular objects that may—but never fully do—satisfy it. Or, the already-mentioned example of 'profession': the modern notion of profession implies that I experience myself as an individual who is not directly 'born into' his social role— what I will become depends on the interplay between the contingent social circumstances and my free choice; in this sense, today's individual has a profession of an electrician or professor or waiter, while it is meaningless to claim that a medieval serf was a peasant by profession. The crucial point here is, again, that, in certain specific social conditions (of commodity exchange and the global market economy), 'abstraction' becomes a direct feature of actual social life, the way concrete individuals behave and relate to their fate and to their social surroundings.

The second argument against universal human rights is homologous to the first one. It is just that the class bias is replaced by the cultural bias: while human rights pretend to be universal, they secretly privilege a Western set of values, so that their global imposition equals Western cultural imperialism. A recent conflict in India is instructive with regard to this point. The Hindus organized widespread demonstrations against McDonald's after it became known that, before freezing their potato chips, McDonald's was frying them in beef fat; after the company conceded the point, guaranteeing that all potato chips sold in India would be fried only in vegetable oil, the satisfied Hindus happily returned to munching the chips. Far from undermining globalization, this protest against McDonald's and the company's quick answer signal the perfect integration of the Hindus into the diversified global order. The point is not only that the global market thrives on the diversification of demands, but that, at a purely formal level, the Hindus' defence of their tradition is already inscribed in the logic of modernity, that it is already a 'reflected' gesture: the Hindus have chosen (to remain faithful to) their tradition, thereby transforming this tradition into one of the many options available to them. A closer analysis should take into account the gap between the literal and the metaphoric dimension of the Hindu protest against McDonald's chips: it is clear that this protest functioned as a metaphoric stand-in for the global discontent with the Western cultural imperialism. We can thus imagine two further versions (not taking into account the third one: what if McDonald's were to lie, continuing to use the beef fat, and the Hindus were to believe the company? Is it not that, in this case, everybody would have been satisfied?):

What if, after getting the assurances that McDonald's truly stopped using the beef fat, the Hindus would somehow feel frustrated? By complying with their literal demand, McDonald's prevented them from articulating their more fundamental protest against Western cultural imperialism?

What if, after McDonald's had truly stopped using the beef fat, the Hindu press had continued to spread the lie that it was still being used, and what if this lie had triggered a popular revolt against cultural imperialism with some actually emancipatory results? Is it not that, in this case, an obvious lie would have served as the means of articulating a more global truth? (Recall also the similar cases of the trial of an African-American murderer: even if he really did commit the crime, the sentence is somehow 'wrong', since it serves to sustain racist attitudes towards African-Americans.)

The 'respect' for Indians is thus unremittingly patronizing, like our standard attitude towards small children: although we do not take them seriously, we 'respect' their innocuous customs in order not to shatter their illusory world. When a visitor reaches a local village with its customs, is there anything more racist than his clumsy attempts to demonstrate how he 'understands' the local customs and is able to follow them? Does such behaviour not bear witness to the same patronizing attitude as the one displayed by adults who adapt themselves to their small children by way of imitating their gestures and their way of speaking? Furthermore, what about practices such as the burning of wives after their husbands' death, which is part of the *same* Hindu tradition as

sacred cows? Should we (the tolerant Western multicultural-
ists) also respect these practices? Here, the tolerant multiculturalist is compelled to resort to a thoroughly Eurocentrist
distinction, a distinction totally foreign to Hinduism: the
Other is tolerated with regard to customs which hurt no
one—the moment we touch some (for us) traumatic dimension, tolerance is over. In short, tolerance is tolerance for the
Other in so far as this Other is not an 'intolerant fundamentalist'—which simply means in so far as it is not the real Other.
Tolerance is 'zero tolerance' for the real Others, the Other in
the substantial weight of its *jouissance*. We can see how this
liberal tolerance reproduces the elementary 'postmodern'
operation of having access to the object deprived of its substance: we can enjoy coffee without caffeine, beer without
alcohol, sex without direct bodily contact, up to virtual reality,
i.e. reality itself deprived of its inert material substance—and,
along the same lines, we even get the ethnic Other deprived
of the substance of its Otherness . . .

In other words, the problem with the liberal multiculturalist is that he is unable to uphold a true indifference towards
the Other's *jouissance*—this *jouissance* bothers him, which is
why his entire strategy is to maintain it at a proper distance.
This indifference towards the Other's *jouissance*, the thorough
absence of envy, is the key component of what Lacan calls the
subjective position of a 'saint'. Like the authentic 'fundamentalists' (say, the Amish) who are indifferent, not bothered
by the secret enjoyment of Others, true believers in a (universal) Cause, like Saint Paul, are pointedly indifferent towards
local customs and mores which simply do not matter. In contrast to them, the multiculturalist liberal is a Rortyan 'ironist',
always maintaining a distance, always displacing belief onto
Others—Others believe for him, in his place. And although

he may appear ('for himself') to reproach the believing Other for the particular content of his belief, what effectively ('in itself') bothers him is the form of belief as such. Intolerance is intolerance towards the Real of a belief. He effectively behaves like the proverbial husband who in principle concedes that his wife may get a lover, only not *that* guy, i.e. every particular lover is unacceptable: the tolerant liberal concedes in principle the right to believe, while rejecting every determinate belief as 'fundamentalist'. The ultimate joke of the multiculturalist tolerance is, of course, the way the class distinction is inscribed into it: adding the (ideological) insult to (politico-economic) injury, the upper-class Politically Correct individuals use it to reproach lower classes for their redneck 'fundamentalism'.

This brings us to the more radical question: is the respect for the other's belief (say, the belief in the sacredness of cows) really the ultimate ethical horizon? Is this not the ultimate horizon of the postmodern ethics, in which, since the reference to any form of universal truth is disqualified as a form of cultural violence, what ultimately matters is only the respect for the other's fantasy? Or, to put it in an even more pointed way: OK, one can claim that lying to the Hindus about the beef fat is ethically problematic—however, does this mean that one is not allowed to argue publicly that their belief (in the sacredness of cows) is already in itself a lie, a false belief? The fact of 'ethical committees' popping out all around today points in the same direction: how is it that ethics all of a sudden became an affair of bureaucratic (administrative), state-nominated committees which are invested with the authority to determine what course of action can still count as ethically acceptable? The 'risk society' theorists' answer (we need committees because we are confronting new situations in which it is no longer possible to apply old norms, i.e. ethical committees are the sign of 'reflected' ethics) is clearly insufficient: these committees are the sign of a deeper malaise (and, at the same time, an inadequate answer to it).

The ultimate problem with the multiculturalist 'right to narrate' is that it refers to the unique particular experience as a political argument: 'only a gay black woman can experience and tell what it means to be a gay black woman', etc. Such a recourse to the particular experience which cannot be universalized is always and by definition a conservative political gesture: ultimately, everyone can evoke his unique experience in order to justify his reprehensible acts. Is it not possible for a Nazi executioner to claim that his victims do not really understand the inner vision which motivated him? Along these same lines, Veit Harlan, *the* Nazi film director, around 1950 despaired about the fact that Jews in the US did not show any comprehension for his defence for making *The Jew Süss*, claiming that no American Jew can really understand what his situation was in Nazi Germany—far from justifying him, this obscene (factual) truth is the ultimate lie. Furthermore, the fact that the greatest plea for tolerance in the history of cinema was made in a defence against the 'intolerant' attacks on the celebrator of the Ku Klux Klan says a lot about the extent to which the signifier 'tolerance' is very much a 'floating' one, to use today's terms. For D. W. Griffith, *Intolerance* was not a way to exculpate himself for the aggressive racist message of *The Birth of a Nation*: quite the contrary, he was smarting from what he considered 'intolerance' on the part of groups that attempted to have *The Birth of a Nation* banned on account of its anti-Black thrust. In short, when Griffith complains about 'intolerance', he is much closer to today's fundamentalists decrying the 'politically correct' defence of universal rights of women as 'intolerant' towards their specific way of life, than to today's multiculturalist assertion of differences.

Consequently, the legacy to be reinvented today is the politics of truth. Both liberal political democracy and 'totalitarianism' foreclose a politics of truth. Democracy, of course, is the reign of sophists: there are only opinions; any reference of a political agent to some ultimate truth is denounced as 'totalitarian'. However, what 'totalitarianism' regimes impose is also a mere semblance of truth: an arbitrary Teaching whose function is just to legitimize the pragmatic decisions of the Rulers. We live in the 'postmodern' era in which truth-claims as such are dismissed as an expression of hidden power-mechanisms—as the reborn pseudo-Nietzscheans like to emphasize, truth is a lie which is most efficient in asserting our will to power. The very question, apropos of some statement, 'Is it true?', is supplanted by the question 'Under what power conditions can this statement be uttered?' What we get instead of the universal truth is the multitude of perspectives, or, as it is fashionable to put it today, of 'narratives'; consequently, *the* two philosophers of today's global capitalism are the two great Left-liberal 'progressives', Richard Rorty and Peter Singer—honest in their radical stance. Rorty defines the basic coordinates: the fundamental dimension of a human being is the ability to suffer, to experience pain and humiliation—consequently, since humans are symbolic animals, the fundamental right is the right to narrate one's experience of suffering and humiliation. Singer then provides the Darwinian background: 'species-ism' (privileging the human species) is no different from racism: our perception of a difference between humans and (other) animals is no less illogical and unethical than our one-time perception of an ethical difference between, say, men and women, or blacks and whites.

Lenin's wager—today, in our era of postmodern relativism, more relevant than ever—is that universal truth and partisanship, the gesture of taking sides, are not only not mutually exclusive, but condition each other: in a concrete situation, its *universal* truth can only be articulated from a thoroughly *partisan* position—truth is by definition one-sided. This, of course, goes against the predominant doxa of compromise, of finding a middle path among the multitude of conflicting interests. If one does not specify the *criteria* of the different, alternative, narrativization, then this endeavour courts the danger of endorsing, in the Politically Correct mood, ridiculous 'narratives' such as those about the supremacy of some aboriginal holistic wisdom, of dismissing science as just another narrative on a par with premodern superstitions. The Leninist answer to the postmodern multiculturalist 'right to narrate' should thus be an unashamed assertion of the right to truth.

This brings us to the heart of the matter: the question to be raised by a philosopher is 'What kind of implicit understanding of what is being-human, of human freedom, etc., is contained in the proposed notion of human rights?' As the experience of our post-political liberal-permissive society amply demonstrates, human rights are ultimately, at their core, simply the rights to violate the Ten Commandments. 'The right to privacy'—the right to adultery, done in secret, where no one sees me or has the right to probe into my life. 'The right to pursue happiness and to possess private property'—the right to steal (to exploit others). 'Freedom of the press and of the expression of opinion'—the right to lie. 'The right of free citizens to possess weapons'—the right to kill. And, ultimately, 'freedom of religious belief'—the right to celebrate false gods. Of course, human rights do not directly condone the violation of the Commandments—the point is just that they keep open a marginal 'grey zone' which should remain out of reach of (religious or secular) power: in this shady zone, I can violate the Commandments, and if power probes into it, catching me with my pants down and trying to prevent my violations, I can cry 'Assault on my basic human rights!' The point is thus that it is structurally impossible, for Power, to draw a clear line of separation and prevent only the 'misuse' of the Right, while not infringing upon the proper use, i.e. the use that does *not* violate the Commandments.

Therein resides the weak point of the much-praised new global morality, celebrated today as the sign of a new era in which the international community will be able to enforce a minimal code preventing sovereign states from engaging in crimes against humanity even within their own territory. In an essay apropos the NATO bombing of ex-Yugoslavia significantly titled 'Kosovo and the End of the Nation-State', Vaclav Havel tries to bring home the message that the NATO bombing of Yugoslavia:

places human rights above the rights of the state. The Federal Republic of Yugoslavia was attacked by the Alliance without a direct mandate from the UN. This did not happen irresponsibly, as an act of aggression or out of disrespect for international law. It happened, on the contrary, out of respect for the law, for a law that ranks higher than the law which protects the sovereignty of states. The alliance has acted out of respect for human rights, as both conscience and international legal documents dictate.

Havel further specifies this 'higher law' when he claims that 'human rights, human freedoms, and human dignity have their deepest roots somewhere outside the perceptible world.

[. . .] while the state is a human creation, human beings are the creation of God.' If we read Havel's two statements as the two premises of a judgement, the conclusion that imposes itself is none other than that the NATO forces were allowed to violate the existing international law, since they acted as a direct instrument of the 'higher law' of God Himself—if this is not a clear-cut case of 'religious fundamentalism', then this term is devoid of any minimally consistent meaning. Havel's statement is thus the strongest assertion of what Ulrich Beck, in an article in *Die Süddeutsche Zeitung* in April 1999, called 'militaristic humanism' or even 'militaristic pacifism'. The problem with this term is not that it is an Orwellian oxymoron, reminding us of 'Peace is war' and similar slogans from his *Nineteen Eighty-Four*, and which, as such, directly belies the truth of its position (against this obvious pacifist-liberal criticism, I rather think that it is the pacifist position—'more bombs and killing never brings peace'—which is a fake, and that one should heroically *endorse* the paradox of militaristic pacifism). It is also not that, obviously, the targets of bombardment are chosen not out of pure moral consideration, but selectively, depending on unadmitted geopolitic and economic strategic interests (the Marxist-style criticism). The problem is rather that this purely humanitarian-ethic legitimization (again) thoroughly *depoliticizes* the military intervention, changing it into an intervention into a humanitarian catastrophe, grounded in purely moral reasons, not an intervention into a well-defined political struggle. In other words, the problem with 'militaristic humanism/pacifism' resides not in 'militaristic', but in 'humanism/pacifism': in the way the 'militaristic' intervention (into the social struggle) is presented as a help to the victims of (ethnic, etc.) hatred and violence, justified directly in depoliticized universal human rights.

Consequently, what we need is not a 'true' (demilitarized) humanism/pacifism, but a 'militaristic' social intervention divested of the depoliticized humanist/pacifist coating.

A report in the *New York Times* by Steven Erlanger, from the days before the NATO bombing, on the suffering of the Kosovo Albanians renders perfectly this logic of victimization.[1] Already its title says it all: 'In One Kosovo Woman, an Emblem of Suffering'—the subject to be protected (by the NATO intervention) is from the outset identified as a powerless victim of circumstances, deprived of all political identity, reduced to bare suffering. Her basic stance is that of excessive suffering, of traumatic experience that blurs all differences: 'She's seen too much, Meli said. She wants a rest. She wants it to be over.' As such, she is beyond any political recrimination—an independent Kosovo is not on her agenda, she just wants the horror over: 'Does she favor an independent Kosovo? "You know, I don't care if it's this or that," Meli said. "I just want all this to end, and to feel good again, to feel good in my place and my house with my friends and family." ' Her support of the foreign (NATO) intervention is grounded in her wish for all this horror to be over: 'She wants a settlement that brings foreigners here "with some force behind them". She is indifferent about who the foreigners are.' Consequently, she sympathizes with all sides in an all-embracing humanist stance: 'There is tragedy enough for everyone', she says. 'I feel sorry for the Serbs who've been bombed and died, and I feel sorry for my own people. But maybe now there will be a conclusion, a settlement for good. That would be great.' Here we have the ideological construction of the ideal subject-victim to whose aid NATO comes: not a political subject with a clear agenda, but a subject of helpless suffering, sympathizing with all suffering sides in the conflict, caught in the madness of a local clash that can only be pacified by the intervention of a benevolent foreign power, a subject whose innermost desire is reduced to the almost animal craving to 'feel good again' . . .

At a different level, the same goes for our Western societies. Our courts know the measure of imposing the 'order of restraint': when someone sues another person for harassing him or her (stalking him or her, making unwarranted sexual advances, etc.), the harasser can be legally prohibited from knowingly approaching the victim within 100 yards. Necessary as this measure is in regard to the obvious reality of harassment, there is nonetheless in it something of the defence against the Real of the Other's desire: is it not obvious that there is something dreadfully violent about openly displaying one's passion for another human being to this being him- or herself? Passion by definition hurts its object, and even if its addressee gladly agrees to occupy this place, he or she cannot ever do it without a moment of awe and surprise. Or, to vary yet again Hegel's dictum 'Evil resides in the very gaze which perceives Evil all around itself': intolerance towards the Other resides in the very gaze which perceives all around itself intolerant intruding Others. One should especially be suspect about the obsession with sexual harassment of women when it is voiced by men: after barely scratching the 'pro-feminist' PC surface, one soon encounters the good old male-chauvinist myth about how women are helpless creatures who should be protected not only from intrusive men, but ultimately also from themselves. The problem is not that they will not be able to protect themselves, but that they may start to *enjoy* being sexually harassed, i.e. that the male intrusion will set free in them a self-destructive explosion of excessive sexual enjoyment . . . In short, what one should focus on is what kind of notion of subjectivity is implied in the obsession with the different modes of harassment? Is it not the 'narcis-sistic' subjectivity for which everything others do (address me, look at me . . .) is potentially a threat, so that, as Sartre put it long ago, 'l'enfer, c'est les autres'?

And is not this the case even with the growing prohibition of smoking: first, all offices were declared 'smoke-free', then flights, then restaurants, then airports, then bars, then private clubs, then, in some campuses, 50 yards around the entrances to the buildings, then—in a unique case of pedagogical cen-sorship, reminding us of the famous Stalinist practice of retouching the photos of party members—the US Postal Service removed the cigarette from the stamps with the photo-portrait of blues guitarist Robert Johnson and of Jackson Pollock, up to the recent attempts to impose a ban on lighting up in the street or in a park? Christopher Hitchens was right to point out not only that at least the medical evi-dence for the threat of 'passive smoking' is extremely shaky, but that these prohibitions themselves, intended 'for our own good', are 'fundamentally illogical, presaging a supervised world in which we'll live painlessly, safely—and tediously'. Is what this prohibition targets not again the Other's excessive, risky *jouissance*, embodied in the act of 'irresponsibly' lighting a cigarette and inhaling deeply with an unabashed pleasure— in contrast to Clintonite yuppies who do it without inhaling (or who have sex without actual penetration, or food without fat, or . . .)? What makes smoking such an ideal target is that the proverbial 'smoking gun' is here easy to target, providing a politically correct agent of conspiracy, i.e. the large tobacco companies, and thus disguising envy of the Other's enjoyment in the acceptable anti-corporate clout. The ultimate irony of it is not only that the profits of the tobacco companies have not yet been affected by the anti-smoking campaigns and legislations, but that even most of the billions of dollars the tobacco companies agreed to pay will go to the medico-pharmaceutical industrial complex, which is the single strongest industrial complex in the US, twice as strong as the infamous military industrial complex.

In the magnificent chapter II. C ('You Shall Love Your Neighbour') of his *Works Of Love*, Kierkegaard develops the claim that the ideal neighbour that we should love is a dead one—the only good neighbour is a dead neighbour. His line of reasoning is surprisingly simple and logical: in contrast to poets and lovers, whose object of love is distinguished by its preference, by its particular outstanding qualities, 'to love one's neighbour means equality': 'Forsake all distinctions so that you can love your neighbour.' However, it is only in death that all distinctions disappear: 'Death erases all distinctions, but preference is always related to distinctions.' A further consequence of this reasoning is the crucial distinction between two perfections: the perfection of the object of love and the perfection of love itself. The lover's, poet's, or friend's love contains a perfection belonging to its object, and is, for this very reason, imperfect as love; in contrast to this love:

precisely because one's neighbour has none of the excellences which the beloved, a friend, a cultured person, an admired one, and a rare and extraordinary one have in high degree—for that very reason love to one's neighbour has all the perfections [. . .] Erotic love is determined by the object; friendship is determined by the object; only love to one's neighbour is determined by love. Since one's neighbour is every man, unconditionally every man, all distinctions are indeed removed from the object. Therefore genuine love is recognizable by this, that its object is without any of the more definite qualifications of difference, which means that this love is recognizable only by love. Is not this the highest perfection?

To put it in Kant's terms: what Kierkegaard tries to articulate here are the contours of a non-pathological love, of a love which would be independent of its (contingent) object, a love which (again, to paraphrase Kant's definition of moral duty) is not motivated by its determinate object, but by the mere *form* of love—I love for the sake of love itself, not for the sake of what distinguishes its object. The implication of this stance is thus weird, if not outright morbid: the perfect love is *thoroughly indifferent towards the beloved object*. No wonder Kierkegaard was so obsessed with the figure of Don Juan: do Kierkegaard's Christian love for the neighbour and Don Juan's serial seductions not share this crucial indifference towards the object? For Don Juan, the quality of the seduced object also did not matter: the ultimate point of Leporello's long list of conquests, which categorizes them according to their characteristics (age, nationality, physical features), is that these characteristics are indifferent—the only thing that matters is the pure numerical fact of adding a new name to the list. Is, in this precise sense, Don Juan not a properly Christian seducer, since his conquests were 'pure,' non-pathological in the Kantian sense, done for the sake of it, not because of any particular and contingent properties of their objects? The poet's preferred love object is also a dead person (paradigmatically the beloved woman): he needs her dead in order to articulate his mourning in his poetry (or, as in courtly love poetry, a living woman herself is elevated to the status of a monstrous Thing). However, in contrast to the poet's fixation on the singular dead love object, the Christian as it were treats the still living neighbour as already dead, erasing his or her distinctive qualities. The dead neighbour means: the neighbour deprived of the annoying excess of *jouissance* which makes him/her unbearable. It is thus clear where Kierkegaard cheats: in trying to sell us as the authentic difficult act of love what is effectively an escape from the effort of authentic love. Love for the dead neighbour is an easy feast: it basks in its own perfection, indifferent towards its object—what about not only 'tolerating,' but loving the other *on account* of its very imperfection?

Is this love for the dead neighbour really just Kierkegaard's theological idiosyncrasy? On a recent visit to San Francisco, while listening to a blues CD in a friend's apartment, I unfortunately uttered a remark: 'Judging by the colour of her voice, the singer is definitely black. Strange, then, that she has such a German sounding name—Nina.' Of course, I was immediately admonished for Political Incorrectness: one should not associate someone's ethnic identity with a physical feature or a name, because all this just bolsters racial clichés and prejudices. To my ensuing query about how, then, one should identify ethnic belonging, I got a clear and radical answer: in no way, by means of no particular feature, because every such identification is potentially oppressive in constraining a person to his or her particular identity . . . is this not a perfect contemporary example of what Kierkegaard had in mind? One should love one's neighbours (African-Americans, in this case) only in so far as they are implicitly deprived of all their particular characteristics—in short, in so far as they are treated as already dead. What about loving them *for* the unique sharp-melancholic quality of their voices, *for* the amazing libidinal combinatorics of their names (the leader of the anti-racist movement in France two decades ago was named Harlem Desir!), that is to say, *for* the idiosyncrasy of their modes of *jouissance*?

In what, precisely, does this deadness consist? On today's market, we find a whole series of products deprived of their malignant property: coffee without caffeine, cream without fat, beer without alcohol . . . And the list goes on: what about virtual sex as sex without sex, the Colin Powell doctrine of warfare with no casualties (on our side, of course) as warfare without warfare, the contemporary redefinition of politics as the art of expert administration as politics without politics, up to today's tolerant liberal multiculturalism as an experience of Other deprived of its Otherness (the idealized Other who dances fascinating dances and has an ecologically sound holistic approach to reality, while features such as wife-beating remain out of sight . . .)? Virtual Reality simply generalizes this procedure of offering a product deprived of its substance: it provides reality itself deprived of its substance, of the resisting hard kernel of the Real—in the same way decaffeinated coffee smells and tastes like real coffee without being real, Virtual Reality is experienced as reality without being so.

Is this not the attitude of the hedonistic Last Man? Everything is permitted, you can enjoy everything, *but* deprived of the substance which makes it dangerous. (This is also Last Man's revolution—'revolution without revolution'.) Is this not one of the two versions of Lacan's anti-Dostoevsky motto 'If God doesn't exist, everything is prohibited'? (1) God is dead, we live in a permissive universe, you should strive for pleasures and happiness—but, in order to have a life full of happiness and pleasures, you should avoid dangerous excesses, so everything is prohibited if it is not deprived of its substance; (2) If God is dead, superego enjoins you to enjoy, but every determinate enjoyment is already a betrayal of the unconditional one, so it should be prohibited. The nutritive version of this is to enjoy directly the Thing Itself: why bother with coffee? Inject caffeine directly into your blood! Why bother with sensual perceptions and excitations by external reality? Take drugs which directly affect your brain! And if there is God, then everything is permitted—to those who claim to act directly on behalf of God, as the instruments of his will; clearly, a direct link to God justifies our violation of any 'merely human' constraints and considerations (as in Stalinism, where the reference to the big Other of historical Necessity justifies absolute ruthlessness).

Today's hedonism combines pleasure with constraint—it is no longer the old notion of the 'right measure' between pleasure and constraint, but a kind of pseudo-Hegelian immediate coincidence of the opposites: action and reaction should coincide, the very thing which causes damage should already be the medicine. The ultimate example of it is arguably a chocolate laxative, available in the US, with the paradoxical injunction: 'Do you have constipation? Eat more of this chocolate!', i.e. more of the very thing which causes constipation. And is not a negative proof of the hegemony of this stance the fact that true unconstrained consumption (in all its main forms: drugs, free sex, smoking . . .) is emerging as the main danger? The fight against these dangers is one of the main investments of today's 'biopolitics'. Solutions are here desperately sought which would reproduce the paradox of the chocolate laxative. The main contender is 'safe sex'—a term which makes one appreciative of the truth of the old saying 'Is having sex with a condom not like taking a shower with a raincoat on?' The ultimate goal would be here, along the lines of decaffeinated coffee, to invent 'opium without opium': no wonder marihuana is so popular among liberals who want to legalize it—it already *is* a kind of 'opium without opium'.

And one cannot avoid this deadlock by way of distinguishing the 'common' hedonism and the allegedly 'higher' spiritual self-fulfilment. The lesson of the recent events in Bhutan, the model for Shangri-La, is here very instructive. In 1998, the Dragon King of Bhutan defined his nation's guiding principle as Gross National Happiness: as a country ruled by spirituality, Bhutan should reject the Western materialist principle of Gross National Product as the measure of the success of society's development, and, rather, let itself be guided by the quest for spiritual true happiness. Debates ensued about what is happiness: a delegation from the foreign ministry sent abroad to investigate whether happiness could be measured, finally found a Dutch professor who, after a lifelong study, reached the conclusion that happiness equals $10,000 a year, the minimum on which one can live comfortably . . . The problem, of course, is the very concept of 'Gross National Happiness': what one can measure in one way or another is its opposite, a 'Net National Happiness' defined in precise positive quantified terms, and the gap which separates the two is filled in by what Lacan called 'object small a', the object-cause of desire which can disturb any direct correlation between (Net) Happiness and actual happiness. It is this 'X factor' which accounts for the strange result of a recent opinion poll in which a large sample of citizens of different countries was asked how happy they feel: the highest score was reached in Bangladesh, a poor, overpopulated country which every year suffers catastrophic floods, and the lowest score by Germany, one of the few countries with a surviving Welfare State mechanism and one of the usual contenders for the top post in the competition for the highest quality of life. What this means is not that one should renounce universality in politics, endorsing the 'deep' insight into how there are no universal standards—in Kantian terms, the conclusion should just be that one should not search for universality at the level of 'pathological' (contingent and contextually dependent) notions such as 'happiness'.

The structure of the 'chocolate laxative', of a product containing the agent of its own containment, can be discerned throughout today's ideological landscape. There are two topics which determine today's liberal tolerant attitude towards Others: the respect of Otherness, openness towards it, *and* the obsessive fear of harassment—in short, the Other is OK in so far as its presence is not intrusive, in so far as the Other is not really Other . . . In strict homology with the paradoxical structure of chocolate laxative, tolerance of this coincides with its opposite: my duty to be tolerant towards the Other effectively means that I should not get too close to him, not intrude into his/her space—in short, that I should respect his/her *intolerance* towards my over-proximity. This is what is more and more emerging as the central 'human right' in late-capitalist society: the right not to be 'harassed', i.e. to be kept at a safe distance from the others. A similar structure is clearly present in how we relate to capitalist profiteering: it is OK *if* it is counteracted with charitable activities—first you amass billions, then you return (part of) them to the needy . . . And does the same not hold more and more even for democracy and human rights: human rights are OK if they are 'rethought' to include torture and a permanent emergency state, democracy is OK if it is cleansed of its populist 'excesses' and limited to those 'mature' enough to practise it . . . This same structure of chocolate laxative is also what makes a figure such as George Soros ethically so repulsive: does he not stand for the most ruthless financial speculative exploitation combined with its counter-agent, the humanitarian worry about the catastrophic social consequences of the unbridled market economy? Soros's very daily routine is a lie embodied: half his working time is devoted to financial speculations, and the other half to 'humanitarian' activities (providing finances for cultural and democratic activities in post-Communist countries, writing essays and books) which ultimately fight the effects of his own speculations . . .

Two motifs characterize today's ideological constellation: that of the reduction of humans to bare life, to *homo sacer* as the object of expert caretaking knowledge; and that of the respect for the vulnerable Other brought to extreme, of the attitude of narcissistic subjectivity which experiences itself as vulnerable, constantly exposed to a multitude of potential 'harassments'. Is there a stronger contrast than the one between the respect for the Other's vulnerability and the reduction of the Other to 'mere life' regulated by administrative knowledge? But what if these two stances nonetheless rely on the same root, what if they are the two aspects of one and the same underlying attitude, what if they coincide in what one is tempted to designate as the contemporary case of the Hegelian 'infinite judgement' which asserts the identity of opposites? What the two poles share is precisely the underlying refusal of any higher Causes, the notion that the ultimate goal of our lives is life itself. Nowhere is the complicity of these two levels clearer as in the case of the opposition to the death penalty— no wonder, since (violently putting another human being to) death is, quite logically, the ultimate traumatic point of biopolitics, the politics of the administration of life. To put it in Foucauldian terms, is the abolition of the death penalty not part of a certain 'biopolitics' which considers crime as the result of social, psychological, ideological, etc. circumstances: the notion of the morally/legally responsible subject is an ideological fiction whose function is to cover up the network of power relations, individuals are not responsible for the crimes they commit, so they should not be punished? Is, however, the obverse of this thesis not that those who control the circumstances control the people? No wonder the two strongest industrial complexes are today the military and the medical, that of destroying and that of prolonging life.

Nowhere is this complicity more clearly observable than in the case of war, with 'militaristic pacifism' as the ultimate case of the chocolate laxative: war is OK in so far as it really serves to bring about peace, or democracy, or to create conditions for distributing humanitarian help. It is against this background that one should judge the recent war in Iraq. One of Jacques Lacan's outrageous statements is that, even if what a jealous husband claims about his wife (that she sleeps around with other men) turns out to be true, his jealousy is still pathological. Along the same lines, one could say that, even if most of the Nazi claims about the Jews were true (they exploit Germans, they seduce German girls . . .), their anti-Semitism would still be (and was) pathological, since it represses the true reason *why* the Nazis *needed* anti-Semitism in order to sustain their ideological position. And, the same should be said today apropos of the US claim that 'Saddam has weapons of mass destruction!'—even if this claim is true (and it probably is, at least to some degree), it is still false with regard to the position from which it is enunciated.

What one should resist apropos Iraq is thus the temptation of false pragmatism: 'A terrible dictator was overthrown, and why should that be bad?' Or, a more elaborate version: 'After the Communist attempts to do good, which ended with catastrophic results, is it not preferable to do something which is perhaps wrongly motivated (by oil, imperialist hegemony), but whose actual result is good?' Michael Ignatieff recently wrote: 'For me the key issue is what would be the best result for the Iraqi people—what is most likely to improve the human rights of 26 million Iraqis? What always drove me crazy about the opposition [to war] was that it was never about Iraq. It was a referendum on American power'. The same point was made by Paul Berman: 'What we need to do is try and persuade people that this is not a war about Bush but about totalitarianism in the Middle East.' One should counter such statements with a naive question: do Ignatieff and Berman seriously believe that the US attack on Iraq was motivated by the desire 'to improve the human rights of 26 million Iraqis'? Even if the improvement of life for Iraqis may be a welcome 'collateral damage' of the overthrow of Saddam's regime, can any serious analysis permit itself to forget the global context of the attack on Iraq, the new rules of international life that were exemplified and imposed by this attack? *This*, not any sympathy for Saddam, and also not any abstract pacifism, was what moved millions in Western Europe to demonstrate against the war. In their recent *The War Over Iraq*, William Kristol and Lawrence F. Kaplan wrote, 'The mission begins in Baghdad, but it does not end there. [. . .] We stand at the cusp of a new historical era. [. . .] This is a decisive moment. [. . .] It is so clearly about more than Iraq. It is about more even than the future of the Middle East and the war on terror. It is about what sort of role the United States intends to play in the twenty-first century.' One cannot but agree with that: it is effectively the future of the international community that is at stake now—the new rules that will regulate it, what the new world order will be.

On 11 September, 2001, the Twin Towers were hit. Twelve years earlier, on 9 November, 1989, the Berlin Wall fell. The date 9 November announced the 'happy nineties', the Francis Fukuyama dream of the 'end of history', the belief that liberal democracy had, in principle, won, that the search is over, that the advent of a global, liberal world community lurks just around the corner, that the obstacles to this ultra-Hollywood happy ending are merely empirical and contingent (local pockets of resistance where the leaders did not yet grasp that their time is over). In contrast to it, 9/11 is the main symbol of the end of the Clintonite happy nineties, of the forthcoming era in which new walls are emerging everywhere, between Israel and the West Bank, around the European Union, on the US–Mexico border. The prospect of a new global crisis is looming: economic collapses, military and other catastrophes, states of emergency . . .

The true dangers are thus the long-term ones. Are we aware that we are in the midst of a 'soft revolution', in the course of which the unwritten rules determining the most elementary international logic are changing? The exemplary role of the 'war on terror' prisoners held in Guantanamo resides in the fact that their status is directly that of *homo sacer*: there are no legal rules regulating it, they find themselves literally in a legal void, reduced to bare life. And is not the brutal intervention of the Russian police into the Moscow theatre, killing more of their own people than of the Chechen 'terrorists', a clear indication of the fact that we are *all* potentially *homo sacer*: it is not that some of us are full citizens while others are excluded—an unexpected state of emergency can exclude *every one* of us. This parallel is more tell-tale than it may appear: in August 2003, it was reported that the Russian government plans to revive one of the most ominous features of Stalinism, local committees keeping an eye on people and reporting any 'unusual' activities or persons—do some recent initiatives from the US not point in the same direction? Along the same lines, back in 2002, John Ashcroft unveiled a new and expanded mission for the Neighbourhood Watch Program. Up to now, Neighbourhood Watch has been a fairly low-key crime-prevention tool focused on break-ins and burglaries; now, the Bush administration has earmarked it for a broader role—surveillance in the service of the 'war on terrorism'—asking neighbourhood groups to report on people who are 'unfamiliar' or who act in ways that are 'suspicious' or 'not normal'.

However, when we focus on such measures, one should thoroughly reject the standard liberal attitude of criticizing them principally as a threat to individual freedoms, in accordance with the boring alternative 'how much freedom should we sacrifice in our defence of freedom against the terrorist threat?'—at this level, one should fully and shamelessly endorse the good old 'totalitarian' motto of the Jacobins: 'No freedom for the enemies of freedom!' Is, from a radical emancipatory perspective, 'freedom' effectively the highest and untouchable point of reference? Is, on the contrary, the notion of freedom not so deeply caught in structurally necessary ambiguities that it should *always* be viewed with basic suspicion? Every old Leftist remembers Marx's reply, in the Communist Manifesto, to the critics who reproached the Communists for the undermining of family, property, etc.: it is the capitalist order itself whose economic dynamics is destroying the traditional family order (incidentally, a fact more true today than in Marx's time), as well as expropriating the large majority of the population. In the same vein, is it not that precisely those who pose today as global defenders of democracy are effectively undermining it?

More than a year ago, Jonathan Alter and Alan Derschowitz proposed to 'rethink' human rights so that they include torture (of suspected terrorists). In *The Future of Freedom*, Fareed Zakaria, Bush's favoured columnist, already draws a more general conclusion: he locates the threat to freedom in 'overdoing democracy', i.e. in the rise of 'illiberal democracy at home and abroad' (the book's subtitle). The immediate lesson from his book for Iraq is clear and unambiguous: yes, the US should bring democracy to Iraq, but not impose it immediately—there should first be a period of five or so years in which a benevolently authoritarian US-dominated regime would create proper conditions for the effective functioning of democracy . . . We know now what bringing democracy means: it means that the US and its 'willing partners' impose themselves as the ultimate judges who decide if a country is ripe for democracy—along these lines, Rumsfeld stated in April 2003 that Iran should not become a 'theocracy', but a tolerant secular country in which all religions and ethnic groups will enjoy the same rights—one is tempted to add here: 'What about demanding the same from Israel?' The further paradox of Zakaria's argument is that there is one case which should serve as its perfect example—that of China. Is the opposition between China and the late USSR not precisely the opposition between the authoritarian regime destined to create the conditions for capitalist development and a too fast shift to democracy which misfired? So should Zakaria not support the notorious crackdown on Tien-An-Men square?

The exemplary economic strategy of today's capitalism is outsourcing—giving over the 'dirty' process of material production (but also publicity, design, accountancy, etc.) to another company via a subcontract. In this way, one can easily avoid ecological and health rules: the production is done in, say, Indonesia where the ecological and health regulations are much lower than in the West, and the Western global company which owns the logo can claim that it is not responsible for the violations of another company. Are we not getting something homologous with regard to torture? Is torture also not being 'outsourced', left to the Third World allies of the US who can do it without worrying about legal problems or public protest? Was such outsourcing not explicitly advocated by Jonathan Alter in *Newsweek* immediately after 9/11? After stating that 'we can't legalize torture; it's contrary to American values', he nonetheless concludes that 'we'll have to think about transferring some suspects to our less squeamish allies, even if that's hypocritical. Nobody said this was going to be pretty.' This is how, today, the First World democracy more and more functions: by way of 'outsourcing' its dirty underside to other countries.

The danger of this 'soft revolution' can be best exemplified by the strange logic of how we accommodate ourselves to catastrophes. In his 'Two Sources of Morality and Religion', Henri Bergson describes the strange sensations he experienced on 4 August 1914, when war was declared between France and Germany: 'In spite of my turmoil, and although a war, even a victorious one, appeared to me as a catastrophe, I experienced what [William] James spoke about, a feeling of admiration for the facility of the passage from the abstract to the concrete: who would have thought that such a formidable event can emerge in reality with so little fuss?' Crucial here is the modality of the break between before and after: before its outburst, the war appeared to Bergson 'simultaneously probable and impossible: a complex and contradictory notion which persisted to the end'; after its outburst, it all of a sudden became real *and* possible, and the paradox resides in this retroactive appearance of probability:

I never pretended that one can insert reality into the past and thus work backwards in time. However, one can without any doubt insert there the possible, or, rather, at every moment, the possible inserts itself there. Insofar as unpredictable and new reality creates itself, its image reflects itself behind itself in the indefinite past: this new reality finds itself all the time having been possible; but it is only at the precise moment of its actual emergence that it begins to always have been, and this is why I say that its possibility, which does not precede its reality, will have preceded it once this reality emerges.

The encounter of the real as impossible is thus always missed: either it is experienced as impossible but not real (the prospect of a forthcoming catastrophe which, however probable we know it is, we do not believe will effectively occur and thus dismiss as impossible), or as real but no longer impossible (once the catastrophe occurs, it is 'renormalized', perceived as part of the normal run of things, as always already having been possible). The gap which makes these paradoxes possible is the one between knowledge and belief: we *know* the catastrophe is possible, probable even, yet we do not *believe* it will really happen. And is this not what is happening today, right in front of our eyes? A decade ago, the public debate on torture or the participation of the neo-Fascist parties in a West European democratic government was dismissed as an ethical catastrophe which is impossible, which 'really cannot happen'; once it happened, it retroactively grounded its own possibility, and we immediately got accustomed to it . . . *his* is the true threat today.

Response to Slavoj Zizek, 'Against an Ideology of Human Rights'

Michael Ignatieff

In what conditions, Zizek asks, do individuals experience themselves as subjects of universal human rights? He gives a standard Marxist answer: in a society in which commodity exchange predominates. Zizek's claim that human rights begin with commodity capitalism isn't worth much as history. A more apposite historical explanation would be that human rights originate as a response by humanist theorists to the European religious wars of the sixteenth and seventeenth centuries. In a thinker such as Hugo Grotius, for example, natural law figures as a way of theorizing the possibilities of social cooperation for a world of states and peoples sundered in two by the Protestant schism. Capitalism doesn't have all that much to do with the story, but since Zizek doesn't show any sustained interest in the historical story, I shall not pursue it here.

Human rights are the rights people have by virtue of being human, and the need to articulate these rights and defend them arises in two basic conditions: when dependent or subject peoples are abused and lack any remedies within their state to defend themselves, or when they have rights within their states but these are ignored or violated by their own authorities. Thus people experience themselves as the subjects of human rights—and make claims against others—when they are being beaten, tortured, abused, imprisoned, humiliated, expelled; in short, when they experience unmerited cruelty.

Zizek doesn't have anything to say about cruelty, or about the ways in which being treated with cruelty leads people to seek a language of justice to ground an entitlement to remedy. Such a language is to be found in human rights. While the idea of human rights originates in Western liberal democratic societies it has become a universal language because it validates individual and collective claims to dignity and justice.

Zizek admits that rights, once proclaimed in the abstract, have been taken up by a succession of excluded groups— working men without property, women, blacks, colonial peoples, and now gay individuals—because rights language has a 'symbolic effectivity' all its own. Zizek wants to think of human rights as being the ideological export of an oppressive liberal imperial elite, but the reality is at least more complicated. The global diffusion of human rights owes at least as much to its 'symbolic effectivity' on behalf of the oppressed.

It is true, as Zizek says, that human rights is a very abstract kind of humanism indeed. But this doesn't have very much to do with capitalism, its abstract, quantifying, 'everything has its price' mode of thought. Human rights remain abstract—as statute law does not—because there are so few enforceable remedies for human rights claims. Human rights remain verbiage because states do not want to enforce them, and resist attempts by other states to enforce them across borders. Explaining non-enforcement requires thinking about the powerful groups within states that resist enforcement. Landed proprietors do not want farm labourers to have property in land; tyrants do not want their opposition to have rights defensible at law; patriarchal men do not want women to work outside the house or have the vote. Everywhere human rights provide the central legitimizing claim for determinate social struggles: the Palestinian claim to land; the Israeli counter-claim to their own territory; the female claim to equality; the claim by gays for equality of marriage rights.

Zizek has nothing to say about the place of human rights in validating these struggles. Because he has nothing to say about these struggles, he has nothing to say about what human rights are for, what they do, and why they have value.

One would have thought struggle would appeal to Zizek, but he prefers to use the term *jouissance*. This term allows him to set up an opposition between *jouissance*—forbidden and emancipatory pleasure—and the liberal Puritans and their chocolate laxatives and anti-smoking campaigns. The real object of Zizek's bile is liberals. In his text, liberals are hypocritical tyrants: preaching tolerance but contemptuous of social difference, defending freedom yet imposing the clamp of political correctness on all political discussion. Needless to say, Zizek is all for sticky and emancipatory pleasures, while liberals are all for prohibition. This is liberalism caricatured from the Left and it has no more truth than the liberalism caricatured from the Right.

Reading Zizek one would have no idea that there are liberals—John Stuart Mill or Isaiah Berlin, for example—who were as opposed to bullying political correctness as he is. Mill's *On Liberty* and Berlin's *Two Concepts of Liberty* were perfectly clear that liberty is not liberty unless individuals are free to go to hell, i.e. to seek Zizek's *jouissance*, in any way that does not actively harm anybody else.

Zizek's dislike of liberalism draws from two musty nineteenth-century museums of anti-liberal prejudice: Marx's contempt for bourgeois democracy and Nietzsche's contempt for all forms of liberal pragmatism.

Democracy, Zizek rants, 'is the reign of sophists'. Then, quoting that arch-sophist, Vladimir Ilych Lenin, he calls for a realm of truth in politics, backed up by a right to truth. Lenin does not figure here by accident. Zizek is devoutly Leninist in his argument that 'human rights are ultimately, at their core, simply the rights to violate the Ten Commandments'. Thus the right to privacy shields adultery, freedom of the press validates a right to lie, freedom of religious belief entails the right to celebrate false gods. All this is spoken like a true commissar. Vladimir Ilych and his epigones did away with all rights on exactly this sort of reasoning.

Rights do two things, neither of which Zizek seems to grasp. First, they set limits to government power, and arose, historically, from specific historical struggles to create a limited, i.e. constitutional government. Second, they set out the rules for civil society, for the interaction of groups and individuals. The chief of these rules is tolerance. Zizek sees liberal tolerance as a synonym either for indifference or for condescension. Zizek doesn't like Western forms of multicultural tolerance because they lack warmth, good feeling, mutual *jouissance*, and so on. In his mind, something disreputable clings to the very idea that people might not want to spend time together and prefer instead the distance of live and let live. His irony about liberal multiculturalism seems to express nostalgia for an 'emancipatory' communitarianism that, had he thought about it for a second, might turn out to be more hostile to errant individual pleasure than anything his censorious liberals could devise.

The polemic against liberal tolerance is so poorly argued and structured that it is anybody's guess what Zizek believes it has to do with the ideology of human rights or with his polemic against liberal interventionism in Kosovo and Iraq. As far as one can gather, Zizek wants to say that intolerance at home breeds intolerant liberal interventionism abroad.

Zizek doesn't mind the coercive use of force—no erstwhile Leninist wants to be seen as a pacifist—but he hates the humanism, incarnated in Vaclav Havel, which tries to legitimize force in the language of conscience. The problem with Zizek's position is that it simply isn't possible to ignore the human rights violations of the Milošević regime in Kosovo or Saddam Hussein in Iraq if one wishes to understand why intervention occurred in these places at all. One can maintain that without the abuses committed by Milošević and by Hussein, the interventions in question would not have occurred, without being committed to the claim that the abuses were the 'real' or originating reason why they occurred. Other geo-strategic factors were unquestionably in play besides human rights. In Kosovo, the US intervened to reassert US leadership over the NATO alliance in Europe. In Iraq, the intervention was driven by false intelligence about the extent of Saddam's weapons of mass destruction, by a desire to create a pro-American regime at the head of the Gulf and so on.

At no time did those who supported the Iraq war on human rights grounds fail to see that these other factors were the more important motive. Zizek makes much of our naivety, but while we may have been mistaken, we were not naive. We supported the war because we believed its consequences would improve the human rights of ordinary Iraqis, even as we understand that these consequences were secondary to the intentions of those who initiated the war.

Moreover, the human rights record of the Saddam regime was crucial to assessing whether his acquisition of weapons of mass destruction made him dangerous. Had Saddam not gassed and tortured his people, as well as invading two neighbouring states, the US intervention would not have occurred.

The fact that he used chemical weapons against his own people was central to the assessment of whether he should or should not be overthrown by force. No one on my side of the argument supposed that human rights arguments were sufficient in themselves, or that they motivated those in positions of power. What we did suppose was that a regime that gasses its own people is a danger to the international system. Human rights was thus central to the assessment of regime dangerousness, and it was on this basis that we decided to support the operation. Needless to say, events in Iraq—the ongoing insurgency, the terrorist attacks on civilians, the many failures of the US occupation—have failed to deliver any obvious or demonstrable improvement in the human rights situation in Iraq. Yet it remains the case, at least with me, that I could not have joined the millions of Europeans marching against the war in February 2003, for their position, in its consequences if not in its intentions, would have left Saddam and his regime in power. I thought this was saving your own moral skin at the expense of others, and I thought it was better to take the risks of intervention instead than leave the Iraqi people under a tyranny of indefinite duration. Certainly, Zizek is right to be concerned about the nefarious use of human rights arguments by powerful states as a legitimizing cover for invading other states. But of equal concern is an abstract and entirely rhetorical commitment to human rights which stops short of taking any actual historical risk to defend them when they are being systematically abused.

3

Strangers in Our Midst: In Search of Seven Pillars of Wisdom

Ali A. Mazrui

The year 2004 marks the ninetieth anniversary of the out-break of World War I which resulted in the collapse of Islam's last great imperial order. The story of Islam's relationship with the Western world in the last one hundred years can be viewed as a transition from the final collapse of the Ottomans to the spectacular rise of the American empire.

The decision of the Young Turk Triumvirate to enter World War I on the side of Germany and Austria unleashed forces which were going to affect the Muslim world for the rest of the twentieth century and beyond.[1] As the Ottomans were being defeated, Lord Balfour, then British Foreign Secretary, issued his historic Balfour Declaration expressing British support 'for the establishment in Palestine of a national home for the Jewish people'. The declaration was affirmed in a letter from Arthur James Balfour to Lionel Walter Rothschild, the second Baron Rothschild, a leader of British Jewry.[2] Lord Balfour little realized that he was setting the stage for the most enduring conflict between Muslims and Westerners since the eighth crusade led by King Louis IX in the thirteenth century.[3] Some have even argued that the Arab and Muslim struggle against political Zionism is the belated nineteenth crusade for the control of the Holy Land. In some of the medieval crusades Muslims and Jews were on the same side against the Christian invaders. From the Balfour Declaration onwards the new crusade has been a case of support for Jewish occupation and displacement of Muslims. After all, the Balfour Declaration was a friendly exchange between a Christian aristocrat (Balfour) and a Jewish aristocrat (Rothschild) at the expense of an Arab people.

Enter T. E. Lawrence, otherwise known as Lawrence of Arabia![4] He had been commissioned into the British security forces in 1914 and was officially attached to the Hejaz Expeditionary Force under the command of General Wingate. His mission was to unite the Arabs, not against the emerging force of Zionism but against the older adversary of Ottoman occupation. Lawrence promised the Arabs that if they united and revolted against the Turks, Arab freedom and a united Arab nation would be supported by Great Britain.[5] T. E. Lawrence was sincere in wanting to help the Arabs become a free and united people. But Lawrence's country, the United Kingdom, was far less sincere. Great Britain encouraged the Arab revolt against the Ottomans as one of the strategies of winning World War I. Once the Ottoman Empire collapsed, Arab countries became the loot of the victorious European powers. Much of the Arab world fell under European rule either as outright colonies, or as protectorates, or as Mandates of the League of Nations.[6] That included Palestine, which fell under British administration, ostensibly answerable to the League of Nations. The ghost of Lord Balfour hovered over the British mandate in Palestine. British trusteeship failed to protect the freedom and integrity of the Palestinian people—with long-term disastrous consequences for the history of the world.

Had Lawrence's dream of a united Arab nation materialized, perhaps Palestine would never have been partitioned. Alternatively, if Lawrence and Great Britain had failed to destroy the last great Muslim empire in history, subsequent relations between Islam and the West might have been less acrimonious. What the Arabs had needed was liberation from the Turks without recolonization by the British, the French and subsequently the Americans. The Arabs did succeed in jumping out of the Ottoman frying pan—but only to fall into the fires of Euro-American domination.

According to Lawrence, freedom itself is 'the seven-pillared worthy house', a structure of glory resting on seven pillars. But Lawrence knew that in the Bible the seven pillars upheld the house not of Freedom but of Wisdom. In the words of the Book of Proverbs (9: 1): 'Wisdom hath builded a house: she hath hewn out her seven pillars.'[7] Lawrence wrote his book, *Seven Pillars of Freedom* partly at All Souls College, Oxford. He had lost much of his draft at Reading Station, while changing trains in the Christmas season in 1919.[8] Three years later All Souls hosted Lawrence to help him complete his book. This remarkable stranger among the Arabs was only one of the actors who helped to change the relationship between the Arabs and the West. But perhaps Lawrence was the most romantic of all the relevant actors. To use his own words:

All men dream but not equally. Those who dream by night in the dusty recesses of their minds wake in the day to find that it was vanity: but the dreamers of the day are dangerous men, for they may act their dream with open eyes, and make it possible. This I did. I meant to make a new nation, to restore a lost influence, to give twenty millions of Semites the foundations on which to build their national thoughts.[9]

Lawrence saw the Arab liberation fighters as responding to what he called 'the inherent nobility of their minds'. Lawrence felt that the Arabs were betrayed for the sake of what he called 'the British petrol royalties in Mesopotamia', an old name for

Iraq. Lawrence lamented, 'We pay for these things too much in honour and in innocent lives . . . Arab help was necessary to our cheap and speedy victory in the East, and that better to win and break our word than lose.'[10] Lawrence tried to reject honours and rewards for his role in the Arab revolt.[11] He was so ashamed of the British adulation of 'Lawrence of Arabia' that he even changed his name for a while to T. E. Shaw.[12] While the British and the French were fragmenting the Arab world, a British imperial presence was astride Iraq, Kuwait, Jordan, and the Gulf as a whole, in addition to the older British occupation of Egypt. A French imperial presence was astride Syria and Lebanon, as well as the older French colonization of the Maghreb in North Africa. As for the legacy of the Balfour Declaration, it was increasingly interpreted as a green light for Zionist ambitions in spite of Lord Balfour's proviso that 'nothing shall be done which may prejudice the civil and religious rights of existing non-Jewish communities'.[13]

The old allegory of the camel and the Arab's tent assumed the dimensions of a political allegory. It was cold in the desert at night. The camel begged the Arab to permit its head to enter into the tent for shelter and warmth. The Arab thought compassionately about a stranger in distress. Then the camel asked for shelter in the tent for its neck. Then the camel's shoulders begged for shelter. By the time the camel was asking for shelter for its second hump, there was little room left in the tent for the original Arab occupant in the tent. The camel was the Zionist movement. The tent was Palestine. Lord Balfour was being invoked to strengthen the Zionist movement. Hundreds of thousands of Palestinians were subsequently displaced! A new heritage of hate was created.

The collapse of the Ottoman Empire had also resulted in the collapse of the Islamic caliphate for the first time in thirteen centuries. Turkey, which had been the strongest link of Muslim solidarity under the Ottomans, became instead the strongest expression of neo-Muslim secularism under the new Turkish Republic. The ending of the caliphate deprived Muslims of a global institution of shared allegiance. The political secularization of Ataturk's Turkey also deprived the Muslim *ummah* of the strongest Muslim military power in the Middle East.[14] The negative long-term consequences of World War I for the Muslim world continued to pile up.

But it was not just the Ottoman Empire which collapsed after World War I. It was also the German Empire in Africa under the Kaiser. And just as Ottoman rule in the Arab world was rapidly replaced by British and French imperialism, so was the German empire in Tanganyika, Ruanda-Urundi, South West Africa, Cameroon and Togoland rapidly replaced by mandates administered by Britain, France, Belgium, and White South Africans.[15] Like Arab subjects of the Ottoman Empire, African subjects of German colonies fell out of the frying pan of one empire into the fires of an alternative imperial order.

By the end of the twentieth century all of Africa and most of the Arab world were at least nominally independent of old-style colonialism. But a whole new phenomenon had emerged—a different kind of empire under the United States of America.[16] The end of the Cold War had ended older concepts such as 'balance of power'. The world had lost its global checks and balances. The United States had become the mightiest power in human history. It certainly had more military might than the next ten countries added together. Economically it is in a class by itself. It is taking more than a dozen European countries to constitute a union which could adequately challenge the economic influence and power of the United States. This mighty country was still a democracy at home in spite of the recent erosion of civil liberties since September 11th.[17] Domestically the United States does have a system of checks and balances. But externally the United States has become an empire, only marginally subject to checks and balances. Domestically the American system is still predicated on rights. Internationally American behaviour is predicated increasingly on might.

The greatest military casualties of the new Pax Americana are Muslims. The greatest economic casualties of an American-led globalization are Africans. The rules and priorities of a globalizing international economy are leaving Africans more and more marginalized. The erosion of rules in the use of military power is leaving Muslim countries more and more vulnerable to Pax Americana. In the face of this new international disequilibrium, humanity needs a new Global Ethic. There is a compelling need for new criteria of right and wrong across civilizations. One approach is to rediscover the seven pillars of wisdom and redefine them in the context of the new imbalances in the world system.

In this chapter, I use the term 'strangers in our midst' to refer to people who we do not regard as part of the 'we' in the we/they equation. Their identity is perceived as different— either by race, religion, ethnicity, nationality, gender, or some other criteria of differentiation. The search for a global ethic is partly a search for how to deal with 'strangers in our midst' ethically and in solidarity. The human race needs to identify seven principles. Every civilization in the world has elements which can be used to consolidate those principles of a global ethic. In this chapter I shall use two civilizations as case studies—Islamic and African values. How can these two civilizations contribute to the pillars of the new global ethic?

Seven Pillars of a New Global Ethic

1. Tolerance and Minimization of Violence

Which of the values of Africa and Islam are supportive of tolerance? Both Africa and the Muslim world seem to be conflict-prone. Does not conflict signify a breakdown in tolerance? The behaviour of every people is only partially determined by the ethical standards of its culture. Some cultures are born intolerant, some become intolerant, and some have intolerance thrust upon them. How much of the violence in the Muslim world is native-born and how much has been thrust upon Muslims?

At the present time, there are three Muslim countries under military occupation—Iraq, Afghanistan, and Palestine. There are other Muslim populations forcefully and sometimes brutally integrated into wider state systems. This includes the Chechens under Russian occupation, the Kashmiris under Indian rule, and the ethnic Albanians in Kosovo under international trusteeship with no hope of self-determination. In the last three years at least two hundred thousand Muslims have been killed in Afghanistan, Iraq, Gujarat, Kashmir, Palestine, and Chechnya. In the period since the 1991 Gulf War, we may have to add a million more killed by United Nations sanctions in Iraq and by Serbian brutalities in Bosnia, Kosovo, and elsewhere, and by the merciless Israeli occupation of the West Bank and Gaza. Counting the number of dead in the world as a whole since 1990, Muslims are a people more sinned against than sinning.

But there is a lot in the ethical code of Islam which recommends forgiveness and compensation rather than revenge. In chapter 2, *Surat el Baqara*, the Qur'an does not recommend turning the other cheek. It does allow for the legitimacy of retaliation (*Al-Qisas*) if the injustice is clear, but the sura recommends compensation and forgiveness as a better alternative. For instance:

> O believers, ordained for you is retribution
> For the murdered
> (Whether) a free man is (guilty)
> Of (the murder of) a free man, or a slave of a slave
> Or a woman of a woman
> But he who is pardoned some of it by his brother
> Should be dealt with equity
> And recompense (for blood) paid with a smile.   (2: 178)[18]

Indeed, the same sura goes on to emphasize: 'Saying a word that is kind, and forgiving is better than charity that hurts' (2: 263).[19] And when the Prophet Muhammad conquered Mecca from the ruling Quraysh, he did not issue playing cards of the fifty most wanted Quraysh. He did not imprison thousands as some conquerors have done. The Prophet Muhammad conquered Mecca, granted amnesty to all Quraysh who entered the sacred mosque for asylum, or stayed peacefully in their homes, or found their way to the home of the paramount Quraysh leader, Abu Sufyan—Muhammad's former enemy.[20] As for the importance of asylum in Islam, it is captured in when the Islamic calendar begins. The Islamic calendar does not begin from when the Prophet Muhammad was born (the year 610 CE), but from when he secretly left Mecca in search of asylum in a safer place. The Hijjrah from Mecca to Medina in the Miladiyya year 610 was a quest for religious refuge. The whole Islamic calendar is therefore a celebration of asylum.[21]

In Africa's ethical code, tolerance is partly captured in Africa's short memory of hate. While Islam recommends compensation and forgiveness as a better response than retaliation, Africanity recommends a return to normality without hate after each conflict.[22] The Nigerian civil war of 1967–70 ended without reprisals and without an African equivalent of the Nuremberg trials.[23] Ian Smith unleashed a racial war on Zimbabwe and lived to sit in Zimbabwe's parliament and criticize the successor black regime.[24] Nelson Mandela lost twenty-seven of the best years of his life under a white racist regime, and emerged ready to have afternoon tea with the widow of the architect of apartheid, Mrs Verwoerd.[25] Jomo Kenyatta was imprisoned by the British and denounced by a British Governor as a 'leader unto darkness and death'. He emerged from detention and turned Kenya towards a pro-Western orientation in which it has tragically persisted. Kenyatta even published a book entitled *Suffering Without Bitterness*.[26] Africans fight deeply and passionately, sometimes ruthlessly, in defence of either their identities or their values. But when the fighting is over, African cultures have a low level of hate-retention. Potentially this could be part of Africa's contribution to the principle of tolerance in the global ethic.

2. Optimization of the Economic Well-Being of the People

The Muslim world has been privileged to have a disproportionate share of the oil wealth of the human race. Saudi Arabia is a country which accommodates the holiest sites of Islam (Mecca and Medina), but it is also a country which is blessed with the world's greatest oil reserves.[27] Iraq, which accommodates some of the holiest sites of Shia Islam, also accommodates the second largest oil reserves in the world. And the Organization of Petroleum-Exporting Countries is at least two-thirds Muslim in composition.[28] Traditional Islam is basically pro-profit but anti-interest. The oil wealth of the

Muslim world challenges Muslim believers to find out where legitimate economic returns end and illegitimate usury and exploitation begin. Ancient laws of *zakat* (religious tax) and *sadaqah* (charity) may need to be transformed for the age of petroleum. But the blessing of oil-wealth can also be the curse of vulnerability to the global strategy of the American empire.

African economic ethics go back to the concept of *ujamaa* in Julius K. Nyerere's prescription for post-colonial Tanzania. While the West in the twentieth century had evolved the concept of the welfare state, Africans had evolved even earlier the concept of the welfare tribe. Long before welfare socialism in Britain, Africa had developed a de facto system of collective responsibility for orphans, for the infirm, for the aged, and for the needy. African communities had historically looked after their most vulnerable members. From former German East Africa (Tanganyika), Julius K. Nyerere expanded this African sense of family (*ujamaa*) into the basis of the modern socialist ethic of sharing.[29] In this chapter, we go a step further and globalize *ujamaa* into an ethic for the human family as a whole.

3. Social Justice: Race

It is a struggle to reduce ethnic and racial inequalities and a quest for a more humane equilibrium. If in terms of political violence in the world Muslims are a people more sinned against than sinning, Africans are similarly so in terms of racial prejudice and discrimination. Black people across the centuries have been humiliated, enslaved, colonized, castrated, marginalized, and spat upon. The tormentors of black folks have sometimes been Muslims, sometimes Christians, sometimes others. Blacks have been racial victims par excellence.

The Qur'an tells Muslims that when confronting injustice,

reparation is often better than revenge. But black people are only just beginning to mention the word 'reparations' for outright enslavement or for the obscenities of apartheid. In 1992 a summit meeting of the Organization of African Unity appointed a Group of Eminent Persons to explore the modalities and strategies for claiming reparations for black enslavement. One of the biggest problems faced by this Reparations Committee is the relative lack of support from Africans themselves for the reparations crusade.[30] In terms of the global ethic perhaps there should be reparations for black people, just as there have been reparations for the Jewish people. But reparations can take different forms. For the Jews it consisted of capital transfer from Germany to Jewish survivors and to the State of Israel.[31] For black people another form of reparation could be skill-transfer—a major global effort in genuine capacity-building among devastated black people. A third kind of reparation could be *power sharing*—increasing African power in those institutions which have extra power over Africans. There should be increased African representation in the governing bodies of the World Bank and the International Monetary Fund, and a permanent seat for Africa on the Security Council.[32] These measures would constitute an attempt to empower Africans after centuries of enfeeblement. A new kind of black empowerment is symbolized by Secretary of State Colin Powell and National Security Adviser Condoleeza Rice of the United States. These are descendants of slaves who have come to wield power among white people who had once enslaved their ancestors. In other words, one form of reparation is the empowerment of black people in countries which had previously traded in slaves or practised slavery.

One day in the future, Africans and Arabs would need to

negotiate what kind of reparations are feasible for the Arab slave trade. Among the factors which make the Arab slave trade a different system is the Arab lineage system, which regards a child as Arab if the father is Arab, regardless of who the mother is. Thus Sheikh Saad Abdallah Salim al-Sabah has been Prime Minister of Kuwait though descended from a black mother. Anwar Saadat was President of Egypt and was not faulted for having a black mother. Prince Bandar bin Sultan could be a long-lasting distinguished Saudi Ambassador in Washington DC and be genealogically half African. There are millions of people of mixed blood in the Arab world who are classified as Arabs. This is vastly a different system from the United States where a child is black if either parent is black, even if the father is a White Anglo-Saxon Protestant (a WASP). In the royal houses of Kuwait and Saudi Arabia, where some of the princes have African mothers, which prince would pay reparations to which? A wholly different formula would have to be devised if any reparations were to be negotiated in the future concerning the Arab slave trade.

As for the position of the Islamic religion on the race question, it is arguable that Islam is the most racially egalitarian of all three Abrahamic religions—Judaism, Christianity, and Islam. Judaism has a doctrine of 'the Chosen People' which has often been genealogically interpreted. European Christianity has a long history of racial segregation, including the racial segregation of churches. Such church segregation has persisted to the present day in the United States.[33] To the best of our knowledge the twelve disciples of Jesus were all genealogically Hebrew. But the Prophet Muhammad's disciples—the Sahaba—were multicultural in composition, including the famous black Sahaba, Bilal son of Rabah, who was the first to call believers to prayer at the great Kaaba in Mecca when

Muslims reconquered it from the Quraysh. Bilal was a companion of the Prophet Muhammad, and is widely revered today as the first black man to embrace Islam.[34] The Qur'an tells Muslims that they have been created into nations and tribes mainly so that they could know each other:

> O men, we created you from a male and female
> And formed you into nations and tribes
> That you may recognize each other.   (49: 13)[35]

And the Prophet Muhammad is reported to have said to his followers, more explicitly: 'An Arab is not superior to a non-Arab, nor a red man to a black man except through piety and virtue'.[36]

Islam thus brings to the global ethic a doctrine of racial egalitarianism which goes back fourteen centuries. Where the historical record of Islam is less impressive is with regard to the fourth pillar of wisdom—equality between men and women. Let us turn to this issue of gender in the experience of both Muslims and Africans.

4. Social Justice: Gender

In addition to the disciplines of the clock, the calendar, the numerals, and the letters, has Islam also introduced into black Africa a new discipline of gender? Indigenous cultures in Africa gave more roles to women than Islam did, while Islam gave more rights to women than indigenous culture had.

On the whole, the gender discipline of Islam in black Africa had been negative. Under Islamic influence the roles of women in black Africa have become more restricted as compared with indigenous culture. But the rights of women in inheritance have improved further under Islam than under indigenous traditions. Women are owning more under Islam than under native customary law. But what about the role of women in the wider Islamic experience? Africans should pay attention to trends in the wider Muslim world.[37] Although the Prophet Muhammad's widow Ayesha set the precedent of Muslim women in combat roles on the battlefield, there is general consensus among Muslim jurists that killing women or children is beyond the pale.[38]

This has to be seen in the context of three varieties of sexism evident in human behaviour, not uniquely Islamic. Benevolent sexism is a form of gender discrimination which selectively favours the otherwise disadvantaged gender. For example, when in 1912 the captain of the Titanic decided that the limited space on the lifeboats was to be reserved for women and children, that was a form of benevolent sexism with which most cultures would agree. The safety of women and children came first.[39] Most cultures would also agree that while women may have a duty to die for their faith or for their country, women do not have a duty to kill for their faith or their country. Even in the West drafting women for direct combat has been culturally repugnant. Forcing women to go and kill has tended to be avoided in most cultures, including Western and Islamic, at least until recently.[40] In spite of Ayesha's role in the Battle of the Camel, benevolent sexism in Islam has spared women obligatory combat roles. African Muslim women have similarly been demilitarized, except perhaps in Somalia from time to time.

In addition to benevolent sexism, there is benign sexism. This benign sexism is of differentiation rather than of discrimination. A policy of different dress codes for men and women has been part of the sexism of differentiation in Islam.[41] There are different rules of modesty for male and female. In most cultures women are expected to cover more of their bodies than men.[42] The Swahili *buibui* is part of the local female dress code.

In addition to benevolent sexism and benign sexism, there is the third version of malignant sexism. This is the kind of gender discrimination which results in sexual exploitation, economic marginalization, cultural subordination, or political disempowerment. Although many Muslim countries are guilty of such versions of malignant sexism, there are paradoxes in the Muslim world. In no Muslim country are women more liberated than women are in the United States, but in some Muslim countries women have been more empowered than women have been in the United States. Currently, two Muslim countries outside Africa have women as heads of state or heads of government. Indonesia, the largest Muslim country in population, has a woman as President—Megawati Sukarnoputri. In Bangladesh, both the Head of Government and the leader of the Opposition have been women—Sheikh Hasina Wajed and Begum Khaleda Zia have alternated in political power for more than a decade. Two other Muslim countries outside Africa have had a woman chief executive at the top of the political process. Benazir Bhutto has been Prime Minister of Pakistan twice. And Tansu Ciller has been Prime Minister of Turkey, a far cry from the political culture of the Ottoman Empire. All these cases of Muslim women at the top have occurred long before the United States has had a woman president, or Germany a woman Chancellor, or Italy a woman Prime Minister, or Russia a woman President. But Asian Muslims have been ahead of Africans in this empowerment.

While serving as heads of government such Muslim women in those countries have been de facto Commanders-in-Chief.

Were they continuing in the tradition of the Prophet's widow
Ayesha in the middle of the Battle of the Camel way back in
the first century of the Hijrah calendar, the seventh century of
the Christian era? Have any of these Muslim women in power
had to contend with terrorism by fellow Muslims? Bangladesh
has had conflicts, coups, and assassinations over the years, but
neither Sheikh Hasina Wajed in power nor Begum Khaleda
Zia has had to fight terrorism. On the other hand, Megawati
Sukarnoputri in Indonesia has been under enormous pressure
to act against Islamic militants, especially since the devastating
terrorist bombs in the resort town of Bali.[43] Muslims are not
unique in resorting to terrorism in a bid to redress wrongs
perpetrated against them. But terrorism by Muslims gets far
more publicity as a rule than terrorism by others. What all
cultures and all religions are being forced to scrutinize more
closely than ever are the detailed ethics of terrorism. Black
Africa is caught up in the crossfire between Middle Eastern
militancy and the American war on terror.[44] In Eastern Africa,
Uganda has led the way in the political empowerment of
women. It was a Muslim President of Uganda, Field Marshall
Idi Amin, who appointed the first woman Foreign Minister in
Eastern Africa. This was two decades before Bill Clinton
appointed the first woman Secretary of State in American
history. Although appointed by a Muslim Head of State,
Foreign Minister Elizabeth Bagaya of Uganda was not herself
a Muslim. President Yoweri Museveni has since carried
female empowerment in Uganda even further. Uganda under
Museveni has known a woman Vice-President long before
the United States has had one. Yet once again the highest-
ranking Ugandan women have not yet been Muslims. In
Africa as a whole, the political empowerment of Muslim
women still has a long way to go, though military regimes

have sometimes opened more doors to women than have civilian governments.[45]

In the experience of both Muslims and Africans, the gender question is still problematical. But there are pluses as well as minuses in what these two civilizations can demonstrate to a human race still struggling to achieve gender equity.

5. Ecology and the Environment

Let us now turn to the environmental pillar of wisdom—the quest for ecological balance and the protection of the Earth against excessive exploitation and devastation. Muslims have often chosen green as the colour of Islam, partly because green was associated with peace. But from the middle of the twentieth century the colour green has also been adopted by environmental movements, by those who are committed to keep the hills and valleys of the Earth forever green. In this ecological sense we may indeed ask: how 'green' is Islam doctrinally and in practice?[46] And how ecology-friendly is African culture?[47]

Environmentally there is a remarkable contrast between the ancestral homeland of Islam and the ancestral core of sub-Saharan Africa. Islam was born in a region which was ecologically sparse and dry. Equatorial Africa, on the other hand, is a region of lush natural abundance, including equatorial forests. The Arabian peninsular as the birthplace of Islam is a region of limited natural rainfall and limited water supply.[48] Equatorial Africa, on the other hand, is a region of tropical downpours and some of the greatest rivers and lakes on the face of the earth. It is in that sense that the dry geography of Islamic origins and the abundant geography of equatorial Africa have represented striking contrasts in the ecological heritage of the Earth.

There is a related paradox with regard to the geographical origins of Islam. The Arabian lands which were so short of water during the Prophet Muhammad's time were destined to become lands of abundant oil fourteen centuries later. Lands which once celebrated oases of water became lands which celebrated oases of oil.[49] The greatest oil reserves were discovered beneath the ground where the Prophet and his companions once walked. A religion which taught its followers how to clean themselves with sand (*tayamam*) when they ran out of water later discovered God's petro-bounty beneath the sand.[50]

A more negative paradox about petroleum is the extent to which it has often been a threat to the 'greenness' of the Earth. While Arabia itself has been less environmentally damaged by petroleum than, say, Ogoniland in Nigeria, petrowealth in Saudi Arabia has been culturally corrosive.[51] Much of the pristine Islamicity of the Arabian Holy Land has been compromised by grotesque buildings and the glittering names of Western tourist hotels. The days of water shortage in Arabia were more spiritually authentic than the new era of the abundance of oil. Unlike Islam, Africa's traditional religion draws no sharp distinction about where the Creator ends and the Created begins. More clearly in African religion than in Islam, particular rivers and hills may be sacred, particular trees such as the baobab may be worthy of awe.[52] Islam has profane animals (especially the pig) but no sacred animals (such as the cow in Hinduism). African traditional religions, on the other hand, have both sacred and profane animals. Indeed, some African ethnic and clan cultures have totems which identify with particular animals (e.g. the owl totem for a clan, or a totem of the hippo or monkey).[53]

Sometimes the struggle against environmental degradation

and the struggle for morally accountable economies are inseparable. Particularly poignant in 1995 was the plight of the Ogoni people of Nigeria and the brutal fate of Ken Saro-Wiwa in the full glare of a Commonwealth conference in New Zealand.[54] The environment of the Ogoni villagers was devastated by the oil industry in their areas—and Ken Saro-Wiwa and eleven others were executed partly for protesting in ways unacceptable to the military in Nigeria.[55] The green revolution has also sought to protect the dwindling legacy of wild animals against the greed of hunters, poachers, and corrupt politicians. But is there also a danger that as far as Westerners are concerned, 'one hippo is worth two Hutus!'? In other words, are the agricultural and pastoral needs of Africa's expanding populations being sacrificed to the whims of nature lovers?[56]

There is a genuine dilemma. In many African countries, independence for African people has meant less freedom for African animals. Widening political horizons for African people have coincided with narrowing physical horizons for African animals. Post-colonial African authorities have been far less effective in protecting African animals than the colonial authorities had been. What nature lovers sometimes forget is that post-colonial African authorities have been less effective in protecting African people too. The cost of learning how to govern ourselves has sometimes been high. But we do need to learn self-government in any case. It is a stage we have to go through. On the other hand, the African animals have been lucky that the post-colonial era has coincided with the new ecological revolution. Post-coloniality has coincided with the rise of the green movements. While some human beings are indeed fast depleting the heritage of the Earth, other human beings are on greater ecological alert than ever before in history. Alexander Pope's couplet has been given a new ecological meaning: 'All are but parts of one stupendous whole | Whose body Nature is and God the Soul'.[57]

The environmental depletion is worse today than ever in history, but the environmental defenders are more active than ever before in history. On balance the Asian and African environments have suffered because of independence, but they would have suffered even more if the era of independence had not coincided with the newly energized environmental consciousness worldwide. The ethical revolution of environmentalism is partly helping to discipline the earlier ethical revolution of race. The struggle for the rights of people of colour is by no means over yet. But now there is concern for the rights of the leopard and the rhino, the rights of fish in the rivers and oceans, the green rights of valleys and hills. These two are 'strangers in our midst', deserving asylum.

The environmental revolution and the gender revolution are interlinked at various points. But they are interconnected most poignantly through the issue of population and the whole culture of having and rearing children. It is to this area of convergence between gender, population, and environment that we must now turn.

Many African countries have been witnessing their population double every twenty years. According to the latest *World Development Indicators*, in 2001 it was estimated that children under 15 years of age accounted for 44 per cent of the population of sub-Saharan Africa—as compared with 34.6 per cent in South Asia and 31.3 per cent in Latin America and the Caribbean.[58] Infant mortality is still very high. If we compare the performance on this measure of two poor regions with booming populations, South Asia and sub-Saharan Africa, the progress is depressing. Between 1980 and 2001, South Asia's infant mortality rate fell from 115 per thousand to 71 per thousand. In the same period, sub-Saharan Africa's rate fell from 118 to 105 per thousand. Sub-Saharan Africa's infant mortality rate is the highest in the world.[59] Africans have many children for a variety of reasons, including, on the one hand, the assumption that children are an insurance for old age when parents will need to be looked after and, on the other hand, the belief that children are (in African tradition) a passport to immortality beyond the grave: We are not dead as long as our blood flows in the veins of the living. This is the phase of *Sasa*: the living dead still being remembered by their descendants. Genes are a memory of ancestry.

6. Inter-Faith Relations: Gains and Losses

No global ethic is sustainable without involving the great religions of the world. How has the preceding century affected the chances and quality of inter-faith dialogue? In order to answer that question we need to return to the long-term consequences of World War I and the mission of T. E. Lawrence in the Middle East—the subject with which we opened this chapter.

We mentioned earlier that the collapse of the Ottoman Dynasty marked the last of the great Muslim empires in world history. It led to the end of the caliphate, which had been a symbol of Muslim solidarity for thirteen centuries. It led on to the secularization of Turkey, thus depriving the Muslim Middle East of a great military power. And in the course of World War I, and with the prospect of Ottoman defeat, Lord Balfour issued his momentous Declaration about a national home for the Jews. How World War I ended was one of the major causes of World War II. The humiliating conditions imposed on Germany created the sense of outrage there which facilitated the rise of Hitler.[60] In World War I, Germany had lost her African empire. In World War II under Hitler, Germany sought to create an empire in Europe.

How have these events affected inter-faith dialogue? Hitler's slaughter and brutalization of the Jews severely damaged relations between Christian churches and the Jews in the short run. But in the longer run the scale of the Holocaust and the martyrdom of the Jews under the Nazis brought Jews and Christians in the Western world closer together than they had ever been since the days of the Roman Empire. It is unlikely that Mel Gibson's film, *The Passion of the Christ*, would affect the *rapprochement*. One healthy reason for the Christian–Jewish drawing together was a heightened Western awareness of the evil dangers of ethno-religious bigotry. But there was an unhealthy reason also for the Christian–Jewish *rapprochement*. This was the enormity of guilt felt by Western Gentiles—a depth of guilt so great that Western support rapidly grew for the creation of a national home for the Jews, provided such a home was not created on European soil.

The Zionist movement had previously received offers of territory for Jewish settlement in Uganda, Kenya, and South America. These offers of other people's land for a national home for the Jews were made mainly by European leaders. Britain's Colonial Secretary Joseph Chamberlain offered parts of Uganda and Kenya to the Zionist movement early in the twentieth century.[61] What European leaders never offered European Jews was a piece of Europe for the creation of a national home for the Jews. Creating Israel on a piece of German territory after World War II would have been poetic justice indeed. Instead Palestinians paid the ultimate price for the atrocities and brutalities of the Nazis against the Jews. This diversion of 'the Jewish Question' from Europe to the Middle East helped Christian–Jewish *rapprochement* in Europe. Western Gentiles were so afraid of being accused of anti-Semitism that the State of Israel could do no wrong.[62] Never since Hitler's Germany had a state behaved with such impunity towards its neighbours as Israel has in recent decades. Ordinary citizens and the media in European countries have begun to raise their voices against Israel's brutal occupation of Palestine, but one keeps waiting for a public reprimand of Israel from a major Western leader.[63]

Unfortunately, the creation of Israel and its aftermath have created unprecedented stress between Muslims and Jews. Relations between the global *ummah* and world Jewry have probably never been under greater strain in fourteen centuries than they are today. Two major reasons have poisoned Muslim–Jewish understanding. One is the behaviour of the State of Israel. The second is the almost spontaneous tendency of world Jewry to rally behind Israel and attack those who criticize it. As Ian Buruma has said, 'Even legitimate criticism of Israel, or of Zionism, is often quickly denounced as anti-Semitism by various watchdogs.'[64]

Western sense of guilt over the Nazi Holocaust has on the whole helped relations between Christians and Jews, but Western appeasement of the Zionist movement has damaged relations between Muslims and Jews.[65] About ten years separated two documents of momentous consequences for the Middle East—one was, of course, the Balfour Declaration of 1917 and the other was Hitler's *Mein Kampf* of 1927. The Balfour Declaration was controversial but was in the tradition of 'the British fudge'. *Mein Kampf* was a work of evil. But in their vastly different ways the two documents unleashed forces which favoured the long-term aims of the Zionist movement. Israel was indeed created, and the world has never been the same since.

In the days of T. E. Lawrence, Jerusalem was 'sacred but squalid'. In the words of Lawrence of Arabia: 'Jerusalem was a squalid town which every Semitic religion has made holy. Christians and Mohammedans came here on pilgrimage to the shrines of their past, and some Jews looked to it for the political future of their race. These united forces of the past and the future were so strong that the city almost failed to have a present.'[66] Jerusalem is still excessively preoccupied with the past and the future. But it also has a present, however tumultuous and painful.[67]

We have argued that since the days of Lord Balfour and Hitler, relations between Christians and Jews have improved enormously, while relations between Muslims and Jews have deteriorated. But what about relations between Muslims and Christians? There has been some stress on relations between the Muslim world and the West, but the tensions are not between churches and mosques, but between Muslims and Western secular power. In this case the central cause of tension and hate is not Israel alone, but also the United States as a hegemonic power. America's pro-Israeli policies are part of the problem but not the only ones. Increasingly, in the course of the twentieth century the United States became a new kind of empire.[68] The new American empire is one not of occupation, but of control; not a land-hungry hegemony but a resource-hungry colossus. Militarily American might adds up to the military power of the next ten countries added together. According to one estimate, the United States has some 370,000 troops in nearly one hundred and twenty countries, providing it with awesome global reach.[69] In production, the American economy is the indispensable engine of the world economy. Technologically, the US is not only independently triumphant; it is also a major magnet of the technological expertise of the rest of the world. There was a time when the brain drain consisted of talented people migrating physically to the West. But now the technological skills of South Asians can be used by American industry without having to import the South Asians to the United States. The West is buying the brains of India without buying the bodies.[70]

Lord Lugard, Britain's greatest colonial administrator, devised a strategy for British colonial rule in Africa. Lugard called the policy 'Indirect Rule', which became the guiding principle of governance in British Africa. Lugard's idea was that the British should seek to rule Africans through their own 'native authorities' as much as possible. Subject peoples were best ruled through institutions and customs which they understood. But in the final analysis, British rule required the military might of Pax Britannica to keep control.[71] The question arises whether the new American empire is a latter-day case of Indirect Rule. Are 'native authorities' allowed to remain in power, but only as long as they do not stray far from the designs of Pax Americana? The new strategy of regime-change is the latter-day equivalent of destooling a recalcitrant African chief. The foreign policy of the United States seems to be driven by a latter-day Lord Lugard.

Iraq and Afghanistan have been invaded partly to effect regime-change. The United States sought to marginalize Yasser Arafat as a partial regime change in Palestine. Libya has given up its right to pursue weapons of mass destruction, perhaps partly out of fear of regime change. The Bush administration has recommended regime change in Iran. Israel has recommended regime change in Syria. This is becoming a

pattern of destooling uncompliant chiefs.[72] At least as distressing are the Muslim chiefs and emirs who are protected by
the United States against change. Many undemocratic Muslim
regimes derive part of their stability from the United States.[73]
A significant number of Muslim countries are de facto
American protectorates, although their people are against
American control.[74] Anti-Western sentiment in the Muslim
world is just a version of anti-American sentiment. Even the
new Anglophobia in the Muslim world is a derivation of
Blair-phobia—an angry disgust of Tony Blair. Blair seems
to be less afraid of regime change in Britain by the British
electorate than an imaginary regime change in Britain by
American power. The ominous shadow of George W. Bush is
upon Tony Blair.

Mainstream Christian churches in the West are much more
Muslim-friendly today than they were in the days of the
Ottoman Empire. But there are fringe evangelical movements
in the United States which have become more Islamophobic
than ever. The Prophet Mohammad has been given worse
names since September 11th than at any time since the days of
anti-Turkish sentiment at the beginning of the twentieth century.[75] Ironically, the Ottoman Empire had a more humane
system of autonomy for religious minorities (the millet
system) than that practised by any Western power either at
that time or since.

The contradictions have persisted from the old days of the
Ottoman Empire to the new era of the American empire. It is
arguable that while the Ottoman Empire was bad for the
Arabs, it was good for Islam in world affairs. T. E. Lawrence
helped the Arabs against the Ottomans, but he may at the
same time have harmed Islam in the long run. The Ottomans
had kept Turkey Muslim and independent of the West. The

Turkish Republic is making Turkey secular and part of the West. Turkish women have won the freedom to be members of Parliament, but they have lost the freedom to cover their heads with a scarf. Underlying it all is a monumental transition from the era of Lord Balfour as a representative of the old British Empire to George W. Bush as a symbol of the new American empire.

As for relations between Christianity and Islam in Africa, both religions are expanding in numbers and growing in influence. But can they coexist peacefully? Christianity and Islam are divisive in Africa only if they reinforce prior ethnic and linguistic divisions. In Nigeria, almost all Hausa are Muslims, almost all Igbo are Christians, and the Yoruba are split down the middle. Thus Islam reinforces Hausa identity, Christianity reinforces Igbo identity, and Yoruba nationalism unites the Yoruba regardless of religion. Islam and Christianity divide Northern and Southern Sudan mainly because the two regions were already divided by even deeper cultural differences. The two regions belonged to two different indigenous civilizations even before they were either Islamized or Christianized. On the other hand, Muslims in Senegal repeatedly voted for a Christian president. For twenty years Leopold Sedar Senghor, a Roman Catholic, was President of a country which was over 90 per cent Muslim Abdou Diouf. Leopold Senghor was succeeded for another twenty years by a Muslim president of Senegal. The Muslim president had a Roman Catholic First Lady. This degree of ecumenical democracy has not been achieved in the Western world. No Western democracy has ever elected either a Jew or Muslim for President. Joseph Lieberman, a distinguished Jewish Senator in the United States, trailed far behind in his bid for the Democratic presidential nomination in the 2003–4 primaries.

As for the distinguished British Tory Benjamin Disraeli, there is general consensus that he would never have become Prime Minister of Great Britain in the nineteenth century had his father, Isaac D'Israeli, not quarrelled with his Synagogue of Bevis Marks, and then decided to have his children baptized as Christians.[76] After all until 1858, Jews by religion were not allowed even to run for parliamentary elections in Britain, let alone become ministers. By contrast, Tanzania has had a religiously rotating presidency. Julius K. Nyerere, a Christian, was succeeded by Ali Hassan Mwinyi, a Muslim, who in turn was followed by Benjamin Mkapa, a Christian. Will the next Tanzanian president be Salim Ahmed Salim, a Muslim? The religious rotation may indeed continue. Nigeria has not yet developed a religiously rotating presidency. But there are advocates of a regionally rotating Nigerian presidency, alternating between the north and the south. Such regional alternation could, de facto, be a religious alternation in the Nigerian presidency.

Africa had no religious wars before the arrival of Islam and Christianity. But now that Africa has embraced its own Islam and Christianity, the Africans are developing ecumenical attitudes to religion which are far ahead of the rest of the world. The ecumenical spirit of Africa may be part of its contribution to the global ethic and to the sixth pillar of wisdom.

7. Towards Greater Wisdom

The seventh pillar of wisdom is a relentless quest for greater wisdom. An important part of this area of wisdom is the pursuit of creative synthesis. The synthesis may be between ethics and knowledge, between religion and science, and between one culture and another. It is arguable that Islam was historically at its most creative when it was ready to learn mathematics from India, philosophy from ancient Greece, architecture from Persia, science from the Jews, and jurisprudence from the legacy of Rome.

Muslims believe that God's first words to the Prophet Muhammad were indeed about knowledge; and God's first command to the prophet was the imperative *Iqra* ('Read'). These earliest Qur'anic verses linked biological sciences with the sciences of the mind. Moreover, by proclaiming that all knowledge is ultimately from God, these verses warned against the arrogance of pseudo-omniscience among humans. Science was morally accountable:

1. Read in the name of your Lord who created—
2. Created man from an embryo;
3. Read, for your Lord is most beneficent;
4. Who taught by the pen;
5. Taught man what he did not know.
6. And yet man is rebellious.
7. For he thinks he is sufficient in himself.
8. Surely your returning is to your Lord.[77]

Sura Iqra or *Alaq*, 96: 1–8

God 'taught by the pen'. In contemporary terms, 'the pen' could be extended to include teaching by the computer and the Internet. God taught humankind 'what he did not know'. Within the last one hundred years alone this has included splitting the atom, landing a man on the moon, sending a spacecraft to Mars, cloning a sheep, and exploring cyberspace.[78]

The distinctive aspect of early Islam as a civilization was precisely this readiness to synthesize what was best from other cultures. Those early Qur'anic verses stressed that all real knowledge came from God regardless of which human being (*ominsaan*) discovered it. Every successful scientific discovery helped to reveal more of God. This early Muslim readiness to learn from other civilizations declined. By the second half of the Ottoman era in the eighteenth century, the Muslim world was becoming scientifically marginal. By the nineteenth century, the Ottoman Dynasty was widely regarded as 'the sick man of Europe'. The corruption of Muslim rulers, the walls of theological legalism against innovation, the increasing Ottoman tendency to imitate the West rather than learn from the West, had weakened the Dynasty long before it collapsed during World War I.[79] Hypothetically, Ottoman creativity could have been rehabilitated with new and better leadership. But World War I, the Arab revolt, and T. E. Lawrence deprived the Ottomans of any further opportunities to reinvent themselves. Unfortunately the Arab nations which emerged out of Ottoman and European colonization did not fare much better scientifically or technologically. The heavy hand of cultural obscurantism continued to impede Arab advancement.

In this new millennium, *The Arab Human Development Report 2003* criticized 'the alliance between some oppressive regimes and certain types of conservative scholars'—an alliance which seemed to lead to 'interpretations of Islam which . . . are inimical to human development particularly with regard to freedom of thought, the accountability of the regimes to the people and women's participation in public life'.[80] The report on *Arab Human Development* discusses 'the knowledge gap' in the Arab world in spite of petrowealth. According to the report, only 53 copies of newspapers are sold per 1,000 people in Arab countries, compared to 285 in the West. Less than 2 per cent of the Arab population had Internet access. There are only 18 computers per 1,000 people as compared to a global average of 78.3. As for scientists and engineers in the Arab world, there are only 371 in research and development per million resident citizens as compared to a global average of 979 per million. How much of this knowledge gap and intellectual deficit is due to a version of Islam which is no longer responsive to creative cultural synthesis?

In South Asia, Pakistan has broken through the nuclear barrier and succeeded in giving the Muslim world its first nuclear power. In other respects Malaysia had been the most successful Muslim-led country in the world. Yet Prime Minister Mahathir Mohamad used his swansong of retirement in 2003 to call upon fellow Muslims to close the knowledge gap between themselves and such adversaries as the Zionists.[81] Mahathir Mohamad knew only too well that even in Malaysia itself he had had a tough time trying to close the knowledge gap between Muslim Malays and non-Muslim ethnic Chinese. Economically and technologically Malays had still lagged behind their ethnic Chinese compatriots. All evidence suggests that the Chinese had been better at 'creative synthesis of cultures' than the Malays. Paradoxically the Prophet Muhammad had called upon his followers to pursue knowledge 'even as far as China'. That was fourteen centuries earlier. Was the message of Muhammad prophetic for Malay's relations with ethnic Chinese in both Malaysia and Indonesia? Or did the Prophet anticipate Samuel Huntington's worry at the end of the twentieth century about an emerging alliance between Islam and countries of the Confucian heritage?

First the angel Gabriel calls upon the Prophet Muhammad to read in the name of God, who had taught by the pen. Then Gabriel assures Muhammad that all knowledge comes from God anyhow. Then the Prophet calls upon his followers to pursue knowledge as far as China. And on the eve of the twenty-first century, Samuel Huntington worries about an alliance between China and the Muslim world, while others identify active collaboration between North Korea and Pakistan. Is the Prophet Muhammad's prophecy in the process of fulfilment?[82]

The question arises whether the global ethic would be better served by a new multipolar world than by a world with only one superpower. Does the global ethic require global checks and balances which would include the influence of China and the leverage of the Muslim world as well as the power of the West?

As for Africa, its credentials for a global role in the twenty-first century are still in terms of natural resources and intrinsic cultural values, rather than in technological skills. But African thinkers are in disagreement about the relationship between wisdom, on one side, and technical skills, on the other. Philosophers of romantic gloriana emphasize the monumental achievements of Africa's past, ranging from the pyramids of Egypt to the brooding majesty of Great Zimbabwe. Without necessarily realizing it, such thinkers seem to share part of Bertrand Russell's conviction that civilization is the pursuit of luxury. The greatest of Africa's post-colonial gloriana thinkers was Cheikh Anta Diop of Senegal, who emphasized ancient Egypt's pivotal role in the origins of world civilization as a whole. Diop saw the River Nile as the mother of the earliest human achievements.[83] The other major African school of civilizational theory has emphasized not the grand monuments of Africa's structural achievements but the wisdom of being non-technical. In the words of the black poet of Martinique, Aimé Césaire:

Hooray for those who never invented anything!
Hooray for those who never discovered anything;
Hooray for joy, hooray for love;
Hooray for the pain of incarnate tears . . .

Honour those who have invented neither powder nor the compass;
Those who have tamed neither gas nor electricity;
Those who have explored neither the seas nor the skies . . .
My negritude is neither a tower nor a cathedral;
It reaches deep down into the red flesh of the soil.

Eia for those who have never invented anything
for those who have never explored anything
for those who have never subdued anything

[. . .]

Eia for joy
Eia for love
Eia for pain and its udders of reincarnated tears.[84]

Western thought has a subfield called the 'philosophy of science'. What this simplifying school of African thought represents is a philosophy of unscience. As Jean-Paul Sartre pointed out, this African revelling in not having invented either powder or the compass is a proud celebration of non-technicalness. It is a salute to the wisdom of closeness to nature.[85] The greatest African thinker of this simplifying school was also Senegalese. The late Leopold Sedar Senghor, who was President of Senegal from 1960 to 1980, was a philosopher and a poet, as well as a statesman. Senghor argued that while Cartesian epistemology starts from the premise 'I think, therefore I am,' African epistemology starts from the vastly different source of self-awareness—'I feel, therefore I am.' Senghor belonged to the philosophy of unscience, in contrast to his gloriana compatriot, Cheikh Anta Diop.[86]

As we seek to construct a global ethic based on seven pillars of wisdom, we need to listen to those two competing philosophies about the relationship between expertise, on one side, and genuine wisdom, on the other. We need also to listen to Africa's song of self-affirmation as captured in the following poetic prose:

We are a people of the day before yesterday and a people of the day after tomorrow. Long before slavery we lived in one huge village called Africa. And then strangers came into our midst and took many of us away, scattering us to all the corners of the earth. Before those strangers came, our village was the world; we knew no other. But we are now spread out so widely that the Sun never sets on the descendants of Africa. The world is now our village, and we plan to make it more human between now and the day after tomorrow.[87]

Wisdom begins when we understand ourselves. Wisdom matures when we aspire to higher human standards. How we treat strangers in our midst is the ultimate humane standard.

Conclusion

In the face of the new American hegemony, the new pillars of wisdom need to add up to a global ethic. The first of our new pillars of wisdom has to be a quest for tolerance and minimization of violence. Are Africa and Islam conflict prone? Who forged the link between terrorism and political Islam? We have addressed some of those questions. The second new pillar of wisdom is surely the optimization of the economic well-being of the people. How egalitarian are the cultures of Islam and Africa? We have touched upon the political economy of Islam and the African experience. The third new pillar of wisdom is the quest for social justice. It is a struggle to reduce ethnic and racial inequalities and a quest for a humane equilibrium. We have found Islam to be the most egalitarian of the Abrahamic religions. We have found Africa worthy of reparations for centuries of racial injustice. The fourth new pillar of wisdom is a basic gender equality. How have Islam and Africa treated women? We have examined gains and losses for women in Africa and the Muslim world. The fifth pillar of wisdom is a quest for ecological balance. What is strongly needed is a wider responsiveness to ecological conservation, environmental balance, and population policy. There is also the sixth pillar of inter-faith dialogue and cooperation. Islam reaffirms that 'there is no compulsion in religion'. What about tensions with Christians and Jews? There were no religious wars in Africa before Christianity and Islam arrived. The seventh pillar of wisdom is the quest for further wisdom. This is a struggle for new knowledge, restrained by humane wisdom. The Prophet of Islam urged his followers to seek wisdom as far as China. Was the Prophet predicting a future alliance between Islam and modern China?

Perspectives on these new seven pillars of wisdom have to respond to the Middle East as a normative centre of global culture and to Africa as a challenge to the global conscience. Lawrence of Arabia initiated a process. Whither the American empire? How is it affecting the future of Islam and the African condition? The search for greater wisdom continues.

Response to Ali A. Mazrui, 'Strangers in Our Midst: In Search of Seven Pillars of Wisdom'

Iftikhar H. Malik

Ali A. Mazrui offers a persuasive disquisition on numerous interconnected themes, including Islam, British colonial legacies, Pax Americana, African ethos, Orientalism, the Israeli–Palestinian tragedy, and ascendant Islamophobia. His 'Strangers in Ours Midst' could also be read as 'Old Partners, Persistent Rivals'; Islamic, African, and Western values emerge as often complementary and only occasionally conflicting. Mazrui's own life, anchored on several hyphens (pillars!), reflects a successful blend of African, Muslim, and American identities combining academic finesse with passionate humanism.

Mazrui's broad sweep has to be considered in the context of contemporary academic discourse on recent diasporas, economic immigrants, and asylum-seekers. This tends to basket human beings into convenient categories, totally ignoring their complex environments, sentiments, and antecedents. Specialists periodically produce census-based league tables of minorities. Muslims—largely Pakistanis and Bangladeshis in Britain—routinely feature towards the bottom of the ladder, thus fuelling hostility towards them. Serious scholarship may focus on the sociological models underpinning pluralism and multiculturalism but the alarmists—egged on by the tabloids—scapegoat asylum-seekers and immigrants.[1] *Othering*

Islam and spotlighting Muslims by juxtaposing local trends with international conflicts thus serve several purposes, notably neo-racism. Why incur the charge of racism by apportioning blame along the colour line when all this and more can be blamed on Islam? Islamophobia thus incorporates the three age-old determinants of racism: colour, class, and culture. It embodies neo-racism and exemplifies the age-old dictum of divide-and-rule.[2] Most Muslims are non-white, working-class, adhere to a rival religion, and display different cultural norms, all of which makes it easier for them to be scapegoated.

Mazrui has sought some transcendent commonalities between post-industrial societies and Islamic and African experience. His seven pillars foreground the tripartite relationship of T. E. Lawrence, his Arab allies, and imperial Britain, while focusing on some vital current global pre-occupations. The traditional non-Western norms that he cites are not at odds with the more positive attributes of modernity. But, to revert to the historical analogy of World War I, Muslims and Africans are unwilling to accept a subservient role within the expansive tentacles of the new empire, Pax Americana. Celebrity-intellectuals and television pundits such as Niall Ferguson, Simon Schama, Michael Ignatieff, Fareed Zakaria, and Francis Fukuyama have, in their own ways, been *koshering* the Huntingtonian thesis of a conflict between Islam and the West. They consequently recommend reordering the Muslim world through benevolent or 'lite' imperialism. Some unabashedly propose a rerun of the British colonial enterprise using the unprecedented economic and military potential of the US.[3] Professor Bernard Lewis, 'the guru of the Neo-Cons' and a former British military intelligence official turned historian, is the intellectual mentor of these theorists. His books, especially the recent ones, reject the entire Muslim experience as negative.[4] Lewis's long-standing apologia for Israel has developed into fully-fledged propaganda for war on Iraq and Iran. It has also revived Orientalist discourse. His rancorous campaign is caricatured by ideologues such as Daniel Pipes, Paul Berman, V. S. Naipaul, Ann Coulter, Patrick Buchannan, Bernard Henri-Lévy, Oriana Fallaci, Ian Buruma, David Selbourne, Gilles Kepel, and other overnight specialists on Islam. Influential Evangelical groups similarly diffuse hostile attitudes towards Islam. Meanwhile policymakers at the Pentagon and elsewhere have been trying to implement their own discretionary agendas. The Neo-Cons simply divide the world into good and evil (the US leads the forces of universal good). They believe: (1) that the US must use military means to ensure a pliant world and take unilateral action if its allies will not cooperate; (2) that Washington should not be inhibited by global institutions such as the UN or by 'Old Europe'; (3) that the US must focus on the Middle East and global Islam (the term used for this latter entity is 'terror') since oil and Islam together constitute (in their view) the most serious threat to the USA. To these Neo-Orientalists, diaspora Muslims are an important component of the global Islamic threat and have to be controlled even if the means of such control compromises the Muslims' human and citizenship rights.[5]

However, Mazrui's analysis does not fall into the dialectics of a typical anti-American broadside or an apologetic mantra. He seeks a fresh perspective on the supposed dichotomy of tradition and modernity, which routinely posits Islam and the West as antagonistic. These are issues where scholarship itself may become obsessively partisan but Mazrui avoids polemics. Reiterating points of consensus, he rightly revisits in twentieth-century history the foundations of the relationship between the North Atlantic regions and Islam. This marked the beginning of 'the American century', as Congressman Henry Luce subsequently put it, and witnessed the consolidation of the Franco-British imperial hold on the Middle East as the Ottoman caliphate declined. One could pause here and see the cyclic nature of these developments. Compare the decline of Mughal India and Safwid Persia, when Britain and Russia both were able to establish their Asian empires. Like the other two Turkic empires, the Ottoman decline was hastened by internal weaknesses and external interventions—exacerbated in the Ottoman case by rash entry into World War I. T. E. Lawrence presented the waning of Ottoman control to ambitious Arab leaders (for example, Emir Hussein) as offering the possibility of a new Arab caliphate. The Hashemite dynasty entirely failed to grasp that the colonial enterprise would bypass them as it already had other such intermediaries in the Afro-Asian world. Looking at the post-9/11 self-inflicted marginalization of today's Muslim rulers—an inevitable consequence of their lack of legitimacy—I see little difference from the *modus vivendi* of their predecessors, who either waited outside the Palace of Versailles for crumbs from the Western table or simply ignored the forces intent on changing their destinies.

However, at the beginning of the last century, colonialism was not so dismissive of one community of the faithful, a fact that radically transformed the contours of both Muslim politics and Muslim–West relations. The Zionists, thanks to their friends in the British establishment, were promised a new home. The prevailing wisdom suggested that, if millions of Europeans could have four continents at their disposal for resettlement (by displacing several more millions for sale on the open market), a few million Jews might similarly establish their own Zion amongst the Arabs. The Zionist project depended on very primitive associations with Palestine but the disembarking Jews would surely counteract the local *barbarism*. Europe was, in fact, seeking a *final* solution to its *others* and the Palestinians were due no more attention than the Native Americans, African slaves, and Aborigines who had been 'cleansed' under a more powerful but similarly self-righteous 'civilizing' project exported from the North Atlantic. To this day the Balfour Declaration of 1917 has continued its terrible toll in human lives and Arab natural resources. It proved a crossroads for the Arab–Israeli and Muslim–Western relations and unleashed an avalanche of violence and expulsions that continued until the United States assumed full responsibility for ensuring Israeli salience in West Asian politics. Thus in the Muslim perspective the declining British Empire had already initiated the reordering of the Near East for specific purposes which went well beyond the simplistic goals of Lawrence's Arab companions. By comparison, Washington has now assumed the role of a partisan patriarch. And the legacy of this Anglo-American statesmithery goes on delivering fundamentalisms of various hues and shades. It not only heralded the era of unlimited arms sales and resultant violence, but also ensured the safety of authoritarian regimes whose policies of disempowering their own people and wasting resources continue unabated. No matter. Compared with a binding surrogacy to the West, *comprador* opportunism weighs rather lightly in Washington, Paris, Brussels, and London. The democratic imperatives and civic rights of Western society are not exported. They become the routine mantra of columnists and human rights bodies sanctioned by governments which choose to act otherwise.

T. E. Lawrence's pillars of wisdom may merely be the

whims of an anguished soul who found a sense of belonging among the traditionally austere Bedouins. But Professor Mazrui's seven pillars include tolerance, economic well-being, social justice, gender equality and mobility, ecology, interfaith camaraderie, and a continued struggle for wisdom and rationality. Mazrui's exhaustive case studies from the Muslim and African experiences reveal the universality of these values though there are varying degrees of regional emphasis. Highlighting Muslim views on these values, he is neither defensive nor aggressive. (Let us not palter with the terms 'moderate', 'liberal', or 'enlightened' Muslims—contrasted with 'militant', 'fundamentalist', and 'terrorist' counterparts; none of these labels adequately characterizes Muslim societies and their spokespersons.)[6] But in a world of power politics, Mazrui's pillars are like the intricately carved pillars of the Cordova Mosque or the Alhambra Palace, which stand mute before the thronging tourists, nostalgic for the worshippers eliminated centuries back when Spain set out on its Inquisitorial journey.

Reinforcing the *otherness* of a caricatured East is a dangerous mode of thinking. It is, indeed, proving a 'moral Waterloo' of Western values.[7] But the tendency to exceptionalize Islam by attributing some inherent inferiority and rigidity to its creed is an age-old Orientalist pursuit and has never been forsaken. On the contrary, following 9/11 it has assumed even more dangerous proportions.[8] In its current guise, Orientalism combines its historic burden with contemporary geopolitical ingredients. To these is added a strong component of Islamophobia. It occupies a self-awarded moral high ground, is intensely partisan, and perfunctory in exposition. It depends on sexism and a strictly hierarchical view of Muslim societies, a view justifying their control by authoritarian means. The invasions of Afghanistan and Iraq, and the multiple campaigns prosecuted by Israel and Russia against their underprivileged Muslim populaces have as their concomitant the adoption by several states of discretionary policies on travel, immigration, and pluralism.[9] Muslims worldwide are aggrieved at the destruction and denigration of their communities and their heritage, at their poverty, disempowerment, and alienation. But these griefs are ignored both by their rulers and by their backers in the West. The latter simply prioritize their own interests. Western espousal of democracy, human rights, intergender equality, secularist education, and economic progress is viewed by Muslims as a mere smoke screen. They know that in the past Western regimes prosecuted their own interests while moralizing about higher ideals.

It is a widely held belief among Muslims—though one not generally heard in the Western media—that the proponents of Pax Americana, Greater Israel, Hindu Rashtra, an unassailable Mother Russia, or other such nationalisms are united in their hatred and fear of Muslims.[10] Muslims generally perceive in 9/11 the symptom of a larger malaise rooted in Western double standards. Most of them do not support terror but all are affected by retaliatory policies.[11] They increasingly see sinister lobbies working behind the US-led campaign on terror. Seeing Palestinians, Afghans, Chechens, Kashmiris, Gujaratis, Iraqis, Ossetians, Thai Malays, and Moros dying in droves while the Muslim elite remains sidelined, they fear that not only in the Diaspora but also in their traditional homelands their culture, history, and religion are once again threatened. In a return to the methods of Orientalists and missionaries, Islam is (they fear) being stereotyped as a culture of violence, irrationality, sexism, and authoritarianism. And this is absurd. If we except a small number of extremists, Muslims are not preoccupied with conquering the world for Allah. For most of them, the everyday problems of survival are more than enough. Of course, like other evangelical religions, Muslims may idealize a global Islam and a united *ummah*. But they are aware of their own limitations, especially in a world where spirituality, otherworldliness, and devotion are overshadowed by a cut-throat modernity rooted in competition and individual gain. Commentators such as David Selbourne, 'Will' (Harry) Cummins, Paul Berman, or Ian Buruma, and scholars such as Lewis, Pipes, and others may chide the West for losing the battle with a triumphant global Islam and admonish the Left for not having foreseen the rising tide of radical Islam. But these predictions are merely alarmist. The truth about the Islamic world is pervasive poverty, high rates of illiteracy, and authoritarian regimes kowtowing to specific interest groups. We cannot allow the destiny of the world to be left in the hands of Neo-Cons and their Christian–Zionist friends equipped with vast military and economic resources any more than in the hands of radical Muslims who enthuse young men with concepts of holy war and martyrdom. Neither of these represents the best of the distinguished traditions from which they derive.

The exposé of the torture and brutalization of Muslim internees at Guantanamo Bay, Abu Ghraib Jail, Bagram Air Base, and Israel's Facility 1391, and the massacres at Mazar-i-Sharif, Kandahar, Jenin, Rafah, Grozny, Falluja, Qaim, and Najaf have been justified on the basis of a moralizing and racist argument rooted in Orientalism and the enduring denigration of Muslims. These brutal practices (hooding, rape, and sodomization) went on in the full knowledge of many senior officials. The humiliation of denuded Muslim men by soldiers and private contractors, the rape of Iraqi women, making pyramids of nude bodies and posing with corpses proved to be 'an institutionalised feature of America's war on terror'.[12] The well-known Arab writer, Ahdaf Soueif, commenting on the psychological and sexual dehumanization of Iraqi prisoners by Coalition troops, alerted everyone to the West's moral dilemma when she noted that 'The acts in the photos being flashed across the networks would not have taken place but for the profound racism that infects the American and British establishments.' The constant references to the liberation of Iraqis from Saddam Hussein's regime (or of Afghans from the Taliban) were aimed at diluting local resentment, but simply demonstrated that '[Saddam] Hussein is now the moral compass of the west'. These pictures confirmed that both the US and Britain were 'not in Iraq as an act of goodwill' but simply for their own interest.[13] The dehumanizing treatment reminded another former internee, Haifa Zangana, of the trauma that she herself—and her people with her—suffered under Saddam. As she said: 'Iraqis did not struggle for decades to replace one torturer with another.' Echoing the Pushtuns, Palestinians, Kashmiris, Chechens, Malays, and Moros, she further observed: 'We are a proud people welcoming to guests but unforgiving of those who tread with heavy boots across privacy, integrity and history.'[14]

Her words are not those of one rejoicing in recent liberation. Fortunately, she does not stand alone. In 2001–3 the peace movement became a global civil society rebuking the targeting of vulnerable communities across West Asia and elsewhere. The Israeli policy of 'politicide', the daily arrests of many Muslim youths in the diaspora, and the collective punishment to Muslim communities elsewhere strongly suggest that Muslims have become 'the new Jews'. There are, of course, human rights groups determinedly defying neo-racism, Neo-Orientalism, and militarist uni-lateralism.[15] Muslim reformers must perceive them as allies in their demand for the long-overdue democratization of the Islamic world. Democratization is not the only goal of such reform. They also seek—of course—economic well-being, inter-gender equality, and respect for pluralism and ecology—precisely the pillars of wisdom that Mazrui has delineated as part and parcel of African and Islamic traditions.

Part Two
Displacement, Asylum, Migration

4

'A Thousand Little Guantanamos': Western States and Measures to Prevent the Arrival of Refugees

Matthew J. Gibney

> I earned my bread and ate it just like you.
> I am a doctor; or at least I was.
> The colour of my hair, shape of my nose
> Cost me my home, my bread and butter too.
>
> She who for seven years had slept with me
> My hand upon her lap, her face against my face
> Took me to court. The cause of my disgrace:
> My hair was black. So she got rid of me.
>
> But I escaped at night through a wood
> (For reasons of my mother's ancestry)
> To find a country that would be my host.
>
> Yet when I asked for work it was no good.
> You are impertinent, they said to me.
> I'm not impertinent, I said: I'm lost.[1]

In the last lines of his 'Emigrant's Lament', Bertholt Brecht contrasts two perspectives on experience of the refugee. In the first, the view of the person forced from his country, to be a refugee is to be 'lost'. The refugee is forced to eke out an existence in a place where the social and political markers that enable orientation in the world are alien and difficult to decode. In the second, the perspective of the receiving country, the refugee is an interloper, someone from whom any request is 'impertinent', or to employ a word closer to the one Brecht uses in the original German, 'shameless'. He is someone who, betrayed by his own state, is forced to rely on the sufferance of others.

Fifty years after Brecht wrote, refugees in Western nations have gained very clear entitlements. Shamed by the experience of Jews who failed to find refuge from Nazi persecution in the 1930s, and desiring to reckon with rising numbers of people attempting to flee the Soviet Bloc in the aftermath of World War II, Western nations drafted and signed the United Nations Convention Relating to the Status of Refugees in Geneva in 1951. In addition to defining in legal terms just what a refugee was—an individual with a well-founded fear of persecution on the grounds of nationality, race, political opinion, religion, or membership of a particular social group—the Convention carefully spelt out just what refugees were owed by the states that hosted them. Under the Convention, states were obligated to allow refugees to work, gain travel documents, travel freely, and a range of other things. Most importantly, states committed themselves under Article 33 (the non-refoulement clause) not to send refugees back to countries where they would face persecution. As the immigration lawyer David Martin has pointed out, to be recognized as a refugee is now to take on something of a privileged status.[2] For refugees are entitled to a range of protections and rights that set them apart from normal immigrants.

If the claims of refugees can no longer be dismissed as impertinent, one could be forgiven for thinking that, at least in Western states, there are no refugees left to claim anything. Everywhere it seems they have been replaced by 'asylum-seekers'—mere pretenders to the title of refugee. Of course, in a neutral reading, the term 'asylum-seeker' simply refers to a person claiming refugee status whose eligibility for asylum has yet to be decided. But it is not the neutral reading that has been taken up by anxious governments, the populist press, opportunistic governments, anti-immigrant groups, and large swathes of the public over the last fifteen years. It is rather a view in which asylum-seekers are widely characterized as welfare cheats, competitors for jobs, security threats, abusers of host state generosity, and even as the killers of swans.[3]

Just how the asylum-seeker has come to displace the refugee is something I will take up briefly below. But my main focus here will be less on why this transition has occurred than on what it has enabled states to do in policy terms. Few people could be unaware of the way willingness to implement tough measures on asylum has become a touchstone for Western governments of all hues recently. Buoyed by rising numbers of asylum-seekers since the early 1980s, as well as widespread public concern over illegal migration, governments in countries as different as Germany and Australia, the US and Ireland, and Italy and the UK, have implemented a raft of measures designed to make life very uncomfortable for those applying for asylum. While variations remain across countries, in the last decade those seeking refuge have increasingly faced the prospect of detention, denial of the right of work, limitations or exclusion from welfare benefits, diminishing rights to appeal negative decisions, and, ultimately, deportation. To be a refugee, it seems, may be to have access to important rights, but woe betide those who arrive in Western states claiming to be a refugee.

This paradoxical situation has not gone uncontested. Human rights groups, church leaders, academics, and some politicians have protested the restrictionist turn, challenging many aspects of it in the media and the courts. Harsh practices towards asylum-seekers have been condemned as 'deeply troubling' efforts to appease xenophobic and poorly informed publics.[4] Concerns have been expressed that there is a 'surging global rhetoric demonizing asylum-seekers'[5] that may encourage growing levels of anti-immigrant hostility.[6] Others worry that the retrenchment of the rights of those seeking asylum may ultimately erode the rights of citizens in liberal democratic states.[7]

Most concern with recent asylum practices has focused on the treatment meted out to asylum-seekers once they arrive. In Australia and the UK, the use of detention has led to public demonstrations and many legal challenges; detention centres for asylum-seekers, such as Woomera (in Western Australia) and Yarl's Wood (in Bedfordshire, England), have become household names, the former after inmates sewed their lips together to protest government policies. Other aspects of the treatment of asylum-seekers, including more widespread deportation (as in the Netherlands), and limitations on (or deprivation of) welfare payments (as in the UK), also generate vocal concerns by church and human rights groups, amongst others. The focus on how asylum-seekers are treated upon arrival is understandable. Questionable uses of state power are more newsworthy and worrying when they occur under our noses, so to speak. I want to explore here another aspect of the architecture of exclusion, one that has generated less attention and controversy, but which, I think, poses an even more serious challenge to the institution of asylum.

My focus will be on the use of what have been called 'non-arrival measures'. These measures can be differentiated from the other restrictive practices used in recent years by the fact that they aim directly to impede access to asylum. Not content with scaling back the rights of asylum-seekers in the hope of deterring applications, states, through the use of visa regimes, carrier sanctions, and immigration pre-inspection, have moved to bar the arrival of foreigners who might claim protection. We have reached the *reductio ad absurdum* of the contemporary paradoxical attitude towards refugees. Western states now acknowledge the rights of refugees but simultaneously criminalize the search for asylum.

How could a paradox this sharp withstand public scrutiny? At least part of the answer lies in the fact that non-arrival practices have subtly transformed the nature of immigration control in recent years. They have shifted entrance decisions away from state borders to a range of new places (the high seas, consular offices, and foreign airports) and, in so doing, empowered new and sometimes unaccountable actors (airline officials, coastguards, and, ironically, smugglers and traffickers, etc.). Most of the time, the paradoxical nature of state practice is thus conveniently out of the sight of domestic audiences. I want to bring it back into view.

My aim will be to highlight the techniques states use to prevent arrivals, as well as to evaluate ethically how they are justified and what their significance might be. I will also propose ways in which non-arrival measures might be operated so that they are not radically in conflict with the provision of protection for refugees. But before embarking on these tasks, let me say a little bit more about the context in which these measures have developed.

I. The Rise of the Asylum-Seeker and the Fall of the Refugee

When the 1951 Refugee Convention came into existence soon after the end of World War II, Western states had a relatively clear idea of who was a refugee and thus eligible to the entitlements of the Convention. The refugees that concerned Western states were ones congruent (in large measure) with their foreign policy objectives. From the early 1950s to the mid-1970s the status of refugee overlapped almost completely with that of defector. Refugees were those who had fled communist states in Eastern and Central Europe. Not only could these people be relatively easily incorporated into Western countries hungry for large supplies of unskilled and semi-skilled labour, but their very desire for asylum also provided much-needed ideological evidence of the superiority of Western liberal democracy during the Cold War.[8] The motivations of escapees from the Eastern bloc were, consequently, rarely the subject of close examination.

In the 1960s and 1970s, however, the face of the refugee began to change. The volume of people leaving European countries under communist control was far outstripped by refugees in Africa and Asia, emerging as a result of painful struggles for decolonization. With over a million refugees in Africa alone by the early 1960s, the assumption that refugees were an intra-European phenomenon was dramatically called into question.[9] At the same time, other important changes were taking place. After the onset of stagflation in the early 1970s, most Western countries wound down programmes for accepting immigrant labour, thus closing off the major avenue through which the denizens of the world's poorer countries could enter the West.[10] Finally, beginning in the 1960s the contemporary revolution in transportation and communications took off. Relatively fast and cheap modes of intercontinental commercial transportation (particularly but not exclusively by air) had begun to come within the reach of much larger proportions of the world's population. The effect of these changes on asylum began to be felt in the early 1970s, with the growth of people from Africa and Asia claiming to be refugees arriving by jet in European capitals.[11]

How asylum was understood in the West was profoundly changed by these developments. In combination, they suggested the prospect of a truly 'globalized' system of asylum-seeking, driven as much by economic disparities between North and South, as by refugee generating events, strictly defined. Ugandan refugees were now able to claim asylum in London, Sri Lankans in Amsterdam, and Chinese in New York. Moreover, the prospects of improved access to asylum did not apply to refugees alone. Government elites expressed concern that North–South inequalities were becoming a reason for migration in their own right. The British Prime Minister, John Major, warned his EU colleagues in 1992, that 'we must not remain open to all comers, simply because Paris, Rome and London seem more attractive than Algiers'.

Some evidence for such a transformation could be found in a sharp rise in asylum applications. Whereas total asylum claims across Western Europe averaged no more than 13,000 annually in the 1970s, the annual totals had grown to 170,000 by 1985, and to 690,000 by 1992. Between 1985 and 1995, more than five million claims for asylum were lodged in Western states. The numbers were, however, also buoyed by the end of the Cold War which, as well as lifting emigration restrictions on the citizens from Eastern and Central Europe and leading to the brutal war in the former Yugoslavia, deprived Western governments of their traditional rationale— the need to support those fleeing communist regimes—for offering asylum.

These changes, along with low rates of acceptance for refugee status in most European countries, transformed public and official attitudes to those seeking asylum. Increasingly, the term 'asylum-seekers' became shorthand in public and media discourse for 'economic refugees', people taking advantage of the asylum route to escape normal immigration control; immigrants in pursuit of the benefits of welfare state at the expense of citizens; or, especially after 11 September 2001, as potential terrorists or security threats. Many of these views were ungenerous and a thin veil for xenophobic attitudes and political scapegoating. Yet they did point to real changes. Economic migration and movements of refugees fleeing conflict had become increasingly entangled;[12] the incentives for people with implausible claims to asylum were strong given the chances of being removed if their claim was unsuccessful were exceedingly low;[13] and there were a number of high profile events in the US and the UK where asylum-seekers were linked with terrorist activities.[14]

From the early 1990s, Western countries seemed to fall like dominoes to the problem of asylum: Germany in 1992/1993; the US in 1994/1995; Australia in 2001; the UK from 1999 to 2003. In each country a period of panic over rising numbers was greeted by tough new measures: Germany neutered its liberal right of asylum in 1993; the US introduced mandatory detention for asylum-seekers until they could show a 'credible fear of persecution' in 1996; Australia redrew its territorial boundaries for immigration purposes in 2001 in order to limit refugee claims; and Britain introduced a raft of measures including dispersing asylum-seekers, increasing detention, paying welfare benefits in kind, and reducing avenues of appeal from 1999 on.[15] In the midst of these new restrictions, governments continued to reaffirm the moral importance of assisting genuine asylum-seekers.

By the middle of the 1990s, the number of asylum

applicants in Western countries had started to decrease. While approximately 675,000 people applied for asylum in the EU in 1992, the number of applications had dropped to 375,000 by 2001.[16] This fall was partly due to a reduction in the number of refugees worldwide, but not to this alone. The volume of asylum-seekers across the West fell faster than the number of the world's refugees.[17] Through the use of new restrictive policy measures, the potentially liberating effects of globalization on intercontinental movement for those seeking asylum were undercut. Western states had, it seemed, limited the globalization of asylum.

II. Measures of Exclusion[18]

Measures to prevent people arriving at the borders of Western countries have been an important part of these new restrictions. The measures concerned have been many and varied. They have ranged from visa regimes, the use of which is almost as old as immigration control itself, to truly novel measures, like the excision of parts of state territory for immigration purposes, as recently used by Australia. Some measures have been implemented unilaterally; others are subject to coordinated action, often at the level of the European Union. I want now to look more closely at some of these measures, before considering the way in which states have attempted to justify them.

Perhaps the most ubiquitous tool used to prevent arrivals is the visa: a document that provides pre-arrival permission to enter a foreign country. The use of visas to control the movement of individuals from specific countries or categories of entrant (e.g. criminals, the penurious) can be traced back virtually to the beginnings of immigration control itself. In recent years, visa controls have been used directly to prevent the arrival of asylum-seekers. In the UK, for example, rising numbers of Tamil asylum-seekers in 1987 led the government to require for the first time visas of all Sri Lankan nationals. While all Western states used visas against some groups of asylum-seekers, variations abound in the extent of their usage. Australia, for example, requires visas of all foreign nationals. By contrast, Canada, the US, and most EU states usually require visas from citizens of countries that produce large numbers of asylum-seekers or illegal migrants (for example, Afghanistan, Somalia, Sudan, and Iraq).[19] Under the Schengen Agreement, member countries of the EU have harmonized visa requirements in recent years, leading to a situation where the citizens of around 136 countries require visas to enter Europe.[20] It is a mistake to think that visas are only used to control asylum-seekers and illegal immigrants. Concerns about security and the entry of individuals with criminal records have been other justifications for their use. But the growth in the number of countries to whom Western states apply visa restrictions since the 1980s, closely tracks rising concern over asylum.

Visas are most effective when they are used in conjunction with another tool of arrival prevention, carrier sanctions. Carrier sanctions are fines (or other penalties) imposed by states on airline, train, and shipping companies for bringing foreign nationals to their territory without required documentation (e.g. a valid visa or passport). These sanctions effectively transfer migration management to private carriers, who, if they wish to avoid substantial fines, must make decisions on the possession and authenticity of appropriate documents. As Elspeth Guild has recently observed: 'between the possibility to seek protection from a foreign state and the individual fleeing persecution in his or her home state, the

private transport company . . . [has now been] inserted'.[21]
Refugees forced to flee their homeland often lack the time or
ability to access required documentation. Profit-conscious
airlines are reluctant to risk incurring fines for carrying those
who may or may not be refugees, especially when legislation
makes no express allowance for asylum-seekers to be treated
as special cases.[22] The result is a barrier to the entry of asylum-
seekers which the state has no need directly to police. Since
the late 1980s, carrier sanctions have been adopted by most
Western states. Australia, Austria, Belgium, Canada, Denmark,
France, Germany, Italy, and the US impose fines ranging from
€100 for each individual brought to state territory (in the case
of Italy) to a fine of around €7,000 (in the case of Germany for
negligent carriers). A directive harmonizing carrier sanctions
across EU states was formally adopted in June 2001.

The desire to prevent arrivals has also led immigration
officials to operate beyond state territory. Pre-inspection
agreements enable countries to post an advance guard of
immigration officers at the airports, train stations, or ports of
foreign countries so that aspiring entrants can be screened
for suitability and correct documentation before they arrive.
By the end of the 1990s, the UK, Canada, the US, Sweden,
and France had employed immigration staff ('immigration
liaison officers') at selected foreign airports. Australia, the
Netherlands, and Norway, on the other hand, have sent
immigration officials abroad to train airline staff at foreign
airports to recognize fraudulent or incomplete documentation. Early in 2001, on the initiative of Greece, the EU
established a network of Immigration Liaison Officers to
coordinate its immigration control activities. While the implication of such practices for asylum-seekers is generally dire,
few states have been as brazen as the UK in the use of such

measures to stop those seeking protection. As I will discuss in more detail later, in 2001 it sent immigration officials to Ruzyne airport in Prague to prevent Roma from boarding aeroplanes to the UK where, it was believed, they would claim asylum.

While pre-inspection regimes extend migration boundaries, some states have also contracted their boundaries to evade asylum claims. Switzerland, France, Germany, and Spain have all declared parts of their airports international zones. Such zones are established to function as areas in which officials are not obliged to provide asylum-seekers or foreign individuals with some or all of the protections available to those officially on state territory (for example, the right to legal representation, or access to a review process) in order to enable speedy removal from the country. In a similar vein, the US has used Guantanamo Bay for the processing of Haitian and Cuban asylum claimants in order to obviate the need to grant them the constitutional protections held by foreigners on US sovereign territory.[23] Arguably the most radical development along these lines was the Australian government's redefinition of the status of its island territories for immigration purposes. A 2001 law 'excised' Christmas Island, Ashmore Reef, the Cocos Island, and other territories from its migration zone, so that the landing of asylum-seekers on these territories did not engage most of the country's protection obligations. While Australia's obligations under the 1951 Refugee Convention still applied, the more extensive protections and entitlements associated with the country's domestic asylum laws, including the right to seek review of negative decisions, were no longer available to individuals on these territories.[24]

Finally, states have resorted to interdiction to prevent asylum-seekers from accessing national territory. While all interdiction aims to prevent asylum-seekers from reaching the territory (or waters) of the repelling country, the implications for asylum-seekers differ between cases. In some cases, asylum-seekers are indiscriminately turned back to the country from which they departed; in others, some attempt is made to separate out refugees through a preliminary screening procedure, thus reducing the chances of refoulement. Throughout the first half of the 1990s, US policy towards Haitian boat people moved back and forth between these two responses.[25] In other cases still, interdicted asylum-seekers are taken to an offshore territory or to a safe third country with or without the intention of resettlement in the interdicting country if determined to be refugees. Australia used the latter response during the Tampa incident of 2001. The island nation of Nauru was enlisted to host asylum-seekers while their eligibility for refugee status was assessed.[26] In a scene worthy of Jean Raspail's Camp of Saints, the UK government, faced with rising numbers of asylum-seekers in 2001, prepared a plan that considered deploying naval carriers in the Mediterranean to apprehend illegal immigrants to 'deliver a radical reduction in the number of unfounded asylum applications'.[27] The announcement had, to be sure, the flavour of a publicity stunt for the consumption of the highly restrictionist British electorate. But the government's willingness even to float the idea illustrates how the bounds of acceptable discourse and practice have been shifting.

The list of measures I have outlined above hardly constitutes a complete inventory of non-arrival practices. I do not have the space here for such an accounting and, anyway, new techniques are constantly emerging to satisfy what sometimes seems like an insatiable appetite for control. The list does however give an insight into what those who wish to claim asylum in the West are now up against. A globalized world, in which opportunities of intercontinental movement have increased, has been met by an expansion in the sphere in which entrance controls work. The traditional view of entrance control as something operated at the state's territorial borders, train stations, and airports by domestic immigration officials increasingly appears quaint and outdated. It is now beyond the boundaries of the state, on the high seas, in foreign countries, or in vaguely defined territories (like Australia's excised zones) that exclusion from admission occurs.

The implications of this development for the institution of asylum are baleful. Efforts to prevent arrivals strengthen the hand of the state *vis-à-vis* actors that might normally be expected to publicize and challenge rights violations. With the simultaneous export and dispersal of immigration control, the exercise of power becomes extremely difficult for domestic groups to track and oversee. Try as they might, human rights groups lack the resources to observe what goes on at airport counters across the world, let alone to access US Coastguard cutters or British naval carriers, or the visa sections of foreign consulates. Courts may lack the information, the jurisdiction, or the legal basis to question offshore practices that occur at one (or two) steps remove from actual government officials. Asylum-seekers who never arrive cannot recount their experiences. With only mild exaggeration one might say that a thousand little Guantanamos have been created in the last two decades:[28] centres of power where states (and their formal and informal agents) act free from the constraints imposed on their activities by the courts, international and domestic law, human rights groups, and the public at large.

When asked in 2002 whether there existed any legal

avenues by which legitimate refugees might enter the UK, the Minister of State for Immigration, Lord Rooker, answered bluntly, 'No'.[29] One recent estimate claimed that in Germany access to asylum is for 98 per cent of entrants impossible without entering illegally and concealing one's access route.[30] Those desperate for protection are driven to take even great risks to evade controls. One recent report found that, on average, 4,000 asylum-seekers drown at sea every year.[31] Many more seek help with entrance from the one group of entrepreneurs who have profited (albeit illicitly) from the changing boundaries of immigration control: smugglers and traffickers.

III. Justifying Exclusion

Despite these efforts to export border control, non-arrival practices have occasionally received great publicity. When the Australian government refused to let a Norwegian ship, the M.V. Tampa, land on its territory in August 2001, a storm of controversy was unleashed; more recently, in 2004, George W. Bush's statement that the US 'will turn back any [Haitian] refugee that attempts to reach our shore' generated an outcry from human rights organizations.[32] Because the blocking of asylum-seekers cannot always be hidden from view, governments have had to offer some justifications for non-arrival measures—ways, that is, of addressing the paradox of simultaneously supporting asylum but denying access to asylum-seekers. I want now to consider the adequacy of three of the major justifications offered in defence of non-arrival measures.

1. Beyond the Bounds of Responsibility

The most direct route to justifying non-arrival measures is to claim that states have no responsibilities to guarantee the protection of refugees who have not reached their territory. Implausible as this claim might seem, the policies of Western states sometimes appear to be built on this premise. Furthermore, governments have recently argued that it accurately encapsulates their legal responsibilities. For example, in a 1994 case before the US Supreme Court, *Sale* vs. *Haitian Centers Council*, the US government claimed that its practice of intercepting boatloads of people fleeing Haiti (in the midst and aftermath of a military coup) in international waters and returning the occupants (without assessing their claims to asylum) to Haiti was not a violation of the 1951 Refugee Convention or international law generally. In a controversial decision, the Court accepted (by an 8–1 margin) the government's case that the US government's duty not to return refugees (the non-refoulement principle) applied only to refugees within US territorial waters.

Under slightly different circumstances, deliberate action to prevent the arrival of asylum-seekers by the UK has also passed judicial muster. In *European Roma Rights Centre & others* vs. *The Immigration Officer at Prague Airport* (2003) in the UK Court of Appeal, the British government successfully defended its practice of stationing immigration officials at Prague Airport in the Czech Republic in order to prevent Roma boarding flights to Britain where, it was believed, they would claim asylum. In this case, the judges reasoned that the impediments were lawful in part because the 1951 Refugee Convention contains 'no right of access to [the UK] . . . or any other country to claim asylum' (s.37). Moreover, since Roma concerned had not been able to leave their country of residence, the non-arrival practice in question could not be said to involve 'returning' refugees, and thus could not be considered a violation of the non-refoulement principle.

The Convention, the judges found, is concerned 'not with permitting access to asylum-seekers but with the non-return of those who manage to gain such access' (s.37).

Morality is, of course, not the same thing as law. And I shall not enter into the issue of whether judges were right (in the law) to rule in the way they did. The question I want to ask is whether this (supposed) legal limitation on state responsibilities coincides with a moral one. Can a state evade moral responsibility for refugees simply by preventing their arrival? To answer this question it is helpful to begin by considering whence the responsibility to assist refugees derives. Many observers have argued that the duty to aid refugees can be derived from a more general humanitarian responsibility binding on everyone to provide assistance to individuals in need when the costs of doing so are low.[33] In the case of refugees, this general duty falls on states because only they control the good that refugees are in need of—access to a secure and protected territory. Most of the early theorists of international law believed that a state's right to sovereign control carried with it a correlative duty to provide asylum to refugees.[34]

Yet there are many states and many refugees. Unless an account of responsibilities can show how a particular state incurs an obligation to a particular refugee, one is left in a situation where refugees are the responsibility of all states in general, but no state in particular. The first natural law theorists of asylum, writers such as Grotius, Kant, and Vattel, seemed to have assumed that geographical proximity offered an answer to this question.[35] A state had a duty to aid those refugees who arrived at its own borders. A similar assumption was arguably also built in to the 1951 Refugee Convention. The obligation not to return (refouler) refugees was commonly interpreted as applying to those refugees who were in a particular state's territory or at its borders. Neither the early theorists of natural law, nor the Refugee Convention's framers, could have foreseen that this allocation mechanism might be evaded by measures to obstruct arrivals.

Non-arrival measures have rightly been criticized because of the appalling implications they have for the institution of asylum. If every state operated the way Britain and the US claim to be legitimately entitled to do in relation to all refugees, access to asylum would no longer exist (except perhaps through resettlement programmes). Dire as this situation would be, it is hard to blame states if one believes that it is the location of a refugee at (or within) the borders that creates a special responsibility between a particular state and a claimant for asylum. But should we accept this premise?

I think that territorial location is best viewed simply as a shorthand way of expressing a broader idea: that we have a special responsibility to those whose fate lies uniquely[36] in our hands. Obviously, a state has the fate of refugees in its hands when they arrive on its territory (what else could sovereignty mean?) But the relationship between territorial location and controlling a refugee's fate is a contingent one, especially in a world where states are increasingly able to project their power across borders. It is significant that the most influential recent defence of the non-refoulement principle (written in 1983 before the introduction of most non-arrival measures) argues that what is wrong about returning refugees is that it involves the state using 'force against helpless and desperate people'.[37] While its author, Michael Walzer, assumes that the refugees concerned will be at the borders of the state, the grounds he gives for the principle are detachable from this assumption. States also use force on 'helpless and desperate people' when they intercept boats on the high seas or block asylum-seekers (with the help of local police) from boarding flights in foreign airports. One can go even further. It is obvious that when a state uses physical force against asylum-seekers it controls their destiny, and thus ought to shape it in ways that are morally defensible. But it is not only through force that a state controls a refugee's fate. When it considers the visa application of a foreigner in need of refuge a state is equally (and presumably, uniquely) implicated in the person's plight. It makes little difference that the refugee's life chances are being determined by a pen rather than a gun.

If we accept, as I think we should, this broader account of how responsibilities to refugees are formed, then the act of exporting immigration control cannot offer states an escape route from their moral obligations.[38] As states move immigration control outwards across the globe, they become implicated in new ways in the fate of others, and in ways that it is wrong for them to ignore. The irony of this situation has recently been expressed by the political theorist Joseph Carens: 'if we deliberately take steps to make it difficult for potential legitimate asylum claimants to reach our shore', we establish the very 'moral connection we seek to prevent'.[39]

2. Preventing Abuse

A second and perhaps less dramatic claim is that non-arrival measures prevent 'abuse of the asylum system and illegal migration'.[40] It is often claimed that public confidence in asylum requires a reduction in the number of 'bogus asylum-seekers' or economic migrants arriving to claim protection. Many scholars and refugee activists have argued that allegations of asylum abuse are greatly exaggerated by populist media outlets and self-serving politicians.[41] In the UK, for example, where cries of 'abuse' have been widespread, around one-third of asylum-seekers were given Convention refugee status (or another humanitarian status) in 2002.[42] The accuracy of the characterization is also called into question by the countries from which most asylum-seekers arrive. Across Europe since the early 1990s, the largest groups of asylum-seekers have consistently come from the former Yugoslavia, Afghanistan, Iraq, Iran, Romania, Turkey, and Sri Lanka, countries notable for civil conflict or widespread human rights violations.[43] Of course, not everyone leaving these countries is a refugee. But lack of success in gaining refugee status is as often attributable to the narrow interpretation of eligibility for refugee status as it is to a desire to abuse asylum systems.

There are, then, good reasons for being sceptical about abuse claims. Nonetheless, let's put these doubts aside for the moment and take the argument at face value. Can non-arrival measures be justified if they prevent asylum abuse? Visa regimes, carrier sanctions, and pre-inspection at foreign airports all work to prevent the arrival of genuine refugees every bit as much as aspiring immigrants with dubious intentions. While it is not known how many actual refugees are prevented from accessing asylum by these measures, the effects of non-arrival policies are in themselves completely indiscriminate. Most refugees who do arrive at Western states now are forced to break the law to do so, usually with the help of traffickers or smugglers.[44] The best that could be said in defence of states is that refugees are a kind of 'double effect'[45] resulting from the legitimate targeting of economic migrants. They are unintentional casualties in a war to preserve asylum.

But if this were true, one would expect states concerned about asylum to strive to minimize the harm done to refugees, just as we expect civilian casualties to be minimized by states in a time of war. In both cases, the security and bodily integrity of innocent people is on the line. What steps might be taken? The European Council on Refugees and Exiles has recently suggested that states make people fleeing countries marked by 'civil wars or systematic abuses of human rights' exempt from visa requirements to enable them to enter European countries.[46] Another, different, possibility is for the overseas embassies of Western countries to process (or pre-screen) asylum claims in situ, in the refugee's country of origin; asylum-seekers with a credible claim would then be given a visa to travel to Western countries. This latter suggestion is a poor substitute for direct access to another country. Refugees often have to flee their country and have no time patiently to wait out bureaucratic formalities. Yet such a move would at least improve access to protection for some.

Few states have made any real attempt to disentangle refugees (or those with plausible asylum claims) from the web of restrictions. No state that I am aware of applies a general policy of allowing refugee-producing countries visa-free access. Many European countries, including Belgium, Germany, Finland, Spain, and Sweden do not allow asylum to be claimed at their embassies.[47] Indeed, the claim that refugees constitute unintended consequences in efforts to reduce abuse seems an over-generous interpretation of the Western state behaviour. The implementation of visa restrictions closely tracks rising refugee numbers in many countries. Britain, for example, introduced visas for Sri Lankans in 1987, people from the former Yugoslavia in 1992, and Sierra Leoneans and citizens of the Ivory Coast in 1994.[48] A British visa regime was implemented for Zimbabweans in 2003, over the public protestations of UNHCR.[49] Other countries, including Canada, Germany, and Australia (which, as I noted, has a visa requirement for all foreigners), have equally dubious track records. Non-arrival measures may aim to prevent the arrival of economic migrants, but clearly that is not their only aim.

Another reason the 'abuse defence' does not ring true is because governments do so little to inform the public of the downside of non-arrival measures. One would expect that a government reluctantly pushed into using these measures would be keen to highlight the way they harm genuine refugees. After all, even a highly restrictionist public might be prepared to tolerate a little 'abuse' in their asylum system, if they knew the price paid by refugees for stamping it out. But in their eagerness to impress us with falling asylum numbers, governments have edited out of their public pronouncements the consequences of non-arrival practices.[50] The widespread public assumption that there is nothing inconsistent about providing asylum for real refugees and strict exclusionary measures for bogus ones is thus never called into question.

3. Rectifying Injustice

A third and final justification for non-arrival measures has been to prevent countries becoming unfairly burdened. As asylum numbers have risen in recent years, politicians in such countries as Germany, Britain, and Australia have complained that their country is taking more than its 'fair share'[51] of those in need of protection, pointing to the need for 'more just'[52] arrangements. These feelings of injustice commonly reflect more widespread public concerns, and fuel the desire to prevent the arrival of asylum-seekers.

There are indeed substantial differences in the number of asylum-seekers and refugees that states host. Under current international law, the state responsible for protecting (or at least not returning) refugees is determined primarily by where an asylum-seeker arrives to claim protection. This, in turn, is influenced by a range of factors including a country's proximity to a region of refugee outflow, its reputation for welcoming immigrants, etc. As a result, some countries prove more popular destinations for asylum-seekers than others. For example, Germany's liberal asylum laws, long land borders, and large population of ethnic Yugoslavs, made it a common destination for refugees fleeing events associated with the break-up of Yugoslavia in the early 1990s (much to the chagrin of Germany's leaders). Similarly, Cuban and Haitian asylum-seekers and refugees have tended to head for the US and a range of other countries in the Caribbean region (such as the Dominican Republic), largely because of proximity, the presence of compatriots, and because other avenues for asylum are not open.

Are these inequalities across states unjust? There are a number of different standards for assessing asylum 'burdens'.[53] In terms of raw volume, Germany and the US are the only wealthy Western countries in the world's top ten refugee hosting states. All the remaining countries (with one exception) are in either Africa or Asia. If, however, one factors in other considerations, such as the proportion of refugees in relation to GDP, or the size of the national population, Western states have even less to complain about. According to UNHCR figures, in terms of proportion of GDP or of population density, only one wealthy industrial society makes it to the top ten most burdened states. Moreover, adjusted for GDP, the list of largest refugee hosting countries reads like a roll call of some of the world's poorest (and in some cases, most unstable) states: Armenia, Guinea, Tanzania, DRC, and Congo.[54]

This is not to say there is no basis to some of their complaints. The UK and Germany have had fairly high asylum levels compared to other European countries. Germany, for example, took around two-thirds of all asylum-seekers arriving in EU states throughout the 1990s.[55] Yet, if these countries have legitimate complaints against their neighbours, they still appear to be in debt to states in Africa and Asia. Indeed, when refugees leave refugee camps in Iran and Pakistan to travel to wealthy Western states, such as Australia, considerations of interstate justice (the equalization of burdens across states) would appear to require that they be allowed in.[56]

The discussion so far suggests that, considered globally, Western states are going to find it difficult to defend non-arrival measures on the grounds of justice. But the case against these measures is even stronger because their use tends merely to exacerbate current unfair distributions. Non-arrival measures lock refugees into their region of origin by ensuring that they do not have the documentation or permission (e.g. visas) necessary to leave. As most refugee-producing countries are in the South, and as these are already the countries with the highest refugee burdens, non-arrival measures merely cement existing injustices. To paraphrase the words of one recent observer, they contribute to 'burden shifting' rather than 'burden sharing'.[57]

IV. Humanizing Non-Arrival Measures

I hope now to have shown that the major justifications for non-arrival measures used by states do not resolve the paradox I identified at the beginning of this chapter. States have moral duties to asylum-seekers that they have prevented from arriving at their borders. Furthermore, non-arrival measures promote neither the interests of genuine refugees, nor lead to greater justice in the provision of asylum across states. Yet it might be said that there is another defence open to states: dismantling non-arrival measures would lead them to incur costs in excess of what could be demanded by the humanitarian principle. States have tended not to emphasize infrastructural, social, and political costs as a justification for recent restrictive practices. They have largely preferred to concentrate on questioning the integrity of claimants for asylum. Might it be, however, that getting rid of non-arrival measures is above and beyond the call of moral duty?

While we cannot know for certain what consequences would result from the demise of non-arrival measures, there is a real possibility that the number of asylum-seekers would rise substantially (if not, why should we be so concerned with these measures?[58]). There are a number of reasons for this: demand for entry into Western states currently far outstrips the availability of legal places; most Western states are highly unsuccessful at removing failed asylum claimants, more inclusive policies might thus serve as a magnet for people with weak or baseless claims; and it is unlikely that other states could be brought to agree on simultaneously dismantling control measures. If numbers did rise substantially, so would asylum processing costs and pressure on public infrastructure (schools, housing, health services, etc.) Public anxiety over asylum and immigration would also be likely to increase, especially if the growing number of entrants appeared uncontrolled or demand-driven. Of course, before most of these costs began to be felt, relaxed control measures would have become politically unfeasible. Any government in the current political environment presiding over large, short-term increases in asylum numbers would find itself dangerously unpopular with large sections of the electorate.

This is, it should be stressed, only one possible scenario for what would happen if non-arrival measures were dismantled. It is, however, the outcome that most concentrates the minds of governments in Western states, and it is a highly plausible one. It suggests the possibility of an impasse: non-arrival measures mock the principle of asylum, but states have powerful reasons not to dismantle them.

Yet even if we accept that this scenario is credible, there are good reasons for believing that things are not as deadlocked as they might at first seem. To begin with, the 'costs' faced by states are partly a social and political construct that governments play an important role in shaping.[59] For example, public attitudes towards asylum-seekers (and thus the likelihood of social conflict) can be influenced by the way political leaders characterize asylum-seekers. When exaggerated, alarmist and, frankly, racist portrayals of asylum-seekers in the electronic and print media are reinforced (or even left unchallenged) by political elites, it is not surprising that governments find themselves dealing with intolerant publics. In a different vein, governments may have some control over demand for entry from economic migrants. Policies that increase economic opportunities and living standards in poorer countries can address people's need to migrate, and thus pressure on asylum systems from those with weak claims. No government, it is true, has the power in the short term simply to eliminate the costs associated with the entry of asylum-seekers. The changes mentioned will take long-term commitment to bear fruit. Nonetheless, an understanding of costs as constructed provides a reason for not succumbing to fatalism in terms of what states can do.

Another reason to be dubious of the description of deadlock is that it relies on a dramatic contrast between the current state of affairs of growing use of non-arrival measures and an alternative scenario involving their complete abolition. At the risk of stating the blindingly obvious, there may be choices falling between these two options: ways of operating non-arrival measures that ensure that avenues to asylum are kept open.

I have already hinted at some of the elements of a com-promise. States could, first of all, allow refugees to apply for asylum at their foreign consulates. This would enable those prevented from leaving their state still to seek protection.

Since this will not be a suitable option for many refugees, Western states should, secondly, consider supporting, through financial and logistical help, the establishment of asylum pro-cessing centres in safe countries within major regions of forced migration outflow. These centres would allow those facing problems reaching Western states an opportunity to present their case for entry in a secure environment without having to make long, difficult, and dangerous journeys. A Western state could then arrange to resettle (with or without the help of other states) those who receive refugee status.[60] It is important to emphasize that I am not suggesting the establishment of places to which asylum-seekers who reach Western states could be deported. This would simply add another non-arrival measure to the mix (albeit one that held out the opportunity of eventual asylum). Rather, I am propos-ing sites that would provide a non-compulsory alternative for those asylum-seekers who otherwise would incur the expense and danger of long voyages to Western states with the dubious help of smugglers or traffickers. There are benefits to Western states, too, in this proposal. Refugees would arrive pre-screened, and the problems associated with the arrival of asylum-seekers with weak claims would be reduced.

Thirdly, states should waive visa requirements on those countries that face serious human rights violations and produce refugees on a large scale. In order to achieve this task, the international refugee organization, UNHCR, could provide a regular list of eligible countries, adjusting it to reflect the situation therein. States could, if they agreed, also construct principles for the distribution of responsibilities between themselves. They might decide, for example, which state would create visa openings for which refugee generating country (say, the UK for Somalia, or France for Algeria). These openings could reflect historical or cultural affinities between the refugees and the potential host state. They could also be operated so as to acknowledge considerations of fairness in the distribution of refugees and asylum-seekers between participating states (by ensuring proportional numbers of asylum-seekers entered participating states). The new attitude to visas would not mean that everyone who arrives with a visa would be granted asylum. But it would provide more people currently excluded by non-arrival measures with a chance to claim refugee status.

Taken together these three changes would challenge the most morally dubious aspects of non-arrival measures. Their implementation would not require a commitment to the complete dismantling of non-arrival measures with the full (social, political, and financial) costs of such a move. Those in need of asylum would be provided with new avenues for access to the West. States would probably find themselves facing more refugees and claimants for asylum than they currently do (that, I think, is the point!). But they could be reasonably confident that those arriving would be refugees, either because their status was determined before stepping on the state's soil, or because they would come from countries well known to be refugee source countries. Rather than building up walls that indiscriminately block unwanted economic migrants from poor countries, asylum-seekers, and refugees, Western states would have established something more akin to a sieve:[61] control procedures that offer states the chance to sift through aspiring entrants before arrival to identify refugees and asylum-seekers. The paradox at the heart of current Western policies—the simultaneous recognition and undermining of the rights of refugees—would thus be lessened, if not eliminated.

Conclusion

Is there any reason to believe that states would actually make these changes? If states currently have a powerful interest in minimizing the number of people claiming asylum, why should we expect this to change?

There have been numerous attempts to explain why states have adopted restrictive policies towards asylum-seekers in recent years. Some observers have stressed the diminishing value of refugees with the end of the Cold War,[62] others have emphasized popular pressures for restriction stemming from changes in the way refugees arrive at state territory,[63] and others still have pointed to the desire of political elites to distract the public's attention from their limited ability to control the economic forces central to the destiny of the citizens they rule over in a globalized world.[64] While each of these explanations helps us to understand restrictionist pressures, they offer little insight in themselves into why measures to control asylum have taken the form they have:

why, that is, states have increasingly expanded border control outwards.

The answer to this question, I believe, lies in large part in the desire of Western states to escape constraints on their treatment of asylum-seekers within their territory imposed by domestic actors: the courts, non-governmental organizations, human rights groups, and sections of the public. These actors are, along with liberal norms these groups articulate and appeal to, part of a broader 'culture of rights' that has developed in Western states, particularly since 1945. This culture has not prevented harsh measures being implemented on those asylum-seekers who have arrived. But it has slowed down their implementation, and made practices such as detention, deportation, and the removal of welfare rights extremely expensive for states and liable to legal challenge under domestic and international law.[65] The exportation of border controls is thus a kind of backhanded compliment to those domestic actors that have challenged the restrictionist direction of policies toward asylum-seekers.

If this is an accurate explanation for the proliferation of non-arrival measures, then the way forward for those interested in protecting refugees seems clear. They need simultaneously to spread the culture of rights abroad and to work to create a political environment more receptive to asylum-seekers and refugees at home. This may be a clear task but no one could pretend it is an easy one. Human rights organizations, the courts, and national media often lack the resources, authority, or ability to act beyond the territory of their own state. Public discussions of asylum and migration, more generally, often degenerate into prejudice, political manœuvring, and unfounded anxiety. I have no special insight into how these problems might be resolved. But I do believe that a key step in the creation of this culture both abroad and at home must involve the relatively simple step of shining the light of publicity on what states do beyond their borders.

Publicity may not in itself offer an answer to key social and political questions. It provides no way of resolving the genuine difficulties states face in responding to forced migrants in a world characterized by grave injustices and huge inequalities. But by revealing the inconsistencies between how refugees are treated at home and abroad; following the transfer of power from state officials to private actors; and tracking the fate of those individuals turned away or prevented from entering, it can inform us of the hypocrisies and true costs of current courses of action. Forty years on from Brecht's observations, the refugee has once again become lost—this time from our sight. Exposing the reality of non-arrival measures may be one way of bringing the refugee back into view.

Response to Matthew J. Gibney, 'A Thousand Little Guantanamos'

Melissa Lane

The title of Matthew Gibney's essay, A Thousand Little Guantanamos', darkly recasts a remark made by Michael Walzer in his brief but influential discussion of refugees. According to Walzer, far from free movement at the neighbourhood level being a model for instituting free global migration, the former is made possible only on the basis of control of immigration by the state. Without such state control, he prophesied, 'a thousand petty fortresses' would arise as neighbourhoods and municipalities sought to reassert control over borders at their own levels.[1] Among the many things we can learn from Gibney's trenchant essay is that while current Western immigration policies may eliminate the need for a thousand petty fortresses at home, they increasingly claim to be able to do so only by establishing a thousand petty fortresses for unfortunates abroad. (As Jeremy Waldron has observed, when it is said that a price must be paid for our security, very often that price is paid by someone else.[2]) Contrasting Gibney and Walzer can help us to bring out some further points about the meaning of non-refoulement, points which Gibney does not make but which I think should be congenial to him. After discussing these, I will conclude with some brief reflections on the imagination of political space.

The first point is whether non-refoulement applies only to refugees who have succeeded in reaching at least temporary safety. Although Gibney himself describes Walzer's argument against non-refoulement as based on the fact that it would involve the state 'using force against helpless and desperate people', Walzer actually relied more fundamentally on a different argument. He posited that the principle of asylum applies to refugees who have succeeded in finding refuge in some state not their own, from which they should not then be expelled. Just as those who have made their life in a place should not be expelled from it, so someone who has only just arrived but has 'no other place where he can make a life' must not be expelled either.[3] Non-refoulement on this view would apply only to refugees who have actually arrived. If this were right, it would undermine Gibney's concern with the case of the refugee who has not yet arrived at such a border — for the principle of non-refoulement would not on Walzer's account apply to that case at all.

But surely Walzer was wrong. The justification underlying non-refoulement is not that the person at risk of refoulement has already succeeded in making a life for herself somewhere else, but rather that she should not be returned to any territory under a state authority where her life or freedom would be threatened due to persecution for the political reasons proscribed generally by the 1951 Convention relating to the Status of Refugees. What matters is not what she has managed to achieve here, but what likely fate awaits her there. The wording of Article 33 makes this plain. Contracting states there undertake not to 'expel or return ("refouler") a refugee in any manner whatsoever to the frontiers of territories where his life or freedom would be threatened on account of his race, religion, nationality, membership of a particular social group or political opinion'.[4] If this obligation generates a right to asylum when a refugee is already in or at the borders of privileged state territory, because he or she has in that circumstance nowhere else to go save the place of endangerment, then it should also do so when to keep a refugee at bay by non-arrival measures has the same effect. Should it be argued that in the latter case it is impossible to determine who is and is not a genuine refugee in terms of the 1951 Convention, the only legitimate answer is to modify such measures to allow for the determination to be made. To keep out all asylum-seekers indiscriminately is, as Gibney shows, to make it impossible for genuine refugees to achieve refuge. This cannot be justified even in terms of double effect. That doctrine would apply if, say, keeping our obligation to let in some genuine refugees, we found ourselves forced to repel others. But the intention of non-arrival measures is to keep everyone out precisely in order to bring down numbers of all asylum-seekers in the privileged territory, whether genuine refugees or not. That intention is precisely what is achieved: there is no double-effect about it.

Such an understanding enables us to register just how shocking are the 'non-arrival' measures Gibney describes. For, having unilaterally and tacitly confined the obligation of non-refoulement to refugees who manage to make it 'inside' some relevant bit of privileged space, more and more states are now concentrating their efforts on making it impossible for any refugee to succeed in making it inside at all. In his recent book, Gibney calls this 'a kind of schizophrenia' and an instance of 'organized hypocrisy'[5] and both epithets are richly deserved. Many of the 'non-arrival' policies he details are worthy of Kafka. Imagine that a state claimed to respect the right to jury trial but bricked up all entrances to the courts.[6]

Yet in speaking of not returning refugees 'to the frontiers' of any state where they would be at risk of persecution, Article 33 equally seems to presuppose that the refugees in question have succeeded in leaving their endangering state. So while current state practices of non-arrival—by assuming that obligations of asylum arise only once the refugee is inside some privileged part of the national territory—are too narrow, aspects of Gibney's analysis of the current situation are arguably too broad. People who are still inside their states, applying for visas, are not yet refugees to whom the particular responsibility of non-refoulement applies, despite Gibney's powerful point about the pen being as potentially lethal as the gun. The force of Gibney's analysis is better confined to the moments and sites where, refugees having fled persecution in their countries of origin, they find themselves confronted with force or obstacles designed to prevent them from accessing a place of refuge, which may have the result of leaving them with no option but to return to their place of endangerment.

The question then is whether a given state's taking measures to repel or prevent entry to its privileged territory at such a moment, is tantamount to 'expelling or returning' the refugees to the place of endangerment—for that outcome comes about only if all other states of possible refuge do the same. Gibney's principle of 'uniqueness' does not provide enough help here, because state A does not uniquely hold responsibility for refugee X's fate if it is logically and practically possible (even if unlikely) that state B could step in and offer refuge instead. And in some circumstances, particularly in cases where refugees are being repelled on the high seas, there may be other countries (as in the Pacific near Australia) where they could conceivably go. Instead, what we need to draw on is a notion of complicity. It has been argued that one is complicit when one plays one's part in what one expects will result from what others do.[7] On this account, most states operating non-arrival measures are likely to be found, on the facts, complicit in any resulting refoulement of refugees. Another way to put this is that states bear the imperfect obligation not to act in such a way as could rightly be described as playing their part in the refoulement of refugees as the expected result. If they find this burden too onerous, they have open to them the standard move in coping with imperfect obligations: they could set up institutions to share the burden more equitably.

I conclude by explaining my locution of 'privileged' space or territory. As Gibney shows, many states now claim that the obligation of non-refoulement applies only to sovereign territory which they have deemed to be functionally part of the state for the purposes of immigration law. We may call territory which is deemed functionally part of the state for the purposes of some domain of law 'privileged' with respect to this domain; it is to be contrasted with the de-privileged territories from which standing for these purposes has been stripped away. Gibney gives many chilling examples of such de-privileging for the purposes of immigration, including the Australian island territories and Guantanamo Bay in its previous incarnation as a holding station for those fleeing Haiti and Cuba. (Although in these two cases, as Gibney notes, the privileges stripped away have been those of domestic constitutional protection rather than the 1951 Convention, the attitude of the US government to its present use of Guantanamo is indicative that international treaties are also at risk in such zones.) Additional examples are the embassies or consulates, and the airport zones even on 'home' state territory itself, which have been redesignated as de-privileged for immigration purposes.

These many and varied de-privileged spaces constitute a

new and sinister form of what Neil Ascherson has called 'international space'.[8] Noting that the prevailing image of international space has a cellular structure, of cells (states) abutting other cells, Ascherson remarked that we might also attend, inter alia, to the gaps that appear between the cells and to the vacancies created when cells collapse. But his view of such vacancies was that they would inevitably be brief, as neighbouring cells would soon fill them. Ascherson did not envisage that cells might choose deliberately to evacuate part of themselves, excising part of their territory for some but only some purposes: they carefully retain the sovereign authority to declare that elements of their exercise of sovereign authority do not apply. Matthew Gibney's chapter teaches us that space and territoriality are themselves becoming abstract. No longer are they the terra firma on which our rights are clearly grounded. The de-privileging of territory – ostensibly in order to keep out those seeking asylum—actually results in cutting the ground out from under everyone's feet.

5

The Repositioning of Citizenship and Alienage: Emergent Subjects and Spaces for Politics

Saskia Sassen

Most of the scholarship on citizenship has claimed a necessary connection to the national state. The transformations afoot today raise questions about this proposition in so far as they significantly alter those conditions which in the past fed that articulation between citizenship and the national state. The context for this possible alteration is defined by two major, partly interconnected conditions. One is the change in the position and institutional features of national states since the 1980s resulting from various forms of globalization. These range from economic privatization and deregulation to the increased prominence of the international human rights regime. The second is the emergence of multiple actors, groups, and communities partly strengthened by these transformations in the state and increasingly unwilling automatically to identify with a nation as represented by the state.

Addressing the question of citizenship against these transformations entails a specific stance. It is quite possible to posit that at the most abstract or formal level not much has changed over the last century in the essential features of citizenship. This is not the theoretical ground from which I address the issue. I emphasize the historicity and the embeddedness of both categories, formal membership and the national state. I posit that citizenship and alienage are incompletely theorized contracts between subjects and the state: In locating my enquiry at this point of incompleteness, I allow for the possibility of micro-transformations in both formal and non-formal components of membership. Each of these has been constructed in elaborate and formal ways. And each has evolved historically as a tightly packaged bundle of what were in fact often rather diverse elements. The dynamics at work today are destabilizing these particular bundlings and bringing to the fore the fact itself of that bundling and its particularity. Through their destabilizing effects, these dynamics are producing operational and rhetorical openings for the emergence of new types of political subjects and new spatialities for politics.

More broadly, the destabilizing of national state-centred hierarchies of legitimate power and allegiance has enabled a multiplication of non-formalized or only partly formalized political dynamics and actors. Further specific transformations inside the national state have directly and indirectly altered particular features of the institution of citizenship. These transformations are not predicated necessarily on deterritorialization or locations for the institution outside the national state as is key to conceptions of post-national citizenship, and hence are usefully distinguished from current notions of post-national citizenship. I will refer to these as denationalized forms of citizenship.

Analytically, I seek to understand how various transformations entail continuities or discontinuities in the basic institutional form. That is to say, where do we see continuities in the formal bundle of rights at the heart of the institution and where do we see movement towards post-national and/or denationalized features of citizenship? And where might as yet informal citizenship practices engender formalizations of new types of rights? Particular attention goes to several specific issues that capture these features. One of these is the relationship between citizenship and nationality and the evolution of the latter towards something akin to 'effective' nationality rather than as 'allegiance' to one state or exclusively formal nationality. A later section examines the mix of distinct elements that actually make up the category of citizenship in today's highly developed countries. Far from being a unitary category or a mere legal status, these diverse elements can be contradictory. One of my assumptions here is that the destabilizing impact of globalization contributes to accentuate the distinctiveness of each of these elements. A case in point is the growing tension between the legal form and the normative project towards enhanced inclusion as various minorities and disadvantaged sectors gain visibility for their claim-making. Critical here is the failure in most countries to achieve 'equal' citizenship—that is, not just a formal status but an enabling condition.

The remaining sections begin to theorize these issues with a view towards specifying incipient and typically not formalized developments in the institution of citizenship. Informal practices and political subjects not quite fully recognized as such can nonetheless function as part of the political landscape. Undocumented immigrants who are long-term residents engage in practices that are the same as those of formally defined citizens in the routines of daily life; this produces an informal social contract between these undocumented immigrants and the community. Subjects who are by definition categorized as non-political, such as 'housewives', may actually have considerable political agency and be emergent political subjects. In so far as citizenship is at least partly shaped by the conditions within which it is embedded, conditions that have today changed in certain very specific and also general ways, we may well be seeing a corresponding set of changes in the institution itself. These may not yet be formalized and some may never become fully formalized. Further, social constructions that mark individuals, such as race and ethnicity, may well become destabilized by these developments in both the institution of citizenship and the nation-state. Generally, the analysis in this chapter suggests that we might see an unbounding of existing types of subjects, particularly dominant ones such as the citizen-subject, the alien, and the racialized subject.

A concluding section argues that many of these transformations in the broader context and in the institution itself become legible in today's large cities. Perhaps the most evolved type of site for these transformations is the global city.[1] In this process, the global city is reconfigured as a partly denationalized space that enables a partial reinvention of citizenship. This reinvention takes the institution away from questions of nationality narrowly defined and towards the enactment of a large array of particular interests, from protests against police brutality and globalization to sexual preference politics and house-squatting by anarchists. I interpret this as a move towards citizenship practices that revolve around claiming rights to the city. These are not exclusively or necessarily urban practices. But it is especially in large cities that we see simultaneously some of the most extreme inequalities and the conditions enabling these citizenship practices. In global cities, these practices also contain the possibility of directly engaging strategic forms of power, a fact which I interpret as significant in a context where power is increasingly privatized, globalized, and elusive.

SASKIA SASSEN

I. Citizenship and Nationality

In its narrowest definition citizenship describes the legal relationship between the individual and the polity. This relation can in principle assume many forms, in good part depending on the definition of the polity. Thus, in Europe this definition of the polity was originally the city, in both ancient and medieval times. But it is the evolution of polities along the lines of state formation that gave citizenship in the West its full institutionalized and formalized character and that made nationality a key component of citizenship.

Today the terms 'citizenship' and 'nationality' both refer to the national state. In a technical legal sense, while essentially the same concept, each term reflects a different legal framework. Both identify the legal status of an individual in terms of state membership. But citizenship is largely confined to the national dimension, while nationality refers to the international legal dimension in the context of an interstate system. The legal status entails the specifics of whom the state recognizes as a citizen and the formal basis for the rights and responsibilities of the individual in relation to the state. International law affirms that each state may determine who will be considered a citizen of that state.[2] Domestic laws about who is a citizen vary significantly across states and so do the definitions of what it entails to be a citizen. Even within Europe, let alone worldwide, there are marked differences in how citizenship is articulated and hence how non-citizens are defined.

The aggressive nationalism and territorial competition among European states in the eighteenth, nineteenth, and well into the twentieth centuries made the concept of dual nationality generally undesirable, incompatible with individual loyalties, and destabilizing of the international order.

Absolute state authority over a territory and its nationals could not easily accommodate dual nationality. Indeed, we see the development of a series of mechanisms aimed at preventing or counteracting the common causes for dual nationality.[3] This negative perception of dual nationality continued into the first half of the twentieth century and well into the 1960s. There were no international accords on dual nationality. The main effort by the international system remained rooting out the causes of dual nationality by means of multilateral codification of the law on the subject.[4] It is probably the case that this particular form of the institution of citizenship, centred on exclusive allegiance, reached its high point in the twentieth century.

The major transformations of the 1980s and 1990s have once again brought conditions for a change in the institution of citizenship and its relation to nationality, and they have brought about changes in the legal content of nationality. Mostly minor formal and non-formal changes are beginning to dilute the particular formalization coming out of European history. The long-lasting resistance to dual or multiple nationality is shifting towards a selective acceptance. According to some legal scholars in the future dual and multiple nationality will become the norm.[5] Today, more people than ever before have dual nationality. In so far as the importance of nationality is a function of the central role of states in the international system, it is quite possible that a decline in the importance of this role and a proliferation of other actors will affect the value of nationality.

These transformations may give citizenship yet another set of features as it continues to respond to the conditions within which it is embedded.[6] The nationalizing of the institution, which took place over the last several centuries, may today give way to a partial denationalizing. A fundamental dynamic in this regard is the growing articulation of national economies with the global economy and the associated pressures on states to be competitive. Crucial to current notions of competitive states is withdrawal from various spheres of citizenship entitlements, with the possibility of a corresponding dilution of loyalty to the state. Citizens' loyalty may in turn be less crucial to the state today than it was at a time of people-intensive and frequent warfare, with its need for loyal citizen-soldiers.[7] Masses of troops today can be replaced by technologically intensive methods of warfare. Most import-antly, in the highly developed world, warfare has become less significant partly due to economic globalization. Global firms and markets do not want the rich countries to fight wars among themselves. The 'international' project of the most powerful actors on the world stage today is radically different from what it was in the nineteenth and first half of the twentieth centuries.

Many of the dynamics that built economies, polities, and societies in the nineteenth and twentieth centuries contained an articulation between the national scale and the growth of entitlements for citizens. During industrialization, class forma-tion, class struggles, and the advantages of both employers and workers tended to scale at the national level and became identified with state-produced legislation and regulations, entitlements, and obligations. The state came to be seen as a key to ensuring the well-being of significant portions of both the working class and the bourgeoisie. The development of welfare states in the twentieth century became a crucial insti-tutional domain for granting entitlements to the poor and the disadvantaged. Today, the growing weight given to notions of the 'competitiveness' of states puts pressure on states to cut down on these entitlements. This in turn weakens the reciprocal relationship between the poor and the state.[8] Finally, the growth of unemployment and the fact that many of the young are developing weak ties to the labour market, once thought of as a crucial mechanism for the socialization of young adults, will further weaken the loyalty and sense of reciprocity between these future adults and the state.[9]

As these trends have come together towards the end of the twentieth century they are contributing to destabilize the meaning of citizenship as it was forged in the nineteenth and much of the twentieth centuries. Economic policies and technical developments we associate with economic globalization have strengthened the importance of cross-border dynamics and reduced that of borders. The associated emphasis on markets has brought into question the foundations of the welfare state. T. H. Marshall and many others saw and continue to see the welfare state as an important ingredient of social citizenship.[10] Today the assumptions of the dominant model of Marshallian citizenship have been severely diluted under the impact of globalization and the ascendance of the market as the preferred mechanism for addressing these social issues. For many critics, the reliance on markets to solve political and social problems is a savage attack on the principles of citizenship. Thus Peter Saunders argues that citizenship inscribed in the institutions of the welfare state is a buffer against the vagaries of the market and the inequalities of the class system.[11]

The nature of citizenship has also been challenged by a proliferation of old issues that have gained new attention. Among the latter are the question of state membership of aboriginal communities, stateless people, and refugees.[12] All of these have important implications for human rights in relation to citizenship. These social changes in the role of the state, the impact of globalization on states, and the relationship between dominant and subordinate groups also have major implications for questions of identity. 'Is citizenship a useful concept for exploring the problems of belonging, identity and personality in the modern world?'[13] Can such a radical change in the conditions for citizenship leave the institution itself unchanged?

II. Deconstructing Citizenship

Though often talked about as a single concept and experienced as a unitary institution, citizenship actually describes a number of discrete but related aspects in the relation between the individual and the polity. Current developments are bringing to light and accentuating the distinctiveness of these various aspects, from formal rights to practices and psychological dimensions.[14] They make legible the tension between citizenship as a formal legal status and as a normative project or an aspiration. The formal equality granted to all citizens rarely rests on the need for substantive equality in social and even political terms. In brief, current conditions have strengthened the emphasis on rights and aspirations that go beyond the formal legal definition of rights and obligations.

This is mirrored most recently in the reinvigoration of theoretical distinctions: communitarian and deliberative, republican and liberal, feminist, post-national, and cosmopolitan notions of citizenship. In so far as citizenship is a status which articulates legal rights and responsibilities, the mechanisms through which this articulation is shaped and implemented can be analytically distinguished from the status itself and so can the content of the rights. In the medieval cities so admired by Max Weber, it was urban residents themselves who set up the structures through which to establish and thicken their rights in the space of the city.[15] Today it is the national state that provides these mechanisms and it does so for national political space. But these mechanisms may well be changing once again given globalization, the associated changes in the national state, and the ascendance of human rights. In each of these major phases, the actual content and shape of the legal rights and obligations also changed.

Some of these issues can be illustrated through the evolution of equal citizenship over the last few decades. Equal citizenship is central to the modern institution of citizenship. The expansion of equality among citizens has shaped a good part of its evolution in the twentieth century. There is debate as to what brought about the expanded inclusions over this period, most notably the granting of the vote to women. For some, it is law itself—and national law—that has been crucial in promoting recognition of exclusions and measures for their elimination.[16] For others politics and identity have been essential because they provide the sense of solidarity necessary for the further development of modern citizenship in the nation-state.[17] Either way, in so far as equality is based on membership, citizenship status forms the basis of an exclusive politics and identity.[18]

In a country such as the US, the principle of equal citizenship remains unfulfilled, even after the successful struggles and legal advances of the last five decades.[19] Groups defined by race, ethnicity, religion, sex, sexual orientation, and other 'identities' still face various exclusions from full participation in public life notwithstanding formal equality as citizens. Second, because full participation as a citizen rests on a material base, poverty excludes large sectors of the population and the gap is widening.[20] Feminist and race-critical scholarship have highlighted the failure of gender- and race-neutral conceptions of citizenship, such as legal status, to account for the differences of individuals within communities.[21] In brief, legal citizenship does not always bring full and equal membership rights. Citizenship is affected by the position of different groups within a nation-state.

Yet it is precisely the position of these different groups that has engendered the practices and struggles that forced changes in the institution of citizenship itself. Thus Kenneth Karst observes that in the US it was national law that 'braided the strands of citizenship'—formal legal status, rights, belonging—into the principle of equal citizenship.[22] This took place through a series of Supreme Court decisions and acts of Congress beginning with the Civil Rights Act of 1964. Karst emphasizes how important these constitutional and legislative instruments are, and that we cannot take citizenship for granted or be complacent about it.

There are two aspects here that matter for my argument. This history of interactions between differential positionings and expanded inclusions signals the possibility that the new conditions of inequality and difference evident today and the new types of claim-making they produce may well bring about further transformations in the institution. Citizenship is partly produced by the practices of the excluded. Secondly, by expanding the formal inclusionary aspect of citizenship, the national state contributed to create some of the conditions that eventually would facilitate key aspects of post-national citizenship. At the same time, in so far as the state itself has undergone significant transformation, notably the changes bundled under the notion of the competitive state, it may reduce the chances that state institutions will do the type of legislative and judiciary work that has led to expanded formal inclusions.

The consequence of these two developments may well be the absence of a lineal progression in the evolution of the institution. The expanding inclusions that we have seen in the US since the 1960s may have produced conditions which make possible forms of citizenship that follow a different trajectory. Furthermore, the pressures of globalization on national states may mean that claim-making will increasingly be directed at other institutions as well. This is already evident in a variety of instances. One example is the decision by first-nation people to go directly to the UN and claim direct representation in international fora, rather than going through the national state. It is also evident in the increasingly institutionalized framework of the international human rights regime and the emergent possibilities for bypassing unilateral state sovereignty.

As the importance of equality in citizenship has grown and become more visible, and as the role of national law to giving presence and voice to hitherto silenced minorities has grown, the tension between the formal status and the normative project of citizenship has also grown. For many, citizenship is becoming a normative project whereby social membership becomes increasingly comprehensive and open-ended. Globalization and human rights are further enabling this tension and therewith furthering the elements of a new discourse on rights. These developments signal that the analytic terrain within which we need to place the question of rights, authority, and obligations is shifting.[23] Some of these issues can be illustrated by two contrasting cases described below.

III. Towards Effective Nationality and Informal Citizenship

1. Unauthorized Yet Recognized

Perhaps one of the more extreme instances of a condition akin to effective as opposed to formal nationality is what has been called the informal social contract that binds undocumented immigrants to their communities of residence.[24] Thus, unauthorized immigrants who demonstrate civic involvement, social deservedness, and national loyalty can argue that they merit legal residency. To make this brief examination more specific, I will focus on one case, undocumented immigrants in the US.

Individuals, even when undocumented immigrants, can move between the multiple meanings of citizenship. The daily practices by undocumented immigrants as part of their daily life in the community where they reside—such as raising a family, schooling children, holding a job—earn them citizenship claims in the US even as the formal status and, more narrowly, legalization may continue to evade them. There are dimensions of citizenship, such as strong community ties and participation in civic activities, which are being enacted informally through these practices. These practices produce an at least partial recognition of them as full social beings. In many countries around the world, including the US, long-term undocumented residents often can gain legal residence if they can document the fact of this long-term residence and 'good conduct'. US immigration law recognizes such informal participation as grounds for granting legal residency. For instance, prior to the new immigration law passed in 1996, individuals who could prove seven years of continuous presence, and good moral character, and that deportation would be an extreme hardship, were eligible for suspension of deportation, and thus, US residency. NACARA extended the eligibility of this suspension of deportation to some 300,000 Salvadorans and Guatemalans who were unauthorized residents in the US.[25]

The case of undocumented immigrants is, in many ways, a very particular and special illustration of a condition akin to 'effective' citizenship and nationality. One way of interpreting this dynamic in the light of the discussion in the preceding sections is to emphasize that it is the fact of the multiple dimensions of citizenship which engenders strategies for legitimizing informal or extra-statal forms of membership.[26] The practices of these undocumented immigrants are a form of citizenship practices and their identities as members of a community of residence assume some of the features of citizenship identities. Supposedly this could hold even in the communitarian model where the community can decide on whom to admit and whom to exclude, but once admitted, proper civic practices earn full membership.

Further, the practices of migrants, even if undocumented, can contribute to recognition of their rights in countries of origin. During the 1981–92 civil war, Salvadoran migrants, even though citizens of El Salvador, were directly and indirectly excluded from El Salvador through political violence, enormous economic hardship, and direct persecution.[27] They could not enjoy their rights as citizens. After fleeing, many continued to provide support to their families and communities. Further, migrants' remittances became a key factor for El Salvador's economy—as they are for several countries around the world. The government of El Salvador actually began to support the emigrants' fight to get residency rights in the US, even joining US-based activist organizations in this effort. The Salvadoran government was thus supporting Salvadorans who were the formerly excluded citizens—they needed those remittances to keep coming and they needed the emigrants to stay out of the Salvadoran workforce given high unemployment. Thus the participation of these undocumented migrants in cross-border community, family, and political networks has contributed to increasing recognition of their legal and political rights as Salvadoran citizens.[28]

According to Susan Coutin and others, movements between membership and exclusion, and between different dimensions of citizenship, legitimacy, and illegitimacy, may be as important as redefinitions of citizenship itself. Given scarce resources the possibility of negotiating the different dimensions of citizenship may well represent an important enabling condition. Undocumented immigrants develop informal, covert, often extra-statal strategies and networks connecting them with communities in sending countries. Hometowns rely on their remittances and their information about jobs in the US. Sending remittances illegally by an unauthorized immigrant can be seen as an act of patriotism, and working as an undocumented immigrant can be seen as contributing to the host economy. Multiple interdependencies are thereby established and grounds for claims on the receiving and the originating country can be established even when the immigrants are undocumented and laws are broken.[29]

2. Authorized Yet Unrecognized

At perhaps the other extreme of the undocumented immigrant whose practices allow her to become accepted as a member of the political community, is the case of those who are full citizens yet not recognized as political subjects. In an enormously insightful study of Japanese housewives, Robin LeBlanc finds precisely this combination.[30]

Being a housewife is basically a full-time occupation in Japan and restricts Japanese women's public life in many important ways, both practical and symbolical. A 'housewife' in Japan is a person whose very identity is customarily that of a particularistic, non-political actor. Yet, paradoxically, it is also a condition providing these women with a unique vehicle for other forms of public participation, where being a housewife is an advantage, one denied to those who might have the qualifications of higher-level political life. LeBlanc documents how the housewife has an advantage in the world of local politics or the political life of a local area: she can be trusted precisely because she is a housewife, she can build networks with other housewives, hers is the image of desirable public concern and of a powerful—because believable—critic of mainstream politics.

There is something extremely important in this condition which is shared with women in other cultures and *vis-à-vis* different issues. For instance, and in a very different register, women emerged as a specific type of political actor during the brutal dictatorships of the 1970s and 1980s in several countries of Latin America. It was precisely their condition as mothers and wives that gave them the clarity and the courage to demand justice and to demand bread and to do so confronting armed soldiers and policemen. Mothers in the barrios of Santiago during Pinochet's dictatorship, the mothers of the Plaza de Mayo in Buenos Aires, the mothers regularly demonstrating in front of the major prisons in El Salvador during the civil war—all were driven to political action by their despair at the loss of children and husbands and the struggle to provide food in their homes.

SASKIA SASSEN

Further, and in a very different type of situation, there is an interesting parallel between LeBlanc's capturing of the political in the condition of the housewife and a set of findings in some of the research on immigrant women in the US. There is growing evidence that immigrant women are more likely than immigrant men to emerge as actors in the public domain precisely because of their responsibilities in the household. Regular wage work and improved access to other public realms has an impact on their culturally specified subordinate role to men in the household. Immigrant women gain greater personal autonomy and independence while immigrant men lose ground compared to what was their condition in cultures of origin. Women gain more control over budgeting and other domestic decisions, and greater leverage in requesting help from men in domestic chores. Their responsibility for securing public services and other public resources for their families gives them a chance to become incorporated in the mainstream society—they are often the ones in the household who mediate in this process.[31] It is likely that some women benefit more than others from these circumstances; we need more research to establish the impact of class, education, and income on these gendered outcomes.

Besides the relatively greater empowerment of immigrant women in the household associated with waged employment, what matters here is their greater participation in the public sphere and their possible emergence as public actors. There are two arenas where immigrant women are active: institutions for public and private assistance, and the immigrant or ethnic community. The incorporation of women in the migration process strengthens the settlement likelihood and contributes to greater immigrant participation in their communities and *vis-à-vis* the state. For instance, Pierrette Hondagneu-Sotelo found immigrant women come to assume more active public and social roles, which further reinforces their status in the household and the settlement process.[32] These immigrant women are more active in community building and community activism and they are positioned differently from men regarding the broader economy and the state. They are the ones that are likely to have to handle the legal vulnerability of their families in the process of seeking public and social services for them. This greater participation by women suggests the possibility that they may emerge as more forceful and visible actors and make their role in the labour market more visible as well.[33]

These are dimensions of citizenship and citizenship practices that do not fit the indicators and categories of mainstream frameworks for understanding citizenship and political life. Women in the condition of housewives and mothers do not fit the categories and indicators used to capture participation in political life. Feminist scholarship in all the social sciences has had to deal with a set of similar or equivalent difficulties and tensions in its effort to constitute its subject or to reconfigure a subject that has been flattened. The theoretical and empirical distance that has to be bridged between the recognized world of politics and the as yet unmapped experience of citizenship of the housewife—not of women as such, but of women as housewives—is a distance we encounter in many types of inquiry. Bridging this distance requires specific forms of empirical research and of theorization.

IV. Post-national or Denationalized?

From the perspective of nation-based citizenship theory, some of these transformations might be interpreted as a decline or devaluation of citizenship or, more favourably, as a displacement of citizenship in the face of other forms of collective organization and affiliation, as yet unnamed.[34] In so far as citizenship is theorized as necessarily national by definition these new developments cannot be captured in the language of citizenship.[35] An alternative interpretation would be to suspend the national, as in post-national conceptions and to posit that the issue of where citizenship is enacted is one to be determined in the light of developing social practice.[36]

From where I look at these issues, there is a third possibility, beyond these two. It is that citizenship—even if situated in institutional settings that are 'national'—is a possibly changed institution if the meaning of the national itself has changed. That is to say, in so far as globalization has changed certain features of the territorial and institutional organization of the political power and authority of the state, the institution of citizenship—its formal rights, its practices, its psychological dimension—has also been transformed even when it remains centred in the national state. I have argued, for instance, that this territorial and institutional transformation of state power and authority has produced operational, conceptual, and rhetorical openings for nation-based subjects other than the national state to emerge as legitimate actors in international and global arenas that used to be exclusive to the state.[37]

I distinguish what I would narrowly define as denationalized from post-national citizenship, the latter the term most commonly used and the only one used in the broader debate.[38] In my reading we are dealing with two distinct dynamics rather than only the emergence of locations for citizenship outside the frame of the national state. Their difference is a question of scope and institutional embeddedness. The understanding in the scholarship is that post-national citizenship is located partly outside the confines of the national. In considering denationalization, the focus moves on to the transformation of the national, including the national in its condition as foundational for citizenship. Thus it could be argued that post-nationalism and denationalization represent two different trajectories. Both are viable, and they do not exclude each other.

The national, then, remains a referent in my work.[39] But, clearly, it is a referent of a specific sort: it is, after all, its change that becomes the key theoretical feature through which it enters my specification of changes in the institution of citizenship. Whether or not this devalues citizenship is not immediately evident to me at this point.[40] Citizenship has undergone many transformations in its history precisely because it is to variable extents embedded in the specifics of each of its eras.[41] Significant to my argument here is also the fact discussed earlier about the importance of national law in the process of expanding inclusions, inclusions which today are destabilizing older notions of citizenship. This pluralized meaning of citizenship partly produced by the formal expansions of the legal status of citizenship, is today contributing to explode the boundaries of that legal status even further.

First, and most importantly in my reading is the strengthening, including the constitutionalizing, of civil rights which allow citizens to make claims against their states and allow them to invoke a measure of autonomy in the formal political arena that can be read as a lengthening distance between the formal apparatus of the state and the institution of citizenship. The implications, both political and theoretical of this dimension are complex and in the making: we cannot tell what will be the practices and rhetorics that might be invented.

Secondly, I add to this the granting, by national states, of a whole range of 'rights' to foreign actors, largely and especially, economic actors—foreign firms, foreign investors, international markets, foreign business people.[42] Admittedly, this is not a common way of framing the issue. It comes out of my particular perspective about the impact of globalization and denationalization on the national state, including the impact on the relation between the state and its own citizens, and the state and foreign economic actors. I see this as a significant, though not much recognized, development in the history of claim-making. For me the question as to how citizens should handle these new concentrations of power and 'legitimacy' that attach to global firms and markets is a key to the future of democracy. My efforts to detect the extent to which the global is embedded and filtered through the national is one way of understanding whether therein lies a possibility for citizens, still largely confined to national institutions, to demand accountability of global economic actors through national institutional channels, rather than having to wait for a 'global' state.[43]

V. Citizenship in the Global City

The particular transformations in the understanding and theorization of citizenship discussed thus far bring us back to some of the earlier historical formations around questions of citizenship, most prominently the crucial role played by cities and civil society. The large city of today, most especially the global city, emerges as a strategic site for these new types of operations. It is one of the nexi where the formation of new claims materializes and assumes concrete forms. The loss of power at the national level produces the possibility for new forms of power and politics at the subnational level. The national as container of social process and power is cracked. This cracked casing opens up possibilities for a geography of politics that links subnational spaces. Cities are foremost in this new geography. One question this engenders is how and whether we are seeing the formation of new types of politics that localize in these cities.

If we consider that large cities concentrate both the leading sectors of global capital and a growing share of disadvantaged populations—immigrants, many of the disadvantaged women, people of colour generally, and, in the megacities of developing countries, masses of shanty dwellers—then we can see that cities have become a strategic terrain for a whole series of conflicts and contradictions. We can then think of cities also as one of the sites for the contradictions of the globalization of capital, even though, heeding Ira Katznelson's observation, the city cannot be reduced to this dynamic.[44] Recovering cities along these lines means recovering the multiplicity of presences in this landscape. The large city of today has emerged as a strategic site for a whole range of new types of operations—political, economic, cultural, subjective.[45]

While citizenship originated in cities and cities played an important role in its evolution, I do not think we can simply read some of these current developments as a return to that older historical condition. The significance of the city today as a setting for engendering new types of citizenship practices and new types of incompletely formalized political subjects does not derive from that history. Nor does current local city government have much to do with earlier notions of citizenship and democracy described for ancient and medieval cities in Europe.[46] It is, rather, more connected to what Henri Lefebvre was capturing when describing the city as œuvre and hence the importance of agency.[47] Where Lefebvre found this agency in the working class in the Paris of the twentieth century, I find it in two strategic actors—global corporate capital and immigration—in today's global cities. Here I would like to return to the fact of the embeddedness of the institution of citizenship.

What is being engendered today in terms of citizenship practices in the global city is quite different from what it might have been in the medieval city of Weber. In the medieval city we see a set of practices that allowed the burghers to set up systems for owning and protecting property and to implement various immunities against despots of all sorts.[48] Today's citizenship practices have to do with the production of 'presence' of those without power and a politics that claims rights to the city. What the two situations share is the notion that through these practices new forms of citizenship are being constituted and that the city is a key site for this type of political work and is, indeed, partly constituted through these dynamics. After the long historical phase that saw the ascendance of the national state and the scaling of key economic dynamics at the national level, the city is once again today a scale for strategic economic and political dynamics.

In his effort to specify the ideal-typical features of what constitutes the city, Weber sought out a certain type of city—most prominently the cities of the late Middle Ages rather than the modern industrial cities of his time. Weber sought a kind of city that combined conditions and dynamics which forced its residents and leaders into creative, innovative responses and adaptations. Further, he posited that these changes produced in the context of the city signalled transformations that went beyond the city, that could have a far reach in instituting often fundamental transformations. In that regard the city offered the possibility of understanding far-reaching changes that could—under certain conditions—eventually encompass society at large.

There are two aspects of Weber's *The City* that are of particular importance here. Weber sought to understand under what conditions cities can be positive and creative influences on people's lives. For Weber cities are a set of social structures that encourage social individuality and innovation and hence are an instrument of historical change. There is, in this intellectual project a deep sense of the historicity of these conditions. For Weber, modern urban life did not correspond to this positive and creative power of cities; Weber saw modern cities as dominated by large factories and office bureaucracies. My own reading of the Fordist city corresponds in many ways to Weber's in the sense that the strategic scale under Fordism is the national scale and cities lose significance. It is the large Fordist factory and the mines which emerge as key sites for the political work of the disadvantaged and those without power.

For Weber, it is particularly the cities of the late Middle Ages that combine the conditions that pushed urban residents, merchants, artisans, and leaders to address them and deal with them. These transformations could make for epochal change beyond the city itself: Weber shows us how in many of these cities these struggles led to the creation of the elements of what we could call governance systems and citizenship. In this regard struggles around political, economic, legal, and cultural issues which are centred in the realities of cities can become the catalysts for new transurban developments in all these institutional domains: markets, participatory governance, rights for members of the urban community regardless of lineage, judicial recourse, cultures of engagement and deliberation.

199

The particular analytic element I want to extricate from this aspect of Weber's understanding and theorization of the city is the historicity of those conditions that make cities strategic sites for the enactment of important transformations in multiple institutional domains. Elsewhere, I have developed the argument that today a certain type of city—the global city—has emerged as a strategic site precisely for such innovations and transformations in multiple institutional domains.[49] Several of the key components of economic globalization and digitization instantiate in this type of city and produce dislocations and destabilizations of existing institutional orders and legal, regulatory, and normative frames for handling urban conditions. It is the high level of concentration of these new dynamics in these cities that forces creative responses and innovations. There is, most probably, a threshold effect at work here.

The historicity of this process rests in the fact that under Keynesian policies, particularly the Fordist contract, and the dominance of mass manufacturing as the organizing economic dynamic, cities had lost strategic functions and were not the site for creative institutional innovations. The strategic sites were the large factory and the whole process of mass manufacturing and mass consumer markets, and, secondly, the national government where regulatory frameworks were developed and the Fordist contract instituted. The factory and the government were the strategic sites where the crucial dynamics producing the major institutional innovations of the epoch were located. With globalization and digitization—and all the specific elements they entail—global cities emerge as such strategic sites. While the strategic transformations are sharply concentrated in global cities, many of the transformations are also enacted, besides being diffused, in cities at lower orders of national urban hierarchies. Furthermore, in my reading, particular institutions of the state also are such strategic sites even as there is an overall shrinking of state authority through deregulation and privatization.

A second analytic element I want to extricate from Weber's *The City* is the particular type of embeddedness of the transformations he describes and renders as ideal-typical features. This is not an embeddedness in what we might think of as deep structures because the latter are precisely the ones that are being dislocated or changed and are creating openings for new fundamental arrangements to emerge. The embeddedness is, rather, in very specific conditions, opportunities, constraints, needs, interactions, contestations, interests. The aspect that matters here is the complexity, detail, and social thickness of the particular conditions and the dynamics he identifies as enabling change and innovation. This complexity and thickness also produces ambiguities in the meaning of the changes and innovations. It is not always clear whether they are positive—where we might interpret positive as meaning the creation or strengthening of some element, even if very partial or minor, of participatory democracy in the city—and in what timeframe their positiveness would become evident. In those cities of the late Middle Ages he saw as being what the city is about, he finds contradictory and multivalent innovations. He dissects these innovations to understand what they can produce or launch.

The argument I derive from this particular type of embeddedness of change and innovation is that current conditions in global cities are creating not only new structurations of power but also operational and rhetorical openings for new types of political actors which may have been submerged, invisible, or without voice. A key element of the argument here is that the localization of strategic components of globalization in these cities means that the disadvantaged can engage the new forms of globalized corporate power, and secondly that the growing numbers and diversity of the disadvantaged in these cities under these conditions assumes a distinctive 'presence'. This entails a distinction between powerlessness and invisibility or impotence. The disadvantaged in global cities can gain 'presence' in their engagement with power but also *vis-à-vis* each other. This is different from the 1950s–1970s period in the US, for instance, when white flight and the significant departure of major corporate headquarters left cities hollowed out and the disadvantaged in a condition of abandonment. Today, the localization of the global creates a set of objective conditions of engagement. This can be seen, for example, in the struggles against gentrification—which encroaches on minority and disadvantaged neighbourhoods and led to growing numbers of homeless beginning in the 1980s—and the struggles for the rights of the homeless, or also in demonstrations against police brutalizing minority people. These struggles are different from the ghetto uprisings of the 1960s, which were short, intense eruptions confined to the ghettos and causing most of the damage in the neighbourhoods of the disadvantaged themselves. In these ghetto uprisings there was no engagement with power.

The conditions that today mark the possibility of cities as strategic sites are basically two, and both capture major transformations that are destabilizing older systems organizing territory and politics. One of these is the rescaling of what are the strategic territories that articulate the new political-economic system. The other is the partial unbundling or at least weakening of the national as container of social process due to the variety of dynamics encompassed by globalization and digitization. The consequences for cities of these two conditions are many: what matters here is that cities emerge as strategic sites for major economic processes and for new types of political actors. In so far as citizenship is embedded and in turn marked by its embeddedness, these new conditions may well signal the possibility of new forms of citizenship practices and identities.

There is something to be captured here—a distinction between powerlessness and the condition of being an actor even though lacking power. I use the term 'presence' to name this condition. In the context of a strategic space such as the global city, the types of disadvantaged people described here are not simply marginal; they acquire presence in a broader political process that escapes the boundaries of the formal polity. This presence signals the possibility of a politics. What this politics will be will depend on the specific projects and practices of various communities. In so far as the sense of membership of these communities is not subsumed under the national, it may well signal the possibility of a politics that, while transnational, is actually centred in concrete localities.

Response to Saskia Sassen, 'The Repositioning of Citizenship and Alienage: Emergent Subjects and Spaces for Politics'

Christian Joppke

I fully subscribe to the point of departure of this thoughtful chapter, which is the diagnosis of a 'blurring' of the distinction between citizenship and alienage. But I am less sure about some of the further interpretations given to, and conclusions drawn from, this. According to Sassen, at the 'formal level not much has changed over the last century in the essential features of citizenship'. Instead, 'informal' practices — especially those developed by marginal people (sometimes referred to as 'excluded')—are said to have invested citizenship (and alienage) with new meaning. 'Global cities' are presented as the primary sites of these informal processes. As an example of 'blurred' membership, Sassen refers to the 'effective nationality' of illegal immigrants in the United States, who—in her very apt description—are 'unauthorized yet recognized', formally excluded but increasingly woven into the fabric of society. While I acknowledge the wealth of subtle observations and intriguing connections made in her analysis, I take issue with three central assumptions in it: (1) the privileging of the 'informal' over the 'formal'; (2) the causal impact attributed to the practices of the 'excluded'; (3) and the assumption that 'global cities' are key to the changing forms of citizenship.

1. I was puzzled by the short shrift given to 'formal' changes of both citizenship and alienage.[1] This is probably inevitable given Sassen's preset interest in informal practices, but she does nonetheless quote some crucial formal changes that have undoubtedly altered the quality of citizenship and alienage: on the one hand, the increasing acceptance of dual citizenship and the concomitant weakening of the notion of exclusive allegiance; on the other, the improvements afforded to the status of alien by the international human rights regime. However, there are more, and more important, changes than these. On the side of citizenship, one further important recent change has been the strengthening of the component of *jus soli* over *jus sanguinis* in the birth attribution of citizenship. This proves wrong a key assumption in much writing on nationhood and citizenship:[2] the connection between alleged (ethnic or civic) 'national identities' and (more or less inclusive) nationality laws is much weaker and more peripheral than generally claimed. Whereas political modernity was once associated with the post-feudal *jus sanguinis* citizenship, it is now predominantly associated with *jus soli* citizenship. This is because, in a world of massive international migration, liberal-democratic norms require that all who are lastingly subject to the state's rule should be included in the demos. Note that the same connection between migration and liberal-democratic norms can be mobilized against pure *jus soli* regimes (which existed in Britain and Portugal until 1981, and which still exist today in the United States and Canada). Why should the random fact of birth on the territory of a state entail the lifelong good of citizenship? In their changing laws and policies on citizenship, states are approximating the norm, stipulated by the International Court of Justice in its famous Nottebohm case, that nationality should express a 'genuine connection'

between an individual and the nationality-granting state. Sometimes this may mean emphasizing *jus sanguinis* over *jus soli* citizenship (as in the aforementioned cases of Britain and Portugal). Mostly, however, it today entails the reverse. And all this is entirely unrelated to 'civic' or 'ethnic' traditions of nationhood. A second important formal change is the emergence of as-of-right citizenship. This is part and parcel of the constitutional-rights revolution in the post-war liberal state. It has rendered null and void the (still widely held) theory that under international law states have the 'right' to grant citizenship as they see fit (which largely exempts immigration and citizenship from the anti-discrimination norms of the international human rights regime). In classic texts on nationality law one reads that, because citizenship is a status to which a variety of rights are contingently attached, it cannot itself be a right.[3] From this perspective, the emergence of citizenship as a 'right' is a profoundly paradoxical development—and surely a formal innovation worthy of more detailed examination.

Sassen notes the most important recent change on the alienage side of things: the strong individual rights increasingly attached to alien status. Hannah Arendt's despair over the lot of the stateless as utterly devoid of rights is no longer justified, precisely because of the experience of 'totalitarianism' that she herself had so trenchantly analysed. I believe the major formal upgrading of alien status—or of personhood irrespective of citizenship—stands in an intrinsic and so far largely unexamined relationship to the whittling away of the rights attached to citizen status (the decline of substantive citizenship rights is discussed, though not really accounted for, by Sassen). 'Citizenship' of one of the fortunate north-western states once entailed a significant increase in wealth and security (at least in the short post-war period referred to in France as the *trentes glorieuses*). Of course, compared to the true poorhouses and danger-zones of the earth, it still does, but as welfare states are slimmed down, this is less and less true. In the wake of the constitutional rights revolution, rights have become increasingly procedural and ever less substantive. If everyone has 'rights', it is obvious that their scope and meaning can only be procedural. In turn, this is the best justification for (and inevitable antecedent to) the hollowing-out of substantive citizen rights.

2. In my view, it is doubtful that the improved status of immigrants has resulted from their own actions. Sassen takes the epic stories of political sociology—in which workers, women, and other excluded groups were accepted as equal 'citizens' only through their own campaigning—and extends them to the case of aliens or immigrants. But the former groups were able to obtain equal rights only because they already enjoyed the formal status of citizenship. Immigrants, by definition, do not. Sassen collapses two different meanings of the English word 'citizenship': citizenship as nationality, in the sense of formal state membership; and citizenship as social practice, that is, citizenship as the language that excluded groups have used to fight for their inclusion. If, as Sassen claims, 'citizenship is partly produced by the practices of the excluded', she cannot be referring to citizenship as nationality; she must refer to citizenship as social practice (which incidentally makes her argument circular). But if, as the juxtaposition of 'citizenship' and 'alienage' in her title and lecture suggests, her primary focus is citizenship as nationality, it is, in my view, wrong to argue that the practices of the excluded (such as illegal immigrants) have been the driving force in the stated blurring between citizenship and alienage.

Immigrants simply do not have sufficient political clout for this. Indeed, politicians working on behalf of immigrants are often punished at the ballot box, even in the trans-oceanic 'nations of immigrants'. Independent legal systems combined with civic pressure from non-immigrant sources such as the liberal media, academics, and intellectuals have brought about the significant strengthening of immigrant rights in Western states over the last thirty years. Take the case of illegal immigrants in the United States. The most astounding recognition of their place in society came with the famous Supreme Court decision (*Plyler* vs. *Doe*) granting to the 'innocent' children of undocumented immigrants the right to state education. How courts, which (in the US) were once obstacles to social change (as in the infamous Supreme Court opposition to Roosevelt's New Deal) have (roughly since the 1960s) become vanguards of social change is a separate question, which cannot be pursued here. But the fundamental importance of courts to the alien-rights revolution can hardly be ignored.

Many other examples could be added. None of the significant transformations of citizenship and alienage alluded to in this chapter have resulted from the 'practices of the excluded'. They were achieved by liberal elites and were born not on the street but, for the most part, behind the closed doors of courts and bureaucracies. This may not be comforting to the progressively minded sociologist, but it is a fact, and it calls for a different approach to the citizen/alien problem than that on offer here which, in my view, risks romanticizing the immigrant.

3. It is by now obligatory to elevate the city (especially its 'global' variant) to a new unit of analysis in sociology

and political science. The city, it is alleged, exemplifies our fast-changing world of globalizing markets and diminishing states. I am not convinced. Since the late Middle Ages, cities have been major sites of political, economic, and cultural development—and 'city' is, indeed, the etymological root of 'citizenship'. If the 'global' city embodies our new era, this is only one more variant of the city's pace-setting function; there is nothing new about cities playing a key role in social change. This is not to deny that the global connectivity made possible by new technologies and that is particularly visible in major cities is something new. But if the new forms of 'blurred' membership discussed in this lecture were really limited to cities (which would indeed require that cities replace states as units of analysis), not much would be gained, since they would be invalid outside the city limits. They could not, in that case, carry the liberating potential that is (quite correctly, in my view) attributed to them. In respect of their membership status, the lot of urban undocumented immigrants is no better than that of their rural equivalents. Progressive city mayors may help bring out a friendly regulation here or there, but they do not determine the law of the land.

In her previous work, Saskia Sassen has given us a compelling picture of the 'hour-glass' stratification in global cities, in which the international bottoms and tops squeeze out the national middle. This may be exaggerated, but it catches an important development (that a visit to many a Manhattan restaurant may confirm). However, I do not see how this undeniable reality is causally linked to the changes in the institutions of citizenship and alienage that she describes here.

6

Border Crossings

Caryl Phillips

And then, of course, it happens much as it always happens. The driver turns to me and says, 'Mr Caryl, please you can maybe help me?' I wait for a beat and then he continues. 'I have a form for the visa lottery. I think it is for 2–0–0–5, but I don't know how to fill it. I would like to go out of this place.' Awuje has been driving me for four days now, and I had half-expected this moment from the beginning. But he certainly chose his location well. We are in the small town of Elmina on the West Coast of Africa. The site of one of the largest and most impressive of the slave forts, those troubling edifices from whose dungeons millions of Africans were shipped in conditions of unspeakable misery, across the broad expanse of the Atlantic Ocean and deposited into the new American world.

I smile somewhat helplessly at Awuje, who now pulls a form out of a battered manila paper folder and holds it out for my inspection. I glance at it and immediately see the problem. The form—which includes instructions for filing—has been downloaded from the Internet, presumably by a friend of Awuje's. What my driver does not realize is that this form has to be filled out online. Somewhere in the United States a Department of Homeland Security bureaucrat has made a decision to switch from postal to online filing and, by doing so, he has introduced another level of 'literacy' into the procedure making it even more difficult for the 'huddled

210

masses' to have access to the richest country on earth. I continue to stare at the form and then I see another problem. The online application has to be completed and submitted by 31 December. We are now in late January. Awuje has missed the well-flagged deadline by nearly four weeks, which renders the downloaded material doubly useless. I clutch the well-thumbed visa lottery form and tell Awuje that I will speak to him about it at an unspecified time called 'later on'.

Awuje wishes to do a little border crossing. In his case, from West Africa to the United States of America, where—incidentally—he knows absolutely nobody. And he is not a young man. Far from it. His mass of tightly curled white hair suggests early sixties. The sprightly manner in which he leaves the shade of a tree and runs to the car whenever he sees me coming, suggests late forties. At first I thought he was merely demonstrating his fitness, but I now understand that Awuje is keen to impress upon me just how alert he is to the details of the job. He knows that I will return and he assumes that there will be more employment. However, I have, on more than one occasion, told Awuje that while I appreciate his efficiency, his sprinting does make me feel a little uncomfortable. Really, there is no need to rush, but then again Awuje is rushing not only because he wishes to please me but because he is also keenly aware that he is a man with a greater mass of life behind him than in front of him. In what time he has left he wishes to go to the United States of America to have a chance to better himself. In this sense, he is most certainly in a hurry.

He owns his own car, which in Ghana means that he is doing better than the vast majority of the population. And he keeps his car scrupulously clean, for it serves a double function as both status symbol and his sole means of income. I have already noticed that Awuje seems to have some difficulty

211

reading, and he clearly has no understanding of the Internet, yet my driver has worked assiduously over the years to purchase his second-hand blue saloon. The evidence of the car suggests a disciplined man who has focused on a goal and is now reaping the benefits of having achieved it. What's more, he is a driver with foreign contacts which places him among the elite of Ghanaian drivers. But Awuje wants more, and he is prepared to leave his relatively comfortable life in Accra and journey into the unknown in search of material reward.

Awuje's imagined border crossing will, so he hopes, allow him to prosper economically. If he is lucky enough to reach the Promised Land and get a job, then his border crossing will also help the United States of America for Awuje brings with him a highly developed work ethic. His imagined migration will also allow his native country to prosper, for he plans to remit money to Ghana in order that he might prepare for his return 'home'. One thing Awuje is sure of is that he has no desire to die on American soil. He intends to undertake his border crossing with an imaginary return ticket, but even as he tells me these facts, I find myself wondering about the price of Awuje's ticket and I keep fastening hard onto one word which of itself seems somewhat innocuous, but on closer inspection is often freighted with frustration, confusion, and even despair. That word is, of course, displacement.

I should perhaps explain that because of who I am, and what I do, I can only engage with the term 'displacement' in a personal way. However, this does not mean that I am unaware of the fact that many people think primarily of the word 'displacement' in the less personal context of issues of international order, humanitarian aid, and resettlement strategies. I am also aware of the fact that the socio-political problems associated with this vexed word are being vigorously debated—and taught for credit—at universities all over the world, including Oxford. Similarly, when I use the term 'forced migration', which I will with specific reference to the Atlantic Slave Trade and the African diaspora, this does not mean that I am unaware of its broader usage as a term referring to the movement of people displaced by conflicts, famine, development projects, or environmental and natural disasters. However, the sociological, anthropological, and economic issues which inform most people's engagement with the terms 'displacement' and 'forced migration' are issues of secondary interest to me. For me, 'displacement' and 'forced migration' are terms directly connected to issues of the human heart. I am a writer for whom loss, pain, and memory have long been key locations on my thematic map and this fact, coupled with the migratory impulses which have informed— and continue to inform—my life, render it difficult for me to engage with issues related to migration in any way other than with reference to specific individual human experience.

To be in Ghana, and find myself musing on the word 'displacement', is to force me to think of the life of one man in particular. William Edward Burghardt Du Bois was born in Great Barrington, in the rolling Berkshire hills of South-Western Massachusetts on 23 February 1868, and he died some ninety-five years later in Accra, Ghana. Du Bois was born in the year that Andrew Jackson was impeached, that Ulysses S. Grant was elected president of the United States, and at a time when African-Americans were voting for the first time in the Reconstruction South. During Du Bois's childhood Mark Twain was writing 'Huckleberry Finn', and the newly formed Ku Klux Klan was beginning to make its ugly mark on American life. Du Bois graduated from high school in Great Barrington, the only black student in a class of thirteen, and he went south to Fisk University in Tennessee where he earned a bachelor's degree in 1888. In the same year he was admitted as a junior into Harvard where he famously described his situation—he said, 'I was in Harvard, but not of it.' In 1890 he graduated with a Bachelor of Arts degree, and thereafter entered Harvard's graduate school. Between 1892 and 1894 he studied at a university in Berlin, and in 1894 he returned to the United States where the following year, in 1895, he became the first African-American to receive a Ph.D. from Harvard University. Du Bois subsequently set forth on a remarkable career as a teacher, historian, sociologist, journalist, philosopher, and political activist, a career which ultimately led to his being recognized as the quintessential American Renaissance man.

But Du Bois died in Accra, Ghana in a country he had decided to make his own in 1961 when already ninety-three years of age. Disillusioned by the slow speed and nature of change in the United States of America, and increasingly attracted to the revolutionary principles of the Communist Party, in the very twilight of his life Du Bois determined that he would leave the United States and take up the offer of his friend Kwame Nkrumah, the charismatic president of the recently independent country of Ghana, to come 'home' to Africa. In 1961 a somewhat resigned Du Bois renounced his American citizenship and set sail for Ghana where he intended to direct the Encyclopedia Africana, a project that he had envisaged as early as 1909. Two years later, on 27 August 1963, the day before Martin Luther King's electrifying 'I Have a Dream' speech at the Lincoln Memorial in Washington DC, the 'old man' slipped quietly from this world. The government of his newly adopted country afforded him a state funeral and condolences poured in from heads of state in all corners of the world, including China's Mao Tse Tung and Russia's Nikita Khrushchev. Sadly, the United States government did not acknowledge the passing of its esteemed, but now displaced, former citizen, despite his having served the country with such distinction for the greater part of a century. The day after his state funeral the Ghanaian Times carried a front page editorial under the banner heading 'NANTSEW YIE!' (which in Akan means 'Farewell!'). For the family of the recently departed Du Bois, the official unforgiving American silence must have deafened any expressions of appreciation from Ghanaians and others. Indeed, border crossings can be expensive and troubling.

I have made three migrations all of which have brought me into close proximity with this troubling word, displacement. On 12 July 1958, after a somewhat tedious and often fearful journey across the Atlantic in the lower cabins of a cargo ship, my parents, both of whom were in their early twenties, stepped ashore at Newhaven and looked all around. They had arrived, and finally they were in Britain. I am sure that they both harboured different dreams of how they wished their new British lives to unfold, and the evidence of their acrimonious divorce some few years later would seem to confirm this. However, nearly fifty years ago, on an English summer morning, they stepped ashore—my mother holding me in her arms, my father no doubt already scheming as to what mischief he might get up to. Ostensibly the pair of them had little reason to feel apprehensive about this new world. Tucked away in the inside pocket of my father's only jacket were the British passports which not only suggested, but confirmed, that they belonged.

But this was England in 1958, and within a few weeks of our arrival both Nottingham and London's Notting Hill exploded in scenes of racial violence the likes of which had never before been seen on the streets of Britain. My parents had already travelled north to Leeds, where they soon came face to face with the many difficulties that bedevilled West Indians in Britain during this period. Discrimination in housing and employment was openly practised and commonplace. Pubs and clubs were often segregated, and life was not easy for coloured newcomers. For the first time in their lives my parents were called 'nigger', my mother was spat at in the streets, my father punched; they were shortchanged in shops; offered accommodation that you wouldn't kennel your dog in; and constantly told to go back to the jungle. I was, of course, too young to know what they endured, or how they felt about their welcome in the motherland, but some few weeks ago I sat with my mother and watched a BBC documentary about the arrival of West Indians in the 1950s. As the programme progressed my mother fell increasingly quiet and then she simply left the room. Before she did so she uttered her parting sentence with a quiet dignity that echoed long after her departure. 'I'd forgotten,' she said 'just how awful it was.' I sat for a few moments and then turned off the television.

But my parents were not totally naive. Before embarking on the ship in St Kitts they did have some idea that the streets of Britain were not paved with gold. Letters from friends and relatives became the raw material of village gossip, and not every missive spoke with calypso warmth of Britain as the place to be. Not everybody sang the virtues of English fair play and decency of manners. Uncle Leslie complained that he was called 'Sambo' so often that he began to think it was his middle name. Aunt Monica wrote that the only thing colder than an English January was the look on an Englishman's face when you tried to get a job that involved using the intelligence that God had given to you. And speaking of God, Uncle Vincent could not for the life of him understand why, as he left the church, the vicar shook his hand and said it was nice to see him but please not to come back again next week. These stories made their way back to St Kitts and so, in some senses, my parents were prepared for the possibility that, despite their British passports and shared cultural values, they might, on arrival, feel somewhat out of tune with Britain. And how right they were—yet they stayed.

They stayed because of me. In the years and months that followed, they had other children and, in this sense, the pressure was off me a little because they were now staying because of us. But at least to begin with there was no doubt that these two extremely proud individuals stayed in Britain and took the abuse, the hostility, and at times the hatred, because of their son—me. They were English-speaking Christians who had been educated in the British system and who were, in more ways than one, coming home to Britain. But the truth was they had crossed the water and come to Britain not so they could feel at home, and eat fish and chips, and support a football team, and go down the boozer, and put money on the horses. They came to Britain to get ahead and grow, and to provide me with opportunities that I would never have had on the small island of twelve miles by six that I was born on. This being the case, the anger, hurt, and betrayal that they felt had to be accommodated; the social and cultural rejection had to be absorbed. They did not feel at home, but in the end it did not matter.

In 1990 I was invited to be the Visiting Writer at a private liberal arts college in Western Massachusetts (and, as it turned out, the college was not too far from where W. E. B. Du Bois had been born over a century earlier). The appointment was for just one academic year. Eight years later, in 1998, I resigned and took up another academic post, which I still hold, in New York City. I may be a little slow, but only now am I coming to understand my time in the United States as a migration. It is only recently that I have felt comfortable answering the question 'Where do you live?' with the answer 'New York City', or writing 'USA' against country of domicile on forms that have been officially proffered. In many ways it was the events of September 11th 2001 that helped me to understand the degree to which I had become involved with the United States. Like millions of other New Yorkers, I felt the impact of that day, and the bizarre days that followed, as a participant and not as a global observer. I was shocked to the core, but it was a response that was fed by proprietorial anxiety. What made my response all the more surprising to me is the fact that I have never really felt myself to be at home in the United States. I still prefer the pub to a bar; soccer as opposed to American football; cricket not baseball. I still say 'toma[h]to' and not 'toma[y]to,' spell theatre with an 're,' tune into BBC news, avoid waffles, pancakes, and doughnuts, and watch the EastEnders Omnibus on BBC America on a Saturday afternoon. But the United States does not punish me, or laugh at me, or belittle me for being who I am. I have been able to cross the Atlantic and enter into the society, and my sense of displacement is, in the context of my parents' experience, deeply designer in character.

But this is not, of course, the case for all migrants to the United States. I am a middle-class man, in a middle-class profession, who speaks English, and who can navigate his way around the system. The land of the free and the home of the brave has always offered up 'freedom' and 'home' as deeply relative concepts depending upon who or what you are. I would not be waxing so lyrical about the United States were I a Native American, or Arab American, or Muslim American. In this instance my sense of displacement would not be designer, it would be deeply felt and painful. But I have been fortunate, and I have stayed on in the United States for the same reason that my parents stayed on in Britain; because the country has offered me the opportunity to grow. I used to think such opportunity was limitless in Britain, but soon after my arrival in the United States in 1990 I began to meet British writers, doctors, musicians, filmmakers, newspaper editors, and others who were living in the United States because of the opportunities to grow that the country was affording them. More often than not, these people's decision to live in the United States had little to do with their race, gender, or religion, nor was it connected to prejudice or discrimination here in Britain. The impulse to migrate, in nearly all cases, was connected to the individual's craving to better him or herself, which is precisely why I left in 1990, and why I am still in the United States. As long as growth remains a possibility then displacement, designer or otherwise, is a price that countless millions of migrants, including my parents, are more than willing to pay.

I am also paying the price for my first migration, although I dearly wish that I did not have to. In fact, you are also paying the price for my first migration, everybody reading this is. This was an act of forced migration: the Atlantic Slave Trade. I do not need to rehearse the iniquities of the trade, nor do I need to convince anybody of its fundamental immorality. However, the racial divide in Europe and the Americas between those of African origin and others—most commonly Whites—is directly related to the vigour with which mythologies of racial difference were sown into the consciousness of people, black and white, during the seventeenth, eighteenth, and to some extent the nineteenth centuries. The involuntary migration of millions of Africans is the one border crossing—the one migration—that I regret having undertaken.

In 1997 an African-American journalist named Keith Richburg published a book entitled *Out of Africa* in which, astonishingly enough, he made it clear that he was delighted that the Atlantic Slave Trade had rescued him from an African future. In fact, he gave thanks for the slave trade, and he and others pointed to the diasporan achievement of those of African origin to support a claim that life in the diaspora is preferable to any kind of life in Africa. It is true enough that in music, sport, science, literature, in fact in many, many fields, those of African origin have, having passed out of Africa, made major contributions to Western civilization. But it is surely pernicious to see such achievements as exempla of the benefits of the slave trade and slavery. A triumphant survival of the middle passage? I think not.

No African wanted to leave Africa. None. Including myself. Those of us in the diaspora are all involuntary migrants, people who were forced to leave our land, families, friends, languages, religions, and cultures, and begin anew elsewhere. Forced to do so. Our displacement on arrival in the Americas was profound and it caused a psychic wound which, for countless millions of people of African origin, continues to fester. Today many diasporan people of African origin still feel, to borrow Claude McKay's title to his stirring autobiography, 'A Long Way From Home'. Many diasporan Africans are unhappy, worried, even angry. In fact, a not insignificant number are still trying to 'return' to the land that they were snatched and exiled from. I have sat in countries all over the world and talked with those of African origin who feel unmoored and displaced. And I have also sat in half a dozen different African countries and 'reasoned' with those who have returned, many of whom, to my eyes, never look or feel as though they have truly closed the circle and, having undertaken their reverse 'middle passage', achieved peace. Clearly to force a people to migrate is to risk setting in motion decades or centuries of heartache. Whatever the *raison d'être* for the forced migration, the psychological and spiritual price of such an act is, in my opinion, almost always too high. In the case of the African diaspora, the combined cultural legacy of the Harlem Renaissance is, to my mind, worth nothing when balanced against the anguish of one single African in a male or female dungeon deep in the bowels of Elmina Castle, chained to a now dead and putrefying friend, their mind racked with terror at the thought of what may lie ahead. Cab Calloway can keep singing 'Hi Di Hi De Hi Di Hi', Duke Ellington can keep his band, and Claude McKay and Countee Cullen can hang up their pens. My sympathies are located on the west coast of Africa.

When I think of the failure of forced border crossings I am, or course, thinking biblically. I am also thinking of today, on the West Bank. I am thinking of Iraqi refugees in Lebanon, of Rwanda, Colombia, Kosovo, Burma, Sri Lanka, Afghanistan, in fact, of all the locales in the world where forced migration has more often than not resulted in tens of thousands of people finding themselves in camps whose conditions are an insult to basic human decency. It is easy to forget that people are very often unmoored by traumatic border crossings within the boundaries of their own country. Such is the case in Sudan, where since 1983 nearly 4 million people have been internally displaced, 2 million have been killed, and over a quarter of a million now live in exile beyond their homeland. And the situation is not much better in a country that I visited and wrote about last year; Sierra Leone. At the height of their eleven-year civil war almost half the 4.5 million population was deemed to be displaced, and although many have now been resettled enormous problems still exist. My experience with internally displaced persons and refugees in Sierra Leone served only to confirm my belief that the psychological damage that accompanies forced migrations—either within or across national borders—is far more enduring than physical trauma, and its effects cannot be treated with food rations, plastic sheeting, or artificial limbs.

Yet human beings have a tremendous capacity to absorb the chaos and confusion that comes with migration, forced or voluntary. As I have tried to suggest, it is a natural human impulse to wish to cross borders in search of people and places that might enable one to fulfil one's potential; and a fear of feeling displaced is never going to be a serious obstacle to those who wish to migrate voluntarily. For such people it generally takes a few generations, often less, before the bewilderment and hurt of displacement begin to recede and are replaced by the warm glow of belonging. But not so for those who have been forced to migrate against their will. There ought to be some mathematical equation that we can employ that might enable us to measure the degree of displacement, with voluntary versus forced as one variable, and time as another. The resulting figure would, of course, tell us something about the depth of historical memory.

Diasporan Africans are a long-memoried people. While driving in the hills beyond Accra, Awuje and I passed a large villa surrounded by a high concrete wall. Set atop the wall were large elaborate stone sculptures of lions. The wooden trim just below the roof was painted red, green, and gold, and the signboard by the wall of the compound revealed exactly what was going on. 'Tuff Gong International Recording Studios'. On another board the simple slogan, 'Hit me with Rhythm'. This property, high in the cool hills of Aburi, belonged to the widow of the Jamaican reggae superstar, Bob Marley. Rita Marley had, as her late husband always espoused, found her way back to her roots in Africa. Later on this same day, Awuje dropped me off at the W. E. B. Du Bois Center in Accra, the very place where the great African-American lived and worked, and eventually, having come 'home' to Africa, died at the age of 95. Indeed, we are a long-memoried people.

In 1961, having arrived and taken up Ghanaian citizenship, W. E. B. Du Bois was presented with a large white villa in the residential Cantonments area of Accra by President Kwame Nkrumah. Du Bois's second wife Shirley Graham Du Bois quickly set about transforming the grounds into a lush garden, while her husband busied himself with his writing. Today the house and grounds form the centrepiece of the Du Bois Center, which is an arts complex managed by Sekou Nkrumah, son of the late President. A tall, serious man in his mid-thirties, he tells me that he was educated in communist Romania, which I decide must explain some of his gravity. Sekou escorts me from his office the short distance to the main villa. Here I am able to see the personal library of W. E. B. Du Bois, his academic gowns, private photographs, first editions of his books, letters and papers, but all are falling to pieces and in a terrible state of disrepair. The torn curtains in the villa are hanging sadly from the rails, and out in the grounds things are not much better for the garden is largely denuded. In fact, the whole place is in dire need of paint and maintenance.

The government of Ghana owns the building, and Du Bois's gravesite and tomb, which are also on the land. However, Sekou tells me that it has proved difficult to obtain funding to preserve the valuable evidence of one of the great American lives. I ask him about potential American help, but he smiles then sighs. He tells me that as long as the Ghanaian government claims ownership of the home, the contents, and the gravesite, then Americans have made it clear that they are reluctant to invest in the upkeep and preservation of the Du Bois Center. The professional and personal turmoil which marked the displaced final two years of W. E. B. Du Bois's life, as he moved from the United States of America to Ghana, appears, some forty years later, to have escalated into a squabble over his actual possessions. The end result of this bitter stand-off is the sad, and continued, deterioration of the physical evidence of the legacy of a man who in the early winter of his life felt compelled to cross a border and go to a place where, even for somebody of his rare distinction and achievement, he still felt that he could grow.

Awuje stands outside Elmina Castle and tells me that he wishes to go to the United States of America, but despite the backdrop he speaks without any sense of irony. He views the Atlantic Slave Trade as neither good nor bad, he views it as history and therefore dead and somewhat irrelevant. To those in the diaspora, who continue to be long-memoried, the Atlantic Slave Trade is not only alive, it continues to be painful. The loss and confusion of enduring the Atlantic Crossing lingers to this day, and only a few ever return in order that they might attempt to 'heal' themselves. However, Awuje has absolutely no interest in the psychological needs of displaced Africans in the diaspora. He wishes to go to America for the same reasons that my parents decided to come to Britain, and

I decided to stay in the United States. To grow. And that's just fine. Awuje does not know anybody in the United States, and he has never come face to face with a winter, but he is not afraid of any difficulties that such a move might cause him. In fact, he has already factored in such difficulties as simply part of the price of the ticket. Displacement, whatever. He just wants a chance, that is all, and who can blame him? Voluntary crossing of borders in an attempt to seize such opportunities is one of the oldest and most natural of human instincts; one that we should respect and, when necessary, one that we should vigorously encourage.

Response to Caryl Phillips, 'Border Crossings'

Elleke Boehmer

There are, according to the United Nations, some 100 million people in the world today who qualify as migrants—who live as minorities, in states of unbelonging. In Caryl Phillips's terms, they have 'done a little border crossing': 'Their lives fractured. Sinking hopeful roots into difficult soil,' in the words of the father who has sold his children into slavery in his 1993 novel *Crossing the River*.

Yet for Phillips this 'many-tongued' mass is to be differentiated by a fundamental split, which forms the crux of all he says here. On the one side he places what is sometimes called economic or elective migration, displacement in quest of opportunities 'to grow', or of self-improvement, which is how he describes his parents' migration to Britain, his own to the United States, and the wished-for border-crossing of Awuje, his African driver. This kind of crossing may bring emotional and physical discomfort, and wounding encounters with others, but these have in some sense been opted for, in Phillips's terms, and the discomfort involved will ultimately be overcome. Moreover, this discomfort is shared by the many frenetic border-crossers of the twenty-first-century 'New World Order'.

It is on the opposite side of his distinction that generational pain resides, a rankling historical memory that Phillips believes will never be fully resolved, never go away, that abides. Here we find the world's forced migrants, the majority of the 100 million displaced. Here hunker the victims of (usually) state-generated *commandement*, in the terminology of Achille Mbembe, of those processes that, through the arbitrary deployment of violence and the suspension of all semblance of common law, 'dispose of people' and 'create utilities'.[1] Here are those fleeing war, including civil war, torture, famine by disentitlement, ethnic cleansing; those in Kosovo, the Sudan, Zimbabwe, Sierra Leone, Burma, Afghanistan, Iraq, 'swarming over endless plains'.[2] The multiple further dimensions of the migrant experience which writers—including, prominently, Phillips—have confronted and mythologized in their fiction and poetry—translation, grief, misunderstanding, 'unhomeliness', bad timing, alienation, the carrying and losing of cultural burdens, the retrieval of history, and so on—are not at issue in the chapter. There is this main contrast: either migration is voluntary, in which case migrants will eventually learn to live with their change in location; or there is forced migration, in which the pain of being unhoused will transmit from generation to generation, without ultimate respite. Immigrants 'change faster than the countries they have left behind and they can never go back and be happy'.[3]

Phillips is first and foremost, as he emphasizes, a writer, who engages with 'displacement' through the prism of 'the human heart', his own human heart. In his fiction he is, as he accurately describes himself, 'an explorer of the fissures and crevices of migration'.[4] Off the fictional page, by contrast, he hits hard with a strategically forceful and even advisedly repetitive rhetoric. Some of the points he makes here he has narrated before, but their impact lies in part in the reincantation. Forced migration is an utter historical wrong: it cannot be said often enough. Such perceptions are deeply moulded by his immediate personal experience as a child of the Windrush generation, of economic migrants to 1950s Britain from the West Indies, but also by the historical yet equally personal experience of his 'first migration', the forced displacement occasioned by the Atlantic Slave Trade. For this reason it is crucial that he locates the beginning of the chapter, as he does the Introduction and Conclusion to a recent book of essays *A New World Order* (2002), in Africa, his virtual home, to which he can never, however, because of his history, fully belong. The networks of connection are broken. This is the contrast he wishes to draw for us.

All the same, for a writer who closely embraces, as he puts it, the twenty-first century world in which the claims of 'the migrant, the asylum-seeker . . . the refugee' are non-negotiable, the starkness of the contrast he underlines is noteworthy.[5] Are there not forms of political exile that might inflict the enduring psychological damage he describes, yet that may not have been forced in the same absolute way slavery was forced? Think of the late nineteenth-century Gujerati cane-worker, the man whom poverty pushed into the indenture or *germitya* system taking him to Trinidad, to Fiji, to Mauritius, often on a one-way ticket, forever. Of the Malawian or Zambian miners for whom colonization meant migration under duress to mines far from their village home, and irrevocable, often damaging changes in life circumstances. Or of working-class women across Europe, pressed into domestic service by families in dire need. Will their trauma, too, redound upon future generations in the same kind of way, even though their historical experience evades or transcends the officially recognized categories—Slave Trade, Holocaust, Diaspora? Would they, too, not identify with Langston Hughes's

> keening, his talk
> Of bitter yearnings lost
> Without a place—
> So long,
> So far away?[6]

These are unanswerable, even imponderable questions, though I should take care to emphasize that I am trying like Phillips, to avoid looking at history through 'the narrow prism . . . of pigmentation' in posing them.[7] At base what we—and Langston Hughes—are troubling over is the differential pain—the indiscriminate yet protean violence—inflicted by modernity, by its brutal truncation of 'ancestral' rhythms, its painful production of crossed and mixed identities. The point is that the distinction which Phillips so deeply traces to an extent disregards those subtle shifts of historical register, those differences in voice concerning broken experiences of home, with which his alchemical fiction of loss and partial reconstitution—*Cambridge, A Distant Shore*—stops the heart.

As a sign of this, there is a clear difference between the dichotomies of the chapter—forced v. voluntary migration—and the triads and patterns of threes that shape a significant number of his narratives. 'My Nash. My Martha. My Travis'—the three descendants of slaves whose stories come together to form *Crossing the River*. The three parts of *Cambridge*, framed like *Crossing the River* by a Prologue and an Epilogue: Emily Cartwright's story, the slave Olumide or Cambridge's testimony, and the final official report of his hanging. Or even Phillips's own triangulated comment in an interview with fellow-novelist Graham Swift: 'Displacement engenders a great deal of suffering, a great deal of confusion, a great deal of soul-searching.'[8] In each case the third term signifies not resolution but a transformative or transitional tension. His narrative probes finer temporal and spatial distinctions, more delicate and difficult interstices in the web of history, than is possible in a chapter that seeks to make its central, gutting case.

At the core of the intensely personal burden of Phillips's work lies the fact that he has been throughout his career a deeply ethical writer. Hence his abiding concern with the multiple configurations of displacement, its impact on those who arrive in a strange land, those who receive (or, as the case may be, refuse to receive) the 'arrivants', and on those left behind. Particular moments in his narratives—including also the vignettes from his African travels he mentions here—are placed as symbolic parables teaching lessons for our displaced times. W. E. B. Du Bois's house in Accra, Ghana, his final home, awarded after a long career as an African American public intellectual and activist, is a case in point. Once a place of welcome and respite for Du Bois, who gave up his American citizenship when he 'returned' to Africa in 1961, the house is now the neglected and dilapidated centre of an arts complex. The deterioration is due in large part to the piqued refusal of Du Bois's country of birth—the United States—to take any responsibility for the building or its contents. Returning to the figure of Du Bois across the lecture, placing him against the background of this house, Phillips reminds us that, twenty-one years after the great man's death, his final resting place remains inextricably connected to his former homeland, even in the breach of any admission of relationship.

'England has changed', is the opening line of Phillips's novel *A Distant Shore*, winner of the Commonwealth Writer's Prize for 2004—it has changed because of the new 'strangers' living in its midst.[9] Forced migration represents an indelible sea-change for those forced to move, but it also wreaks irreversible changes upon the community to which the migrants are displaced, changes that they ignore at their peril, at risk of finding themselves equally 'marooned'. As Phillips has said in a comment on the retired music teacher Dorothy in *A Distant Shore*: 'a great number of white British people . . . feel out of tune in as profound a way as any immigrant, who don't feel that their history has been explained to them adequately'.[10]

Phillips's self-appointed task as a writer is to explain that striated history, to explore the rich and convoluted 'variable' of migration time, and, in so doing, to speak compellingly for the values of hospitality and civility. He urges a reciprocal hospitality not only between immigrants and those who receive them in their midst, but also between those who leave a country and those who are left behind. They, too, must 'find the will to begin again, and go on' without either disparaging their homeland, or the ones who have left it.[11] Here, then, once again, we witness the claim that the neglected house in West Africa should have upon America.

7

The New Global Slave Trade

Harold Hongju Koh

It was in the Codrington Library of All Souls, Oxford, that I sat six years ago, thinking about the origins of the modern international human rights movement. In researching that subject, I became fascinated by the work of such nineteenth-century activists as Henri Dunant of the International Committee of the Red Cross, Christian peace activists, such as America's William Ladd and Elihu Burritt, who promoted public international arbitration and permanent international criminal courts, and most of all by William Wilberforce of the British and Foreign Anti-Slavery Society.[1] I came to see these nineteenth-century activists as 'transnational norm entrepreneurs,' who were precursors to such modern figures as Jimmy Carter, Nelson Mandela, Jody Williams of the Global Landmines Movement, Oscar Arias Sanchez of the Nobel Laureates' Initiative to Control Small Arms Transfers, and the sponsor of this lecture—Amnesty International of the anti-death penalty movement—all of whom have devoted themselves to both thinking globally and acting globally to rid the world of various human rights afflictions.

In recalling Wilberforce and his global anti-slavery movement, it is all too easy to conclude that he was dealing with yesterday's problem. The conventional wisdom about slavery and slave trade is that they were common, but now happily extinct, features of the nineteenth-century global commercial system.[2] As most of you know, after the Peace of Utrecht in

1713, British slave traders became the dominant players in the global slave trade, facilitating the transport of some ten million black Africans to the Americas.[3] In the 1800s, however, a powerful British anti-slavery movement grew up, led by William Wilberforce, which came powerfully to influence domestic political institutions within the United Kingdom. The British parliament banned the slave trade, abolished slavery throughout its colonies, and devoted huge diplomatic and military resources to negotiating and policing treaties designed to criminalize the global slave trade. What is most impressive looking back is how the British government backed its moral commitment with both diplomacy and sanctions—the United Kingdom not only helped to conclude the 1841 Treaty of London, the 1862 Treaty of Washington, and the 1890 Brussels Convention, but in the 1840s also devoted nearly a quarter of its warships to suppressing the slave trade.[4] Once the struggle within Britain was won, the British abolitionists turned their attention outwards, and inspired a transnational anti-slavery movement that enlisted partners throughout Europe, Latin America, and the United States, where the matter was finally and famously resolved by our bloody Civil War. Although slavery persisted in parts of Africa, Asia, and the Middle East into the twentieth century, the conventional wisdom goes, slavery has—like smallpox and polio—been systematically eradicated country by country and is now relegated to the dustbin of history.

In this chapter, my sober message is that this conventional wisdom no longer reflects reality. Now and again, the revival of slavery or forced labour in such individual countries as Sudan, Mauritania, or Burma has forced its way into the headlines. But even as I speak, a new, virulent strain of transborder slavery—what I call the New Global Slave Trade—now infects dozens of countries throughout the world. Let me focus my attention on the revival of slave trade across national borders—what the International Labour Organization has called the 'underside of globalization'—namely, the scourge of global trafficking in human beings.

The issue of trafficking is one that has touched my life professionally and personally for more than a decade, in my work as a law professor, as a human rights attorney, and most recently, as Assistant Secretary of State for Democracy, Human Rights, and Labour in the Clinton Administration. As a refugee attorney, I represented thousands of Haitian, Cuban, and Chinese citizens who took to small boats seeking safe haven in the United States, some of whom were victims of traffickers. I served as co-counsel in a New York case involving a group of hearing-impaired Mexican workers, who were lured to the United States, terrorized by their captors, and forced to peddle wares on the streets of New York by day, deprived of food and sleep at night. While in the State Department, I travelled with then Secretary of State Madeleine Albright to the Hill Tribes Institute of Chiang Mai, Thailand, which works to educate indigenous people throughout South East Asia and to create economic alternatives to the dangers of sex trafficking. Some of the young girls I met at that Institute were younger than my own son Will, who is 14 years old.

Let me divide my chapter into three parts: First, how big is the world's human trafficking problem and how did it come about? Second, what can and should we—as responsible citizens, lawyers, scholars, and human rights activists—do about this huge and growing global problem? Third, what kind of anti-trafficking regime could we build and should we be trying to build?

I. The Problem

Let me start by describing the scope and complexity of this global problem. Trafficking in persons involves the forced movement of people across one or more international borders. One definition is 'the recruitment, harbouring, transportation, provision, or obtaining of a person for labour or services, through use of force, fraud or coercion for purpose of subjection to involuntary servitude, peonage, debt bondage . . . slavery', or coerced sex acts.[5] The US State Department's Country Reports on Human Rights Practices identify at least sixty countries in which such trafficking takes place. That number, which is surely a conservative estimate, represents nearly one-third of the countries in the world. Trafficking in human beings is the third-largest criminal industry in the world today, behind drugs and small arms trade. The United Nations estimates that trafficking in persons generates some $7–10 billion a year.

No less a human rights activist than our President, George W. Bush, described the global contours of the problem, when he told the United Nations General Assembly last September:

There's another humanitarian crisis spreading, yet hidden from view. Each year, an estimated 800,000 to 900,000 human beings are bought, sold or forced across the world's borders. Among them are hundreds of thousands of teenage girls, and others as young as five, who fall victim to the sex trade. This commerce in human life generates billions of dollars each year—much of which is used to finance organized crime. . . . Nearly two centuries after the abolition of the transatlantic slave trade, and more than a century after slavery was officially ended in its last strongholds, the trade in human beings for any purpose must not be allowed to thrive in our time.[6]

235

I have publicly differed with my President on many human rights issues since September 11th, but on this, I could not agree with him more.

That so many around the world regularly resort to the exploitation of innocents for personal and monetary gain must be regarded as one of the most brutal forms of evil we confront today. Many policymakers think of human trafficking as a faceless 'problem': a criminal problem, an economic problem, an immigration problem, a public health problem. It is all of that: transborder trafficking is a multi-billion dollar criminal industry that flouts all governmental immigration policies and threatens to spread global disease.

But in this chapter, let me urge you to see trafficking first and foremost as a human rights problem. Global toleration of trafficking is the very antithesis of the Universal Declaration of Human Rights. Trafficking represents one of the most comprehensive challenges to human rights in the world today, for it involves the very denial of the humanity of its victims. Traffickers abuse virtually the entire spectrum of rights protected in the Universal Declaration of Human Rights. By their acts, traffickers deny that all persons are born free and equal in dignity and rights; they deny their victims freedom of movement, freedom of association, and the most basic freedom: to have a childhood. Traffickers profit from arbitrary detention, slavery, rape, and cruel, inhuman, and degrading treatment. They regularly violate any human right that gets in the way of a profit. Traffickers do not respect human rights, precisely because they treat their victims not as humans, but as objects, chattels to be bought and sold.

Trafficking appears not just in Third World settings, but in Washington and New York as well as London. Trafficking takes many forms, from forced prostitution to bonded domestic servitude, from coerced work in sweatshops to the pressing into service of child soldiers. It involves women and children, but also men, victims from every walk of life, every culture, every religion. To show that no country is above trafficking, some 20,000 people a year are trafficked into my own country, the United States. Another primary destination country for internationally trafficked women is the United Kingdom, which yearly receives women from such Eastern European countries as Albania, Bulgaria, Kosovo, Lithuania, Romania, and Russia; such East Asian countries as China and Thailand; and such West African nations as Liberia, Nigeria, and Sierra Leone. Women are trafficked to the UK primarily for domestic servitude and sexual exploitation; male labourers are also trafficked for sweatshop labour and agricultural work. Recent documented examples include the trafficking of a hundred women from remote villages in Brazil to London over a five-year period under debt bondage, an operation on which the trafficker made £5 million profit;[7] the importation of Chinese women by the Triad gang into London, Glasgow, and Manchester;[8] and the importation of some fifty-five Russian women for prostitution into flats in central London under cover of a car import/export business. Most recently, the UK press has been filled with stories about the slave trade that led to the tragic deaths of some nineteen Chinese cockle-pickers on the beach at Morecambe in the north of England.

Practices vary from region to region, but generally speaking, trafficking involves a vicious cycle in which victims are forced or lured from their home countries, shuttled across one or more international borders, and enslaved, with human rights violations occurring at every step of the way. In 'source countries' where trafficking originates—which can be any part of the world, including the United States or the UK—victims of trafficking can include men, women, and children of every age group. A majority are girls and women under the age of 25. Some respond to employment agencies fronting for traffickers and some are sold to traffickers because their families cannot afford to take care of them. A few are tricked into travelling with a so-called 'family friend' or 'uncle' to a large city to go shopping, only to discover too late that they have been kidnapped and ensnared by traffickers in a world of violence and slavery. In almost every situation, traffickers prey upon the hopes and fears of their victims: in the case of the runaway, offering shelter and sympathy; in the case of the poor family, offering a false way out of debt; in the case of those seeking passage abroad, offering the false hope of a better life.

In many cases, victims are sent to 'transit countries', where traffickers make clear that they have no choice but to accept prostitution, debt bondage, or some other form of involuntary servitude. Once a person is in the traffickers' hands, the traffickers regularly use any and all means to ensure their cooperation: typically drugs, violence, sexual assault, threats to victims' families, or threats to turn victims over to unsympathetic local authorities. If victims have identity papers, traffickers often seize or destroy them to ensure compliance. Where money has been exchanged, victims are often told that the cost of transport is greater than expected, and that they will have to work additional months or years to pay back the traffickers.

Traffickers frequently will move victims from safe house to safe house, from city to city, or from country to country. Once victims of trafficking arrive in so-called 'receiving countries', they are often kept in squalid conditions in a state of virtual house arrest. In the victims' world, violence, drugs, and threats about the authorities form part of the brutal daily routine. So too are long hours of forced servitude—whether in a brothel as a prostitute, at gunpoint as a child soldier, or at a sewing machine as a sweatshop worker. Traffickers commonly addict their victims to drugs to subdue and subjugate them. What little compensation comes the victim's way is usually a tiny percentage of actual earnings, with the balance claimed by the trafficker to 'cover' so-called costs such as room, board, and clothing, or to 'repay' the original 'loan'.

Sadly, even the Internet has become a convenient vehicle for promoting the global trafficking and sexual exploitation of women and children. Commercial sex acts are induced by force, fraud, coercion, or by overbearing the will of minor children. Over the web, agents offer catalogues of teenaged mail-order brides, advertise commercial sex tours, and exchange information on the trafficking in women for the purpose of sexual exploitation.

Post-conflict zones and transitional states are ripe targets to become source countries for trafficking. In such zones, organized criminal groups fill power vacuums created by war and unrest to commandeer the services of children as child soldiers, sex slaves, and slave labourers. In cases involving prostitution and pornography, victims are forced to continue working despite disease, meaning that many work throughout pregnancies and despite having contracted sexually transmitted diseases, including HIV. The global HIV crisis has only fuelled the expansion of sex trafficking, with pimps seeking increasingly younger girls and boys in order to market them to customers as 'clean' partners. Healthcare is usually non-existent or provided only by fellow victims, leaving most victims at high risk of further health complications. Tragically, this ensures that many children born to trafficking victims while in captivity will themselves be trafficked through adoption rings, thus ensuring that the vicious cycle will continue.

How should we break this vicious cycle of interconnected human rights violations? To address the problem effectively, we need to focus not just on particular symptoms, but on recurring features of the generic disease.

II. The Approach

With this background, let me turn away from human rights practice to a broader question of human rights theory. In academic work that I began here at Oxford, I have tried to explain why nations do and do not obey international law. The key to understanding whether nations will obey international law, I have argued, is transnational legal process: the process by which public and private actors—namely, nation-states, corporations, international organizations, non-governmental organizations—interact in a variety of fora to make, interpret, enforce, and ultimately internalize, rules of international law.[9] The key elements of this approach are 'interaction–interpret-ation–internalization.' Those seeking to create and embed certain human rights principles into international and domes-tic law should promote transnational interactions, that gener-ate legal interpretations, which can in turn be internalized into the domestic law of even sceptical nation-states.

If we apply this approach to human trafficking, we can break down the problem into five stages:

• First, knowledge—understanding the nature of the global problem.

• Second, networks—creating civil society networks to build a regime to address the problem.[10]

- Third, developing norms and recruiting committed individuals who are willing to promote those norms publicly. Such individuals include credible people from outside the government, (as was William Wilberforce) whom I call 'transnational norm entrepreneurs', and sympathetic people from within governments, whom I call 'governmental norm sponsors'.[11]

- Fourth, 'horizontal process', a shorthand term for legal process that occurs at an intergovernmental level. This horizontal process can transpire either at a formal intergovernmental level or at informal state-to-state gatherings, anywhere that the governments gather to talk about the trafficking issue. The goal is to create a law-declaring forum at a global level that can declare an international norm against trafficking, as well as to build a broader interpretative community that can construe that norm.

- The fifth and final step I call 'vertical process', the process whereby rules negotiated among governments and interpreted through the interaction of transnational actors in these law-declaring fora are brought down vertically into the domestic law of each participating country—'brought home', if you will—and internalized into the domestic statutes, executive practice, and judicial systems.

That, in a nutshell, is how, in my view, international law becomes law that people actually obey: by moving from knowledge, to networks, to norms, to horizontal process, and to vertical process. So if these are the steps toward global regime-building, how should we proceed to address the global regulation of trafficking?

Let me start with the problems of knowledge and networks: Why is it that some one million people a year are enslaved worldwide and almost no one knows about it? The explanations are simple. Victims rarely denounce their traffickers. Trafficked persons are usually far from home, lack official documents, and are threatened into silence by their keepers. Victims hale from the lowest social and economic strata, and their families have little political or economic ability to pressure public authorities to save their loved ones. Amid the poverty, conflict, and political upheaval that cause transborder migration, massive trafficking and human smuggling can be concealed. Many countries deflect responsibility by claiming that all prostitution is consensual sex for money, thus effectively condoning prolonged sexual servitude. Many governments and cultures are simply embarrassed to acknowledge sexual exploitation and trafficking in their own countries, and other governments avoid the subject so as not to embarrass friendly countries where the practice is widely tolerated.

International law first sought to pierce this veil by addressing trafficking in women in a series of ineffectual legal instruments dating back to 1904, when the so-called International Agreement for the Suppression of the White Slave Trade was adopted in Paris by about one hundred governments. Again the dominant transnational norm entrepreneur was a British citizen, Josephine Butler, who persuaded Parliament to oppose the licensing of prostitution.[12] Butler formed the British, Continental, and General Abolitionist Federation to organize and mobilize abolitionist sentiment throughout Europe. But the first treaty narrowly focused on the protection of victims, not the punishment of perpetrators. In 1910, the International Convention for the Suppression of White Slave Traffic, which bound the thirteen ratifying countries to punish procurers, was adopted. This led the drafters of the Covenant of the League of Nations to include 'general supervision over the execution of agreements with regard to the traffic in women and children' within the League's mandate. Under League auspices, two other international treaties were concluded in 1921 and 1933.[13]

By World War II, opponents of the white slave trade had largely succeeded in replacing state licensing of prostitution with a moral prohibition parallel to the contemporaneous efforts to prohibit alcohol. One year after the Universal Declaration was signed, the United Nations combined the four international Conventions into the 1949 Convention for the Suppression of the Traffic in Persons and the Exploitation of the Prostitution of Others (1949 Convention), which continued until recently as the sole dedicated international treaty on trafficking.

But the 1949 Convention, which has been adopted by a mere sixty-nine countries, proved almost entirely ineffective in combating trafficking. Significantly, the Convention does not take a human rights approach, treating trafficked women as vulnerable beings in need of protection from the 'evils of prostitution'. The treaty excludes vast numbers of women from its protection by narrowly defining trafficking as trafficking for the purpose of prostitution. Perversely, the 1949 Convention also allows states to punish the very women who have been subjected to international trafficking by sanctioning their deportation and expulsion. Moreover, the Convention has pathetically weak enforcement mechanisms: although the States Parties theoretically report annually to the United Nations Secretary-General regarding national implementation of the Convention, more than half the parties flout this requirement, and no independent treaty body has been established to monitor the implementation and enforcement of the treaty.

Trafficking finally returned to the international agenda in the early 1970s with the inauguration of the international women's rights movement. The Forward Looking Strategies of the Third World Conference on Women (1985) addressed traffic in women for prostitution and forced prostitution, and the Platform for Action of the Beijing Women's conference called on governments to take appropriate measures to address the root causes of trafficking in women and girls for prostitution and other forms of commercial sex and forced labour. The Declarations concluding both the Vienna World Conference on Human Rights (1993) and the Beijing Women's Conference (1995) treated the issue of 'international trafficking' as a form of gender-based violence and called for its elimination through international cooperation and national legislation.[14]

By the mid-1990s, a network of non-governmental organizations and governmental sponsors had finally put the issue back on the international agenda. Non-governmental organizations such as Human Rights Watch,[15] the Global Alliance Against Traffic in Women, and World Congress Against Sexual Exploitation of Children contributed to form a global Coalition Against Trafficking in Women, a worldwide network against trafficking that began with one secretariat in 1993 and now embraces secretariats in six continents and national coalitions in over fifteen countries.[16] The Coalition in turn organized the International Human Rights Network (IHRN), a coalition of more than 140 NGOs, to advocate for a definition of trafficking that protects all victims, not just those who can prove that they were coerced.

On the governmental side, these advocates enlisted powerful allies in then-US First Lady Hillary Clinton and her husband, Bill Clinton, who in 1998 finally identified trafficking in women and girls as a 'fundamental human rights violation', and tasked his Interagency Council on Women to develop and coordinate US government policy on this issue. America's first woman Secretary of State Madeleine Albright, the first female UN High Commissioner for Human Rights Mary Robinson, the Special Rapporteur for Violence Against Women Radhika Coomaraswamy, and the late US Senator Paul Wellstone of Minnesota all played major roles in giving the issue greater public profile. Simply by speaking out these advocates spurred the global media to give new attention to the issue, and the Internet has greatly magnified the media voice.[17]

What international norms now have emerged from this process of knowledge and network formation? Perhaps the most critical is the understanding that trafficking is never consensual. It is precisely the non-consensual nature of trafficking that distinguishes it from other forms of displacement and migration that are the subjects of chapters in this book. As Radhika Coomaraswamy has pointed out:

While all trafficking is, or should be, illegal, all illegal migration is not trafficking. . . . Although numerous separate abuses are committed during the course of trafficking, which themselves violate both national and international law, it is the combination of the coerced transport and the coerced end practice that makes trafficking a distinct violation from its component parts. . . . The common elements found in all of the trafficking patterns are: (i) the lack of consent; (ii) the brokering of human beings; (iii) the transport; and (iv) the exploitative or servile conditions of the work or relationship.[18]

Moreover Article 7 of the Rome Statute of the International Criminal Court now specifically singles out 'sexual slavery

[and] enforced prostitution' as a crime against humanity punishable by prosecution before that international tribunal.

III. Implementation: Horizontal and Vertical

If these efforts have now produced knowledge, networks, and norms, that leaves two questions: first, what 'horizontal process' has developed to internationalize these norms? And second, by what complementary 'vertical process' can the global norms that emerge from the horizontal process become internalized into domestic legal systems?

Let me start with what I have called 'horizontal process'. After a number of false starts, pressure from the governmental and non-governmental human rights networks began to force the issue of trafficking in persons onto the intergovernmental negotiating stage. Article 6 of the Convention on the Elimination of all Forms of Discrimination Against Women (CEDAW), which entered into force in September 1981, specifically directed states to 'suppress all forms of traffic in women and exploitation of prostitution of women'. Article 35 of the UN Convention on the Rights of the Child, which entered into force in 1990 and is now ratified by every country in the world except Somalia and the United States, required States Parties to 'take all appropriate national, bilateral and multilateral measures to prevent the abduction of, the sale of, or traffic in children for any purpose or in any form'.

To redress the ineffectiveness of these human rights instruments, in the late 1990s, the United Nations made a key process decision: to transport the norm against international trafficking into its emerging international criminal framework, by drafting a convention against transnational organized crime, to be supplemented by an optional protocol on trafficking in persons.[19] Human rights groups supported an expanded definition of trafficking that would apply to all labour sectors in which some form of coercion is present, so as to preserve the ability of women purposefully and voluntarily to migrate in order to work. By the end of the millennium, a new UN Convention on Transnational Organized Crime had been signed in Palermo in December 2000 by 147 nations, and had entered into force by September 2003. Attached to the Convention were three Protocols, including the Protocol to Prevent, Suppress and Punish Trafficking in Persons and to facilitate international cooperation against such trafficking, which now has forty-five parties and 117 signatories, including the US and the UK[20] Critically, this new global regime includes a mutual assessment mechanism, under which parties assess their own and each other's progress in implementing the Convention and its supplemental protocols.

Regional multilateral efforts have also begun to thrive, with the support of the UN High Commissioner for Human Rights. Countries in Asia have begun a special Asian Regional Initiative to Combat Trafficking of Women and Children. The South Asian Association for Regional Cooperation (SAARC) is developing a draft Convention Against Trafficking in Women and Girls. A conference hosted by the OSCE has addressed similar issues. To address the knowledge gap, the UN Global Programme against Trafficking in Human Beings (GPAT) is collecting data on smuggling routes, methods used by organized criminal groups in trafficking, trafficking trends, and information about victims and traffickers. To coordinate intergovernmental efforts, key United Nations and intergovernmental agencies and programmes dealing with trafficking have created a Contact Group on Trafficking that includes the UN High Commissioners for Human

Rights and Refugees, the International Labour Organization, and the International Organization for Migration, as well as a representative from the NGO Caucus on Trafficking to strengthen cooperation between the various international organizations working on trafficking.

That brings me to the fifth and final step: vertical process. How do we bring these international norms home, in the sense of internalizing the global norms that emerge from the intergovernmental process into the rules of domestic legal systems around the world? How do we domesticate these international rules and make them rules to be obeyed locally? Over the years, four local regulatory approaches have been taken to trafficking. First, prohibition, which seeks to criminalize acts associated with trafficking and prostitution. Second and oppositely, decriminalization, which treats sex work as a private matter between consenting adults, and thus treats relationships between traffickers and their victims as outside the criminal law. Third, a sanctions approach, which focuses on imposing sanctions on states that tolerate trafficking, and fourth, an integrated approach, which I favour, which seeks comprehensively to attack all three facets of the problem: preventing trafficking; protecting its victims; and prosecuting those who profit from the new slave trade.

The prohibition approach, the perspective embodied in the 1949 Convention, has been a proven failure. Similarly, the decriminalization perspective simply ignores the non-consensual nature of trafficking. The third approach, which would impose sanctions on countries who participate in trafficking, will rarely work for four reasons:

• First, because trafficking invariably involves source, transit, and receiving countries, mandatory sanctions targeted against any one country or few will have little impact on the transnational problem.

• Second, the primary moving forces behind the problem are not national government officials or policies, but non-state actors. Like their counterparts in international terrorism, organized crime, and narcotics, human traffickers avoid national criminal penalties by shifting their base of operations across borders to reap the highest level of profits. Trafficking thus tends to be a 'bottom-up' and not a 'top-down' problem: the root causes rest in private greed and economic and social conditions, not government micro-management. When foreign government officials are involved or complicit in trafficking, it is usually at the provincial and local level, where the blunt instrument of national sanctions has the least impact.

• Third, when sanctions do work, they do so mainly by supporting the efforts of private institutions who oppose and challenge the governmental and private actions that support trafficking in the first place. But unlike victims of religious or political persecution, for example, victims of trafficking rarely belong to organized groups, and do not enjoy the protection of established transnational institutions capable of speaking out on their behalf. Despite the emerging power of such NGOs as the Coalition Against Trafficking in Women, there is as yet no global anti-trafficking organization with the name recognition and clout of Wilberforce's British and Foreign Anti-Slavery Society.

• Fourth and finally, many affected governments want to deter trafficking, but most lack the resources to do so. A sanctions regime that targets even those countries who are beginning to address the issue could end up discouraging, rather than encouraging, effective international cooperation and an effective international regime to address the problem.

Given the weakness of these alternatives, I believe that an integrated strategy of prevention, protection, and prosecution would best combine future, present, and retrospective strategies to address root causes, humanitarian relief, and criminal investigation simultaneously.

Prevention means attacking the root causes of trafficking worldwide, by fighting poverty and social inequality that leave populations vulnerable to traffickers, and by educating potential victims so that they do not fall prey to traffickers' schemes. In Nigeria, for example, the Obasanjo government has been involved in an aggressive anti-trafficking awareness campaign. Among the many prevention initiatives I participated in while in government was a USAID programme that funded a consortium of NGOs in Ukraine to provide job skills, public education, and mentoring for at-risk women. When the UN stood accused of complicity in trafficking when it emerged that an American International Police Task Force (IPTF) officer—a United Nations policeman charged with monitoring local Bosnian police—had purchased a Moldovan woman from a Sarajevo brothel for 6,000 Deutschmarks, we pressed the UN mission to adopt a zero-tolerance policy for such misconduct, which has since been implemented in Kosovo and South Korea. Two other recent examples of 'bureaucratic internalization' to encourage prevention are a directive issued by the US Department of Defense in early 2004, specifying anti-trafficking education requirements for all servicemen and employed civilians, and language regarding trafficking-related prohibitions for Defense Department contracts. Prevention also means addressing police corruption and complicity, without which trafficking could not flourish.

Protection means redressing the needs of trafficking victims not just by freeing them from slavery, but by providing them with shelter, health services, and resettlement options, and ensuring that they are not punished for what their captors have done. During my time in the US government, for example, the US provided funds in Thailand, Cambodia, Vietnam, and Laos, to help trafficking victims return to their homes and rejoin society. Another programme, funded by the Department of Labor, helped the International Labor Organization work with children in rural Ghana, where they are sometimes sold as domestic or agricultural labourers. More recently, our Department of Health and Human Services has certified victims of trafficking so as to allow them to receive the same services as political refugees. The US Agency for International Development now supports anti-trafficking programme efforts in over forty countries including medical care and victim protection through shelters and counselling. Protection also means legal reform by, for example, revising immigration laws which permit some countries summarily to deport or incarcerate trafficking victims. In Pakistan, for example, discriminatory laws still exist that treat victims like criminals by criminalizing extramarital sex and use victim testimony as admissions of adultery, discouraging victims from bringing forth their cases. Finally, protection means ensuring that local NGO workers who dare to confront trafficking enterprises are not punished for their work. In recent years, members of an anti-trafficking group called La Strada-Ukraine, and an Israeli sex workers' rights organization called We are Worthy received death threats simply for naming companies that had fronted for trafficking operations.

Prosecution of traffickers means encouraging the passage of national anti-trafficking legislation in every country, and instituting law enforcement training so that local prosecutors, police, and immigration officials have the skills to enforce those laws, and pursuing particular arrests and trials. In Laos, for example, there is currently no anti-trafficking legislation, no capacity for arrests and prosecutions, and huge state corruption, and the only international agreement on the subject (with Thailand) excludes children altogether. In Russia, for example, the US has allocated more than $500,000 to outreach and training programmes for law enforcement authorities and victim assistance programmes. In April 2003, President Bush signed into law the PROTECT Act, which makes it a crime for any person to enter the US or for any US citizen to travel abroad for the purpose of sex tourism involving children. The PROTECT Act also makes clear that there is no statute of limitations for crimes involving the abduction or physical or sexual abuse of a child. Sentencing is now going on, for example, in the largest anti-trafficking case in US history, in which a Korean garment factory owner and two others were convicted in Hawaii of enslaving over 250 Vietnamese and Chinese workers in American Samoa. Some new laws usefully require better statistical monitoring to address the ongoing knowledge problem by revealing critical law enforcement data that reveals changes in patterns of trafficking.

But a focus on law enforcement should not drive out a rights-based approach. Successful prosecutions require trafficking victims to take huge risks to testify against their captors. Effective programmes thus require effective government-funded witness protection and victim services programmes to which all trafficking victims have access.

Perhaps most critical in all this work has been the efforts not of governments, but of non-governmental anti-trafficking activists, such as the Geneva-based NGO Trafficking Caucus, which has grown up to lobby international organizations on the best ways to promote legal change. Most impressive has been the work of such local NGOs as WomenAid's UK Anti-Trafficking Network Platform (UKAT), which has risen up to help develop appropriate anti-trafficking strategies to implement in Britain. In Eastern Europe and the former Soviet Union a network of organizations, the La Strada Network, has provided services for victims of trafficking, including psychological counselling, hotlines, medical care, and shelter. To recount just one of a myriad compelling stories, a trafficked Ukrainian woman found herself imprisoned in an Italian brothel with no idea of where she was. Borrowing an inebriated customer's cellphone, she called her mother in the Ukraine, who called La Strada, who in turn called the Italian police. When the police reached the trafficked woman by phone, she described the numbers on a bus going by her window, and using that information, law enforcement authorities found the brothel and finally freed the woman from captivity.[21]

My point is that trafficking may be the underside of globalization, but the tools of globalization are equally available to combat it. In the twenty-first century, we now see at least three global languages: money, the Internet, and human rights. These three global revolutions are synergistically tied to one another. Thanks to the Internet, satellite, cellphones, and faxes, we have the tools now to reach out to almost every place on earth. Information flies across borders on optic fibre. We can now participate in the formation of transnational networks: people and institutions, governments, businesses, and NGOs, who can and do unite around issues with unprecedented speed to bring unprecedented international pressure to bear on government policies. Transnational networks are transforming the way human rights activists do business because they bring NGOs closer to policymakers and policymakers closer to the people. No nation can stop the information revolution nor keep the human rights message from their people.

IV. Conclusion

So in closing let me say, we have a problem: a New Global Slave Trade. But we also have knowledge, we have networks, we have norms. We need to use those norms in an emerging horizontal process to create an international framework of response, and in a vertical process that internalizes those norms in our domestic law.

I know that some of you are thinking, 'This is fantasy. It cannot be done.' Of course, it is one thing for me to stand here and preach to you in the choir, condemning all of these practices that have exploited so many. But how do we get our message through to the places where these practices persist?

The answer lies within each of us. Whether you are businesspeople, lawyers, diplomats, human rights activists, students, or scholars, you are part of an emerging international civil society that is dedicated to the promotion of universal human rights. In the early 1960s, Robert Kennedy put it this way in a speech whose words are now etched on his tomb. He said, 'Each time a person stands up for an ideal, or acts to improve the lot of others he sends forth a tiny ripple of hope, and crossing each other from a million different centers of energy and daring . . . build a current that can sweep down the mightiest walls of oppression and resistance.' He said those words in Capetown, South Africa, during the darkest days of apartheid, in a country that has now been utterly transformed by human rights.

So, please think of yourself not as atomized, isolated individuals, but as individual centres of energy and daring—modern-day William Wilberforces and Josephine Butlers—who can and should join forces to bring down the New Global Slave Trade. And in doing so, please remember the words of the late Reverend Martin Luther King, who once said: 'The moral arc of the universe is long, but it arcs toward justice.'

Response to Harold Hongju Koh, 'The New Global Slave Trade'

Rey Koslowski

In 'The New Global Slave Trade', Harold Hongju Koh describes the grim world of human trafficking but then offers a strategy to combat it. He argues that trafficking is primarily a human rights problem best approached by an analytical focus on transnational legal processes that, in turn, grounds a policy recommendation for an anti-trafficking strategy combining prevention, protection, and prosecution. I am very sympathetic to his general analytical approach and find his implementation strategy eminently reasonable. Therefore, I can offer little in the way of direct critique. Instead, I will place his essay, particularly his analysis of the problem, into a broader context that may provide some additional insights and strategies.

The problem of the global slave trade is broader than the trafficking of human beings across international borders. Koh focuses on the estimated 800,000–900,000 who are bought, sold, or forced across international borders on a yearly basis. This is only part of global slavery today given that many more people are subjected to forced labour and debt bondage but do not cross international borders. Anti-Slavery International was established in London in 1839 and its US sister organization Free the Slaves estimates that there are some 27 million people trapped in new forms of slavery around the world, primarily in South Asia (India, Pakistan, Bangladesh, and Nepal).[1] As opposed to old forms of slavery based on legal ownership in which slaves were maintained largely because of their high purchase costs, relatively low profit margins, and scarce supply, new forms of slavery are typified by avoidance of legal ownership, low purchase costs, high profits, abundance of potential slaves and short-term relationships that are ended by disposal of the slaves once they are used up.[2] Contemporary slavery takes the form of bonded labour, early and forced marriage, forced labour, slavery by descent (also inherited debt bondage), and human trafficking.[3] It is the increasing phenomenon of human trafficking that is, in a sense, bringing new forms of slavery to North America and Europe.

Most media coverage, legislation, and past international treaties on human trafficking focus on the trafficking of women and children into forced prostitution. Although such exploitation of women and children is the most reprehensible variant of trafficking, it is only a part of the trafficking of all forms of labour. For example, a recent study[4] based on cases of trafficking reported in the American media, estimated that at any given time, more than ten thousand, if not tens of thousands, of people work as forced labourers in the United States with approximately half the identified cases being of prostitution and child exploitation but the rest being forced labour in domestic services, agriculture, sweatshops, and food service. Of those forced labourers, the largest group was Chinese, then Mexican and Vietnamese.

Debt bondage and involuntary servitude are defining features of human trafficking as opposed to just smuggling people across borders for a fee. Due to very high smuggling fees, migrants who have been smuggled from China are more likely than other smuggled migrants to enter into debt bondage arrangements backed up by threats of violence against them and their families in China. The 260 passengers of the smuggling ship, The Golden Venture, which washed ashore on a New York beach in 1993, agreed to pay an average fee of $35,000 to be smuggled to the US. The fee for passage from China to New York City in 2004 is as high as $65,000. Typically, customers pay smugglers a down-payment (usually $1,000–1,500) and then family members, relatives, or friends pay the balance of the fee upon arrival and the migrant repays the debt at no or relatively low interest rates. A smaller percentage of migrants become indebted to organized crime groups and loan sharks who charge much higher interest rates and back up debt repayment with enforcers. Generally, the migrants work in garment factories and Chinese restaurants, often up to 80 hours per week and live in very small spaces where it is not uncommon that they share beds by sleeping in shifts.[5]

While in the New York City area, debts might be primarily held by relatives and friends (whose treatment of the migrant may also vary), in American Samoa and the US Territories of the Northern Mariana Islands, Chinese, Taiwanese, and Korean employment agencies, migrant traffickers and unscrupulous subcontractors in the territories exploit migrants through debt bondage arrangements to produce cheaply 'made in the USA' garments which can be sold at high profits.[6] As Koh notes, it was a case of trafficking of sweatshop labour to these territories that produced the largest anti-trafficking case in US history. With fees of up to $65,000 for the promise of work in the US and Europe, the potential for exploitative debt bondage arrangements among smuggled Chinese migrants is all too great. This is reflected in the increasing number of cases of Chinese workers found working in exploitative and dangerous conditions, whether in US sweatshops, Italian shoe factories, or picking cockles along UK beaches.

As the above cases illustrate, human tra
international borders is often a subset of huma
which is itself a part of the broader phenomenoi.
variously termed 'irregular', 'unauthorized', 'undocι
or 'illegal' migration. That is, trafficked individuals ι
forced into prostitution or labour may have initially volι
ily engaged the services of a smuggler to cross internatι
borders illegally but then upon arriving find themseı
coerced into labour through violence directed at them ana
or their families back home. The key difference between
human smuggling and trafficking is coercion, whether through
direct application of physical force or the threat of the use of
force.

It is very difficult to disentangle the processes of human
smuggling from the trafficking of people because these processes are generally handled by networks of intermediaries
rather than end-to-end by the same individual or organization. Consider a typical situation of the late 1990s in which a
young Moldovan woman is told by an Italian trafficker's
Moldovan recruiter that he has friends in Italy that can get her
a job working illegally in an Italian restaurant in Germany.
The recruiter makes arrangements with a series of smugglers
(who may or may not know that he is a recruiter working for
an Italian trafficker) in order to transport the woman to Italy.
The Moldovan woman might be transported across the
Adriatic in an Albanian smuggler's speedboat together with
Turkish men seeking to work in the Netherlands, and Iraqi
Kurds and Kosovo Albanians fleeing persecution and ethnic
cleansing. In the instance of the crossing, all the individuals are
being smuggled as they are simply paying a fee for an illegal
border crossing. However, when the Moldovan woman arrives
in Italy, has her passport seized, and is forced into prostitution,

what on the face of it was an act of human smuggling becomes an act of trafficking for forced prostitution.

Such intermeshing of human trafficking and human smuggling can raise a quandary for policymakers and human rights advocates. Prosecuting the smugglers that transport Moldovan women bound for forced prostitution in Italy may have also stopped Kurdish and Kosovar asylum-seekers from reaching safety. Migrants in search of work are not the only customers for smugglers' services. After the international community turned its back on Europe's Jews at the Evian Conference, many Jews only escaped the Holocaust by paying smugglers who helped them cross the border into Switzerland. During the Cold War, those who helped East Europeans cross the border into West Germany were often considered heroes, even if they accepted payment. For doing the same thing today, one may be prosecuted as a criminal. Referring to those Americans who broke the 1850 Fugitive Slave Law and ran the Underground Railroad to Canada as well as Peter Dupre, a British national who smuggled East Germans and Czechs across the Yugoslav border into Austria, a libertarian activist has made the argument that 'human smuggling is morally good'.[7] Going back to the smuggler's speedboat, yes, the smuggling of the persecuted Kurds and Kosovars may be considered 'morally good' but the simultaneous smuggling of the Moldovan woman destined into forced prostitution is not. Moreover, smugglers may also be human rights violators. In many cases, smugglers have little regard for the safety of their customers as boats are often overloaded and, when pursued by the coastguard, smugglers have thrown babies and small children overboard to force their pursuers to stop for a rescue operation that enables escape.

Not only is trafficking so intermingled with human

smuggling, there are limitations to approaching human trafficking as a human rights problem because trafficking is just as
much an economic phenomenon as human smuggling and
illegal migration are. Human trafficking exists because there is
demand for trafficked labour in receiving countries, whether
in brothels, in sweatshops, or on farms. The greatest shortfall
in the analytical approach and implementation strategy offered
by Koh is that it does not address demand. What about the
employers and consumers of trafficked labour? What about
the johns who purchase sex with trafficked women and
children forced into prostitution?

In an analysis of the demand behind human trafficking,
Kevin Bales makes the argument that 'consumers of trafficked
people operate within a moral economy that allows them to
rationalize this activity'. In contrast, 'human rights are based
on the privileging and then codification of the victim's definitions of an action . . . (but) virtually every action that we
now think of as a violation of human rights was once defined
as acceptable'.[8] Although laws and civilized discourse may
increasingly privilege the victims' definitions of the act of
paid crossing of an international border and debt repayment
through forced labour as a human rights violation, employers
and consumers are increasingly operating in a different moral
economy that tolerates trafficked labour. Johns may accept the
less than enthusiastic performance of women trafficked into
prostitution for the lower cost of the sex sold relative to that of
native prostitutes. Businesspeople who face competitors that
lower costs through exploiting trafficked labour may themselves justify hiring illegal migrant workers. This, in turn,
increases the demand for illegal migrant labour that inspires
desperate people abroad to pay smugglers and be lured by
traffickers.

Part of the problem from a consumer's standpoint is that it is difficult for the consumer to distinguish whether products and services are produced by illegal migrants who overstayed their visas, illegal migrants who paid to be smuggled, or a trafficked migrant in debt bondage. For example, the tomatoes in a meal served in an ethnic restaurant may have been chopped by a smuggled migrant or by a trafficked migrant working 80 hours per week to repay an enormous debt under threat of violence to his family.

Indeed, the tomatoes themselves may have been picked by trafficked labour as became clear from one of the most notorious cases of modern slavery in the United States. Mexicans who were smuggled into the US in the hopes of working in the Southwest were 'sold' to labour contractors who then did not pay the workers and held them against their will to work in Florida tomato fields. A group of workers eventually resisted and found legal assistance, and the labour contractors were successfully prosecuted under a Civil War era antislavery law.[9]

This case is atypical for the vast majority of Mexicans who are smuggled into the US, however, due to increasing smuggling fees (from \$500 in 1995 to between \$2,000 and \$2,500 in 2004)[10] and the entrance of more violent groups into the smuggling business along the US-Mexican border in Arizona, smuggled migrants are increasingly being treated as illegal commodities that are 'stolen' from one smuggler by another to be then delivered to labour contractors. Due to increasing US border control enforcement, it is likely that most illegal migrants now use smugglers[11] and are therefore increasingly at risk of violent treatment when crossing or becoming subject to debt bondage afterwards.

Given that the practices of trafficking are so intertwined

with smuggling, in practical terms, it is often difficult to disaggregate the prevention and prosecution of human trafficking from the prevention and prosecution of human smuggling and illegal migration more generally. Prevention, protection, and prosecution may not be enough if it does not deal with the moral economy of consumer demand for sex with 'exotic' foreign women that fuels a growing industry that capitalizes on vulnerable illegal migrants. Trafficking prevention through poverty reduction might not be enough if the moral economy remains in place that enables the additional 26 million to be enslaved within their own countries. Educating potential victims of traffickers' ploys may not be enough to convince women to stay home when they see the money sent home by those who were smuggled and are working illegally abroad. Given that truly effective measures to stop human smuggling involve major restrictions on employers' access to cheap and compliant illegal migrant labour, one may anticipate significant resistance from powerful interest groups. Given that consumers of cheaper domestic services, restaurant food, fresh vegetables, clothing, and yes, sex services, apparently have little knowledge and/or concerns about the exploitation that goes into the products and services they consume, the moral economy that enables new forms of slavery and trafficking persists and thrives. No matter how much immigration authorities tighten border controls and prosecutors target traffickers and smugglers, as long as there is high demand for illegal migrant labour which inextricably includes the smuggled and the trafficked, it will be very difficult to reduce trafficking.

8

Displacement in Zion

Jacqueline Rose

> I seek to protect my nation by keeping it from false
> limits [. . .] I shall never agree that in this matter it is
> possible to justify injustice by pleading values and
> destinies.
>
> Martin Buber, 'Politics and Morality', 1945

One news item, out of the stream of disturbing news that
pours daily out of Israel–Palestine, particularly caught my eye
in these past weeks. It was the story of Maayan Yaday and her
husband who were hauling their packing cases into their
new home in the tiny settlement of Nezer Hazani just as
Ariel Sharon was making his announcement that he was
planning to make Gaza 'Jew free'. Five years ago, Maayan
Yaday had been Croatian and a Catholic, but with a fervour
made all the more intense by Sharon's 'betrayal', she insisted
that this was her land: Israel and not Palestine: 'Now I am a
Jew,' she stated, 'I understand that this is our land.' What
struck me in this story was not, however, the somewhat sur-
real nature of that claim, but the misplaced energy with
which she defended it. It was precisely because she had been
Croatian and a Catholic that she understood the danger
besetting the Jewish people, with whom her identification
was now total. 'In Croatia', she explained, 'we gave up one
piece of land, then they wanted another piece of land.' For
'they', read Muslims. From Croatia to Palestine, history was
not so much repeating, as simply reproducing itself: 'The

Muslims don't want to stop. They want our souls and they want our blood.'[1]

Although, as it turns out, Maayan Yaday had met her Israeli husband when she was working as a cocktail waitress on a cruise ship, she could still be categorized—and most certainly she sees herself—as a displaced person. 'I was seven years in that war in Croatia [. . .] But people here will not give up like the Croatians and just leave.' She sees herself, that is, as someone who has been forced, under pressure of intolerable political circumstances, to leave her home. That she so fully enters into a religious and historical identification with the land of her exile may, at first glance, seem to make her untypical. After all, isn't one of the main, explicit or implicit, reproaches against refugees, asylum-seekers, and, indeed, most immigrants that they are not, ethnically and culturally, 'one of us', that they do not fit in (unless they are the new Europeans to which Britain may be about to open its doors)? But Maayan Yaday is not alone, I would like to suggest, in her ability—we might call it a need—to transfer one unbearable historical identity into another. Remember that to choose to live in an Israeli settlement is to choose to place yourself more or less directly in a line of fire (it is also a fact that, from the 1930s, emigration to Israel has increased whenever the conflict has intensified).

Last December, Daniel Ben-Simon of *Ha'aretz* newspaper wrote a long feature on the rise of anti-Semitism in France and the breakdown of relations between Muslims and Jews. One schoolgirl, in a Jewish high school located in a suburb of Seine-Saint-Denis, stated 'because of the anti-Semitism, I feel I will always remain a Jew in the eyes of others so I want them to know I am proud to be a Jew and proud of Israel.' This is of course a very different case. This French schoolgirl is turning to her Jewish identity as a legitimate response to hatred. Unlike Maayan Yaday, she is, you might say, making a claim on her own past. There is nonetheless an irony here, as the week before Ben-Simon had written an equally long feature on the increasingly isolated Muslim community of France (reading them one after the other, very naively I wanted all the people from each article to sit in a room with each other). But this young girl is not pondering what might be wrong with her own country. She is also, like although unlike Maayan Yaday, internally if not literally, on the move. Fear generates an identification. With somewhere else. It travels. And, in doing so, it becomes its own fortress. She wants 'them' to know that she is 'proud of Israel'.

How much, I found myself asking, does she know about the nation of Israel? Does she know what the state is perpetrating against the Palestinians in the name of the Jewish people as she speaks? Does she know that 'ethnic transfer' is something now being openly discussed? Today there is a greater displacement and dispossession of Palestinians inside and out the territories than at any time in Israel–Palestine since 1948. Inside Israel, there is rising unemployment and the economy is in crisis. The country is, in the words of David Grossman: 'more militant, nationalist and racist than ever before'.[2] According to Ben-Simon at a meeting in Northern France which I attended two weeks ago, before 2002 a crucial discussion was taking place inside Israel about the relationship between a secular and religious future for the country—or as he put it, between democracy and clerical fascism. Now it has simply stopped. There is no longer any consideration of what kind of a country Israel wants itself, or ought, to be. In response to the second intifada, Arabic has been taken off the school curriculum. And, according to

Varda Shiffer, former chairperson of the Israeli Section of Amnesty International at a meeting on anti-Semitism in London last week, there is—there can be—no discussion of racism. Since racism equals anti-Semitism, it is impossible for a racist to be a Jew.[3]

I would hazard the guess that the schoolgirl in France knows about the suicide bombings. But there was no allusion whatsoever to the conflict in her interview with Ben-Simon. She was simply proud of Israel. It is not for me to judge her; indeed I have every sympathy with her predicament. French anti-Semitism is real. In the past two years, 2,500 French Jews, double the rate preceding the anti-Semitic incidents, have emigrated to Israel. My sense is—and this is of course pure speculation—that should she follow them, her pride in Israel, born on French soil out of fear and hatred, would, like a tiny cherished diamond in the soul, become her claim. And her view of the Palestinians would blend and blur with the colours of the Muslims of France.[4]

I start with these two stories because I think they can take us to the heart of the problem I want to address here. In our analysis of the migration and displacement of peoples, we are talking mainly about the physical movement of bodies across boundaries. I think we would all agree, in a paradox that may well be a defining feature of our age, that these boundaries have become at once increasingly mobile or porous (more and more people on the move), and increasingly entrenched (more and more restrictions and policing of borders). To leap for a moment to a very different historic legacy—when Gillian Slovo spoke at the unveiling of the plaque to Ruth First and Jo Slovo in Camden last year, she simply contrasted the welcome with which her parents had been greeted in Britain as political exiles in the 1960s with Britain's policy on asylum-seekers today (a moment which for me at least more or less stole the show from Nelson Mandela). But in discussion of this dilemma of our times, not enough attention is paid, I want to argue, to the accompanying mobility and immobility of the mind. What happens to a mind on the move? There is a common truism of what goes by the name of postmodern theory that because people today are caught in so many histories and places, likewise identities, miming the uncertainties of nations, are dissolving and unravelling themselves. Both Maayan Yaday, and the French schoolgirl, suggest that it is not the case. There is a baggage of the mind. When you move across a national boundary, you are just as likely to carry your enemies with you. Nothing, as psychoanalysis will testify, is ever simply left behind. We need to understand the peculiar relationship between the shifting sands of migration and the fortress of the soul. Whenever a door in the world is open, a closet of the heart can just as equally well close (the open door is of course at best a mixed blessing for anyone who feels they have been pushed). In a world of teeming diasporas, how, or perhaps we should be asking why, do identities—against the surface drift, as it were—so fiercely entrench themselves?

To answer, or rather ask, this question, I think we need Freud. When I saw the title for the Oxford Amnesty Lectures this year, my mind was predictably drawn to the term 'displacement', which although I suspect was not intended psychoanalytically by the organizers, but geographically and politically, just happens to be coincidentally a key psychoanalytic term. Interestingly for the purposes of this discussion, when it first appears very early indeed in the work of Freud, it signals the mobility—not to say agility—of mental life. The mind has a remarkable capacity to move its psychic energies from one quantity to another: 'in mental functions something is to be distinguished', writes Freud, in 1894, 'which is capable of increase, diminution, displacement and discharge'[5] (note this is three years before *Studies on Hysteria* and close to a decade before he started writing *The Interpretation of Dreams*). As if at this point Freud were genuinely taken unawares— pleasantly surprised might be going too far—by the move- ments that the mind is capable of. It is the basic discovery of psychoanalysis that the mind cannot be held to one place. None of us are ever simply the child of the place where we are meant to be. Displacement gives, if you like, a more fluid, creative, dynamic component to the idea of the unconscious which famously de-centres man from his own mental self- possession (it is probably a purely personal matter which idea—the splitting of the mind, or the perpetual motion of the mind—you find most disorienting).

But as the idea of displacement progresses in Freud's thinking, it starts to change its hue: battens down as it were. It comes more and more to mean substitution. There is some- thing you cannot bear to think about or remember, so you think about or remember something else. A young man recalls, with disarming and enchanting vividness, a lyrical moment from his childhood with a young girl in a bright yellow dress in a field. He does not want to remember that the visit to his young cousin was precipitated by the failure of his father's business.[6] I wake from a dream in terror at a burning house, because I do not want to notice the infant, ignored in the general conflagration, who has been abandoned by her mother in a nearby street in a pram. All this is unconscious— which is why it works so well. We are past masters at getting rid of something unmasterable so that we can panic at the threat, which then becomes as inflexible as our own violent response to it, of something else. You can see perhaps how there is only one short step from displacement to projection. Although I have come half way round the world, in flight from a country where I could never have even set eyes on you, yet you are the one—now, today—who will be answerable for my fear. Whole histories can hang on this turn. From the very beginning, the story of the founding of Israel is full of moments of just such historic displacement. For the early Jewish settlers in Palestine, in flight from the Russian pogroms at the end of the nineteenth century, the barely armed Arab marauders took on the features of mass city rioters buttressed if not incited by the full apparatus of the state.[7] When you move from one nation to another, whatever you find before your eyes, what, or rather who, do you see?

It is, I believe, one of the tragedies of the Israel–Palestinian conflict that the Palestinians have become the inadvertent objects of a struggle that, while grounded in the possession of the land, at another level has nothing to do with them at all. A struggle which makes of them the symbolic substitutes, stand-ins, 'fall-guys' almost, for something quite else. I have become convinced that in political conflicts of any obduracy, nobody is ever playing the part only of themselves. It goes without saying of course—although this too is often a consequence of such primordial, enduring, mostly unspoken displacements— that nobody is ever in the right place.

But if Israel–Palestine has a particular resonance in this context, and indeed for these Oxford Amnesty Lectures, it is because of the immense complexity with which it surrounds the issue not only of displacement but that of rights. Two displaced peoples—the Jewish people and the Palestinians forced—800,000 of them—to leave their land so that the first people can have a home (one displacement leads to another). Two peoples claiming the right to national self-determination, each one supporting that right with another one—the right of return—which definitively pulls the ground from under their antagonist's claim, saps the very foundations on which the first claim rests. The law of return stipulates that any Jew, but only any Jew, throughout the world, including one who was only a matter of months ago a Croatian and a Catholic, has the right to settle in Israel. The right of return of the Palestinians, on which the Geneva Accord is likely to founder—assuming for a moment that it has even the remotest possibility of coming into being—demands that the Palestinians have the right to re-enter a land, in which the majority of citizens believes that to allow this would demographically, as well as politically, destroy the nature of the state (although in fact only 2% of Israelis live on refugee land).[8] Add to this the fact that, although the clash is between two peoples, the right to the land is justified on radically discrepant grounds or histories— one biblical, going back 2000 years, one based up to 1948 on a far more recently lived connection between the native and her soil. In fact even that is a simplification—for the earliest Jewish settlers in Palestine, the right to a state would emerge as much out of the upbuilding of the land as out of the mists of time. 'It was the service to the soil,' Chaim Weizmann, first President of Israel, wrote, 'which determined the right in our favour.'[9]

'I belong here'. The statement is almost impossible to contest—grammatically it consists of a shifter ('I'), a performative ('belong'), and an indexical sign ('here'). It depends for its truth on the moment of utterance, even if it claims an eternity of time. This is my land because this is where I see myself. Now and forever. We have entered the region of the heart. Between two claims for national self-determination there cannot in fact be any arbitration at law. This is Yeshayahu

Leibowitz, the famous Israeli philosopher and dissident, in his 1976 article, 'Rights, Law and Reality':

Fortunate is the people whose conception of its tie to its country is recognised by others, for should this connection be contested, no legal argument could establish it [. . .] Considerations of historical 'justice' are irrelevant. The conflict is not one of imaginary 'rights'. Nor is it a clash between 'Justice and Justice'—since the legal (or moral) category of justice does not apply.[10]

What, we might ask, does it in fact mean to say that nationhood is a 'right'? In chapter 1, Bhikhu Parekh argues that some of the most important exchanges and responsibilities between individual subjects—of loving and caring for example—cannot fall under the mantle of rights or only do so at the gravest cost.[11] He is talking about individuals and the clash between the concept of rights and another very different vision of ethical or virtuous life. The problem posed by Israel–Palestine is different. This is a situation where the idea of rights can be seen tearing itself apart from the outside and from within. Nationhood is not a right, it is a claim; agonistic, most likely to destroy another. Self-determination is a myth, because as a right it depends on the other's recognition. The worst delusion of all perhaps is that of national selfhood. Not just because no nation in the twenty-first century, nor indeed the twentieth, can be anything other than an inmixing of peoples and hence selves (Israel is of course in full panicked confrontation with that reality as I speak). But because the idea of self-sufficiency, in the world of nations, is a complete myth. This is just one of the very many ironies of Israel's original constitution as a nation-state. 'Paradoxical as it may sound,' Hannah Arendt wrote in her 1944 essay 'Zionism Reconsidered', 'it was precisely because of this nationalist misconception of the inherent independence of a nation that the Zionists ended up making the Jewish national independence entirely dependent on the material interests of another nation.' Theodor Herzl, author of *Der Judenstaat*, the founder of political Zionism, 'did not realise', she wrote, 'that the country he dreamt of did not exist, that there was no place on earth where a people could live like the organic national body he had in mind and that the real historical development of a nation does not take place inside the closed walls of a biological entity'. 'As for nationalism,' she remarked, 'it never was more evil or more fiercely defended than since it became apparent that this once great and revolutionary principle of the national organisation of peoples could no longer either guarantee true sovereignty of people within or establish a just relationship among different peoples beyond the national borders.'[12]

To recap then. No national 'right', as in organic and pre-given. No self-determination, as in self-sufficiency, of nations. To which we can add—circling back to my topic— no singular self-hood. Rights, as John Rawls has stressed, although without drawing the implications for his own theory, relies on a fully rational, monochrome, conception of the person. I must know who I am when I claim them. But if the mind is not its own place? If my claim delves into the depths of my own history, trawling through my dreams and nightmares, to create its own law? The image we have of displaced persons tends to be cast in terms of endurance, survival, the fierce adherence of all human creatures to their own life. It bears no investigation of inner worlds. I suggest instead we see peoples on the move at least partly as sleep-walkers, trundling through each other's dark night.

For the rest of this chapter, I want to select moments from the life and writing of three writers who can, I think, help us to explore this question. More honestly, I should say that I simply love all three. Freud is one—David Grossman, the Israeli writer, and W. G. Sebald, the German émigré, are the other two. Two of them are Jewish and two of them move dramatically across national boundaries in the course of their lives. Freud from Vienna to England, Sebald from Germany; Grossman has been in Israel all his life, but in his writing, certainly in his most famous novel, *See Under: Love*, he moves his central character mentally back into the heart of Europe, tracing the lines of displacement and denial that run from the horror of mid-century Europe to the crisis of Israel today. It can be argued that it was the visit of the United Nations Commission to the camps of displaced persons in 1947 that swung the vote to partition in Palestine, without which there might well have been no state of Israel at all (it had been on a knife edge). This makes Israel pure embodied displacement in both the historical and psychological meaning of the term—a new nation arises for the displaced Jews of Europe to wipe out miraculously their historic pain. But even though, or perhaps because the line from the Holocaust to the nation is so obvious, the link is in this sense causal, it is always—Grossman tells us—subject to revision, remains to be read. Each of my writers is, although in radically different ways, the harshest of self-diagnosticians, my answers of sorts to Maayan Yaday and the schoolgirl from Saint-Denis. All three are storytellers, master craftsmen who allow us to glimpse the past as it ferments inside the mind.

When Freud applied the term 'displacement' to the internal migrations of the psyche, he could hardly have expected that by the end of his life it would, in the forced exile of peoples, so hideously concretize itself. He himself would become an exile, leaving Austria as late as he could in the summer of 1938. Even after the Anschluss, he had been reluctant to depart. He was of course a privileged refugee (according to rumour President Roosevelt interceded with the Nazi authorities on his behalf), an elite among elites—unlike his sisters who were left behind. 'Practically everybody who in world opinion stood for what was currently called German culture prior to 1933,' wrote American journalist, Dorothy Thompson, in her 1938 *Refugees—Anarchy or Organisation?*, 'is already a refugee.'[13]

In December 1938, barely six months after going into exile and less than a year before he died, in a little remarked but highly significant moment, Freud wrote recommending Thompson's book to his friend and benefactress, Princess Marie Bonaparte, who had played such a crucial role in getting him, and his library, safely out of Austria.[14] This is worth noting in itself. It's not quite the kind of book one would expect Freud to read, nor was Thompson, one might say, Freud's kind of woman (she had written a scathing review of Freud's *The Ego and the Id* in 1924—clearly he bore no grudges). Thompson was an extraordinary pioneering political journalist. The Director of Publicity for the New York Woman Suffrage Campaign, chief of the Central European News Service before becoming a freelance writer, she achieved notoriety when she succeeded in 1932 in securing an interview with Hitler. Her greatest claim to fame would be her activities on behalf of refugees: 'the dispossessed racial and political minorities' of Europe, nine million of them, according to the blurb of her book: 'There will be more of them tomorrow and even more of them the day after'—four million who had been compelled under political pressure to leave their homes since the end of World War I—'the most pressing of humanity's many problems'.[15] Freud is one of millions. In this almost dying gesture, Freud universalizes his predicament, finds himself making common cause with the refugee.

'As I write this', Thompson begins, 'the news from Europe is distressing in the extreme.'[16] Her book is a plea for an internationally financed programme for mass settlement—a political solution to what she insists is a political problem (her activities on this score are considered to have been influential in the formation of Roosevelt's Advisory Committee on Refugees). 'Horrified humanitarianism', she insists, is not enough.[17] Although her book is dated (how could it not be?), both her plea for international accountability and her indictment of the Great Powers for betraying the Armenians and the Assyrians have much to tell or remind us of today. The Jews are of course central to her analysis. Reluctant to countenance the grimmest outcome of Nazi persecution, she wants the Nazis to be used. Her model for raising finance is the settlement of German Jews in Palestine made possible by means of a trade-and-transfer agreement between the Nazi Government and the Haavara, an organization for the transfer out of the country of the capital of German-Jewish emigrants. Those only 'theoretically interested in the refugee problem', as she puts it, can be left to work out what was uppermost in the minds of the Nazis: 'whether their interest was primarily in increasing their exports, or primarily in getting rid of their Jews'.[18] She is not naive. She knows the deal is sinister. She wants the Jews out of Germany at any cost. Without sentimentality or understatement, Thompson charts the journey—political, geographic, financial—that takes the Jewish people out of the heart of a persecutory Europe and into Palestine.

Thompson believes in the Jewish 'upbuilding' of Palestine. In tones unmistakably resonant of mid-century Zionism, she sees Palestine as redemptive for the Jews: 'There the sons and

daughters of the persecuted Eastern European Jews grow up
to be healthy creatures who do not bear the stigma of their
Jewishness any more, but feel themselves to be happy and
healthy human beings.'[19] In one of his famous, and perhaps
worst moments in *Der Judenstaat*, Herzl had argued that a state
for the Jews would be 'a rampart of Europe against Asia, an
outpost of civilisation as opposed to barbarism'.[20] Thompson
also believes in a form of 'enlightened twentieth-century
imperialism'—her phrase—'a really grandiose scheme for
developing backward territories with displaced Europeans'.[21]
But there is a limit to such benign imperialism and that limit is
Palestine. Contrary to Herzl, for Thompson European gran-
diosity does not finally fulfil itself, but rather crashes, in the
Middle East. Arab resistance to the Jewish presence has made
the dream of mass emigration impossible. There can therefore—'at least for the moment', she writes—be no solution
to the problem of Jewish refugees. Many Jews already in
Palestine or wanting to emigrate may be 'prepared to fight
and die for a country which they consider their homeland'.
(As Herzl put it: 'only the desperate make good conquerors').[22]
But 'unless the difficulties between Arabs and Jews can be
cleared up and a reconciliation effected', Palestine must, she
writes, be considered a 'danger spot for the Jews'. 'All hopes of
anything like mass emigration to Palestine have to be buried.'[23] Ideals can place you in danger. Palestine is no solution
for the Jews. Dorothy Thompson is a pragmatist, but running
under the surface of her analysis is the warning that I like
to think was the one Freud was communicating to Marie
Bonaparte. In a gesture of glorious and truly creative heroism,
escaping the horrors of Europe, the Jews are in danger of
transporting their own legacy of displacement, directly and
perilously, onto the soil of Palestine. The Jews will not be

277

safe—and in this history surely bears her out—in Palestine. In a classic psychoanalytic move, which I am sure was not her intention, Thompson suggests that flight, fortification—your best protection—can turn out to be the worst defence.

In 1930, Freud had written what has become a famous letter to Dr Chaim Koffler of the Jewish Agency who had written to him and other prominent European Jews asking them to criticize British policy in Palestine. In response to the Arab riots of that year, Britain was restricting Jewish access to the Western Wall in Jerusalem and Jewish immigration. Although many readers will already be familiar with this letter, it is an extraordinary one and, I think, worth quoting again:

I cannot do what you wish. I am unable to overcome my aversion to burdening the public with my name and even the present critical time doesn't seem to me to warrant it. Whoever wants to influence the masses must give them something rousing and inflammatory and my sober judgement of Zionism does not permit this. I certainly sympathise with its goals, am proud of our University in Jerusalem and am delighted with our settlement's prosperity. But on the other hand, I do not think that Palestine could ever become a Jewish state, nor that the Christian and Islamic worlds would ever be prepared to have their holy places under Jewish care. It would have seemed more sensible to me to establish a Jewish homeland on a less historically burdened land. But I know that such a rational viewpoint would never have gained the enthusiasm of the masses and the financial support of the wealthy. I concede with sorrow that the baseless fanaticism of our people is in part to be blamed for the awakening of Arab distrust. I can raise no sympathy at all for the misdirected piety which transforms a piece of an Herodian wall into a national relic, thus offending the feelings of the natives. Now judge for yourself whether I, with such a critical point of view, am the right person to come forward as the solace of a people deluded by an unjustified hope.[24]

This is a harsh judgement. The Jewish people are deluded and their hope is unjustified. If Freud was wrong about the hope—there would be a Jewish state in Palestine—he may nonetheless have been right about the delusion (Chaim Weizmann was happy to describe the Jewish desire for a homeland in Palestine as quite mad: 'It is the Zionists' good fortune that we are considered mad; if we were normal, we would not think of going to Palestine, but stay put, like all normal people.')[25] Freud's strongest criticism—'I can raise no sympathy at all'—is directed at the 'misdirected piety which transforms a piece of an Herodian wall into a national relic' ('baseless fanaticism' he calls it, not mincing his words). It is reserved, that is, for the process whereby a people, historically and symbolically burden the land, as the foundation of their claim upon it. Above all the danger resides in that moment or process of substitution. I do not see the people of Palestine; I see the land aglow with my own destiny (Rajeh Shehadeh, the Palestinian lawyer and human rights activist calls this 'pornography of the land').[26]

We all know Israel Zangwill's famous and deadly formula for Zionism: 'A land without a people for a people without a land.' In fact the Arab people were not, of course, invisible as the most cursory perusal of the literature of early Zionism makes clear. To this brute fact, Freud is adding something else. What allows you to ignore the people before your eyes is the force of piety: magical—or as Freud terms it 'omnipotent'—thought. Money—'the financial support of the wealthy'—will not do it alone. In this letter, Freud makes the most careful and resonant distinction between two ways of being in the world, indeed between two forms of Zionism, we could also say. One which—living in the real world—quietly, soberly, works to achieve its ends (the University of Jerusalem, the prosperity of the settlements, by which he means the agricultural work of Jewish immigrants); the other which, recognizing no obstacles, ruthlessly sweeps across the earth and its people. 'It will be Jewish,'—Weizmann again—'whether the Arabs want it or not;' 'There is no power on earth that can stop the Jews from getting to Palestine.'[27] Or in the words of David Ben-Gurion in 1948 (responding to the US proposal to establish international trusteeship over Palestine): 'We are masters of our own fate. We have laid the foundations for the establishment of the Jewish state and we will establish it.'[28]

Freud—'in sympathy with the goals' of Zionism as he makes a point of stating in his letter, as no mere concession I believe—places himself firmly in the rank of those who believed that Jews should travel to Palestine, and make it their home but on condition of not usurping the land and rights of the Arab people. Remember only 2 per cent of Israelis live on refugee land; the Palestinian refugees could, at least technically, return. Those of us who agitate for a more open policy on asylum and immigration would presumably not want to oppose these early migrations of the Jews. To repeat—the problem is not the movement of bodies but thought fastening on and seizing its ground. Migration, therefore, but no national relics. No omnipotence of thought. On the eve of the genocide in Europe, in a gesture which is counter-intuitive to say the least, Freud warns the Jewish people, struggling to survive as a people, not to believe in themselves too much.

David Grossman was born in Jerusalem in 1954, fifteen years after the death of Freud. In between that death and that life, the Jews of Europe are decimated and Israel is born as a nation-state. Both of them, we could say, missed the main event. But for that very reason, Grossman has everything to tell us about a mind struggling to come to terms with a history that no one wants to talk about, and which for that very reason has to be invented inside a psyche which is not, in any obvious sense, its proper place. Freud did not live to see the story he partly warns against. Nor to witness—although this much he could surely have predicted—that in the space of that short fifteen years, it would not just be lived, but repressed.

'Most painful to me', writes the Jewish pro-Palestinian activist and political theorist Sara Roy of her childhood in Israel, 'was the denigration of the Holocaust and pre-state Jewish life by many of my Israeli friends. For them, these were times of shame, when Jews were weak and passive, inferior and unworthy, deserving not of our respect but of our disdain.'[29] On the fiftieth anniversary of the liberation of Auschwitz, Grossman writes in the German newspaper, *Die Zeit*, of the 'cruelty' native Israelis had shown towards the survivors, as if both the event, and the fact of their survival were causes of 'shame'.[30]

In his most famous novel *See Under: Love*, of 1989, the 9-year-old Israeli boy Momik has to call up the Nazi beast from his cellar in order to confront his family's silenced European past. Grossman then spins his whole novel—the story of Anshel Wasserman, Momik's surviving grandfather— out of the boy's later secret research into the Holocaust. Momik's grandfather was assumed to have died in the camps. When he shows up out of the blue as a survivor at the family home on the first page of the novel, he is welcomed as, to say the least, a mixed blessing: 'And then when the new grand-father showed up and Momik's mama and papa screamed and suffered at night worse than ever.'[31] Only the boy who knows nothing of his history can love him. In Momik's recreation of his story, Wasserman survived the camps because, when the Nazis tried to kill him, he miraculously failed to die. At which point the commandant, Neigel, adopts him as a storyteller on the understanding that, for every story he tells, Neigel will oblige by trying once more to kill him (having witnessed the death of his daughter in the camps all Wasserman wants is to die). In this context, 'magical realism' becomes a charged epithet. There is no place in reality—not in the reality of Israel of the first generation—for this story. It has to be conjured out of magical, displaced, time.

Inside the concentration camp that Momik invents in his mind in order to tell his grandfather's story, the Nazi commandant chants like a mantra words that Grossman lifts from Hitler's Berlin speech of 1938: 'Conscience is the business of the Jews.' 'This sentence was interpreted by Jurgen Stroop, the German commander of Warsaw during the rebellion', the narrator comments, 'as follows: "And thus he freed the Nazis from conscience." '[32]

Later in the book, the grandfather responds, accepting the burden of Jewish ethical life: 'Indeed yes, it is a grave responsibility, and a heavy burden we have never forgotten, never [. . .] Sometimes we were the last remaining souls on earth who remembered what a conscience is.' In a rare moment, the narrator intervenes against his own character, telling us to view these words indulgently, as those of a Jew 'doomed to a lifetime of absolute values of morality and conscience', with 'no other weapons at his disposal'.[33] Grossman is struggling not to hand the palm to the Nazis—they win whichever choice you make: reject morality, you become a Nazi, embrace it and they destroy you. As psychoanalyst Jacques Lacan has pointed out, the challenge 'Your money or your life' gives a

false illusion of choice since, disempowered, you lose something of your life in either case. Inside the new nation of Israel,
there is no room for purity of ethical life. 'Enough of Jewish
hyper-moralism', wrote early Zionist Moshe Smilansky in
1908, against the suggestion that the Jewish nation should not
be built without respect for morality and justice.[34] For Israel
to become a nation, rights must take precedence over virtue
(to refer back to Bhikhu Parekh once again).

As I see it, Grossman's tale goes to the heart of a problem at
the core of Israel as a nation today, one which in fact precedes,
even if it was drastically reinforced by, the horrors of the
last World War. He is for me the most subtle analyst of the
dilemma. If an ethical conscience is defined as weakness or
passivity, then what break on power? 'No nation in the
world', Benjamin Netanyahu writes in *A Place Among the
Nations—Israel and the World*, a truly ghastly book which at
least has the benefit of openness, 'will chose to ally itself
with Israel because it has returned to parading the virtue of
Jewish powerlessness' (note 'Jewish' powerlessness, the chapter
is called 'The Question of Jewish Power').[35] This is Assaf
Oron, first Class Reservist and refusenik: 'A loud voice keeps
shouting—we must put morality and conscience to sleep.'[36]
In a letter to the *Guardian* newspaper of August last year, one
Carl Sherer writes from Jerusalem: 'In my Jewish education,
I was taught that with three exceptions, the number one
Jewish moral imperative is to preserve Jewish lives. Ending
Israel's control over another nation was not one of the three
exceptions.'[37]

At the end of his novel, when Wasserman gets to tell his
story, the story he relates is of the miracle child, Kazik, born to
an ageing couple who then ages and dies in accelerated time
(he is 22 hours old when he dies). It is impossible not to read

Kazik as an allegory of the Israeli nation. Grossman has for me
written the supreme novel of displacement. Out of a silence,
he charts the death of a nation that has made its whole rationale the will of the Jewish people to survive. Grossman is one of
the few Israeli writers who is willing to raise as a question
whether, for all its increasing strength and fortification, its
manifest military superiority, its continuing crushing of the
Palestinian people, Israel might be in the process of destroying
itself. During his secret library researches into the Holocaust,
Momik discovers a picture of a Nazi soldier, 'forcing an old
man to ride another old man like a horse'—'deep down
inside he began to sense that these photographs might reveal
the first part of the secret everyone had tried to keep from
him'.[38] 'The soldier,' writes Sara Roy on the Israeli occupation of the West Bank and Gaza, 'ordered the old man to stand
behind the donkey and kiss the animal's behind [. . .]
Throughout the summer of 1985, I saw similar incidents:
young Palestinian men being forced by Israeli soldiers to bark
like dogs.'[39] To displacement we need then to add one more
psychoanalytic concept—the compulsion to repeat. In the
occupied territories the nation finds itself re-enacting
the most shameful moments of its buried past.

It has become something of a truism to say that the
Holocaust is exploited by the state of Israel to deflect criticism
of its policies (one I should say with which I agree). But what
I am inviting you to consider here is different. That is, the
even greater damage done to a national psyche—to any
psyche—when something, far from being vaunted but perhaps as the precondition of its being so terribly misused,
has been silenced or repressed. I am reminded of Roland
Barthes's famous analysis of how fashion pulls clothes so far
from their functional purpose that the reason we wear them

can suddenly return as the surprising, bright idea of a new season: as in 'it will be a long, warm winter this season' to advertise coats (as if the idea that coats were intended to keep you warm could be a glamorous afterthought). The example may seem trivial but it can, I think, help to make a difficult, and of course deadly serious, point. Speaking of something can, paradoxical as it may sound, be a way of not speaking about something. It can be a means to ensure that the true, unbearable, felt humiliation of a catastrophe as it might impact on a nation, not as rationale or apology for state power, but as memory, is still being repressed. Perhaps this is the most disturbing meaning of displacement—when a traumatic history is loudly invoked, with devastating political consequences, almost as a smokescreen for itself.

I am not, I should perhaps stress, suggesting that the Holocaust is not a real traumatic memory for the Jewish people. Nor that a nation does not have a right to legitimate self-defence. But the tragedy of Europe did not simply pass into the nation's mind and it is not simply, as in innocently, being invoked today. Last year, 200 Israeli soldiers serving in Hebron were sent on a visit to Auschwitz to strengthen their resolve. Responding in July last year to questions about the killing of Palestinian children by the Israeli army (in the present conflict, one in five dead Palestinians is a child), the commander in Gaza commented: 'Every name of a child here, it makes me feel bad because it's the fault of my soldiers,' but by the end of the conversation he has—in the words of the interviewer—returned to being 'combative': 'I remember the Holocaust. We have a choice, to fight the terrorists or to face being consumed by the flames again.'[40] There are suicide bombs in which Israeli children have died; they have, as I see it, rightly been described by many not just inside Israel but also by Palestinians and the wider international community as unacceptable crimes. But the flames on the streets of Jerusalem and Tel-Aviv are not the flames of the Holocaust (any more than the Muslims of Croatia are the same as the Arabs of Palestine). Nor do I believe that the building of the wall, targeted assassinations, the destruction of the entire infrastructure of Palestinian life, and the daily humiliation of the people can be justified as a legitimate security response. Something is in excess. For psychoanalysis, something arises in excess when there is something else you cannot bear to think about. What would the situation in Israel–Palestine look like if the commander in Gaza deduced from his 'memory' of the Holocaust, for example, a shared vulnerability of peoples? What kind of a nation would Israel become if the state ceased to promote omnipotence as the answer to historical pain?

I conclude, much more briefly, with W. G. Sebald who in his life and writing brings the art of displacement, in all its ambiguities and multivalence, to the rarest pitch. I know I am not the only reader who has found herself asking if the story of his 2001 novel, *Austerlitz*, of the young Jewish boy sent to England in 1939 on a Kindertransport, is his own. It isn't of course. Sebald is not Jewish. But in this book, and to some degree in *The Emigrants*, Sebald throws himself into the mind of German-Jewish suffering with such understated, desolate, intensity that critics are inclined to cry either miracle or theft. Sebald is, of course, himself an emigrant. He left Germany for England in 1966. Alongside his passion for the earth and contours of the land of his new home, he writes stories of persons lifted out of a past that neither he nor they have left behind. As if moving out of Germany enjoined on him the task of a very peculiar form of remembrance. Something a million miles from being a claim on the past. This is history not as fragment —that would be too easy, too bland; it is memory numbed by the sheer effort of resisting and retrieving itself. Sebald puts himself in the other's place—through Austerlitz he imagines himself as a Jew. As with *The Natural History of Destruction*, which goes into the archives to call up the mostly forgotten and silenced story of the destruction of German cities in the last year of the war, Sebald—not unlike Grossman but from the other side—delves into shame, tells the narrative of his nation in reverse.

Austerlitz speaks to an unnamed narrator whom he meets at stations and in hotels, often by chance, although every encounter also feels like a summons. Austerlitz has chosen this narrator as the vehicle for his own memory of a story he has been in flight from all his life. 'The past', as Daniel Ben-Simon said recently, 'is ahead of us.' The nation's future—I heard him saying—depends on what we will allow, or can bear, the past to be. Sebald, I am tempted to say, writes in the future perfect tense that Jacques Lacan terms the tense of analytic time: not the past of what I once was and am no more [repression], nor what I have been in what I am still [repetition], but what 'I will have been for what I am in the "process of becoming" '.[41] This makes nationhood, like memory, endless (neither redemptive nor retributive, it is not something that can be taken out, brushed down, and used). It is not enough to wear the banner of the dead and claim to speak in their name. If we do not want to disappoint them, as Elizabeth Bowen once famously put it, we must go further. Perhaps we have to go out and meet them. This is from near the end of the book when Austerlitz is trying to remember his father who disappeared shortly after saving his child:

I felt, as I was saying, said Austerlitz, as if my father were still in Paris and just waiting, so to speak, for a good opportunity to reveal himself. Such ideas infallibly come to me in places which have more of the past about them than the present. [. . .] It seems to me then as if all moments of our life occupy the same space, as if future events already existed and were only waiting for us to find our way to them at last [. . .] And might it not be, continued Austerlitz, that we also have appointments to keep in the past, in what has gone before and is for the most part extinguished, and must go there in search of places and people who have some connection with us on the far side of time, so to speak.[42]

'As I was saying, said Austerlitz', 'And might it not be, continued Austerlitz'; 'so to speak'. Memory is as hesitant as it is imperative. In the most intimate details of his grammar, Sebald at once bids memory come and slows it down.

This dull, cruel, urgent pacing of memory seems to me to be crucial. For me Sebald is saying two things that go to the heart of my topic here. There is no limit to the potential for identification—this is displacement in Freud's earliest creative sense. In Sebald's mind any German can become a Jew, and perhaps must try. But all identities are dangerous unless they are given up, qualified—for me the syntax of Austerlitz is the key—at the very moment that they are claimed. Otherwise they will become a fortress, the grounds for a new and killing form of certainty. And no end of dreadful deeds will be enacted in their name.

So let me conclude with fortresses. Not least because at this moment the legality of the security fence in Israel is before the International Court of Justice, condemned this week by Amnesty International in whose name this book is written. But if I end with fortresses it is also because in a way I have been speaking throughout this chapter of nothing else:

fortresses on the ground and in the head. Austerlitz is an architectural historian—he is a lecturer at a London institute of art history—long before he goes in search of his own past. He is obsessed with buildings of war and conquest. Before he gets to the concentration camp in which his parents most likely perished, he tells us, through the meticulous analysis of ramparts and weaponry down the ages, that power is all the more futile the more it tries to entrench itself behind a wall of self-defence. A wall is a false memory—destructive of others and asking to be destroyed. It is also a form of displacement (perhaps the sheerest of them all), since it sidelines, or rather endlessly moves elsewhere, what then becomes—automatically and because he has built it—the defendant's most vulnerable point. This is, as I see it, also Freud's and Grossman's insight. In this passage Austerlitz is commenting on the star-shaped fortresses of Coevorden, Neuf-Brisach, and Saarlouis:

It had been forgotten that the largest fortifications will naturally attract the largest enemy forces, and that the more you entrench yourself the more you must remain on the defensive, so that in the end you might find yourself in a place fortified in every possible way, watching helplessly, while the enemy troops, moving on to their own choice of terrain elsewhere, simply ignored their advers- aries' fortresses, which had become positive arsenals of weaponry, bristling with cannons and overcrowded with men. The frequent result, said Austerlitz, of resorting to measures of fortification marked in general by a tendency towards paranoid elaboration was that you drew attention to your weakest point, practically inviting the enemy to attack it.[43]

And again, on Antwerp in the nineteenth century: 'Although the whole insanity of fortification and siegecraft was clearly revealed in the taking of Antwerp, said Austerlitz, the only conclusion anyone drew from it, incredibly, was that the defences surrounding the city must be built even more strongly than before.'[44] Such defences are living on borrowed time. 'It is often', says Austerlitz, 'our mightiest projects that most obviously betray the degree of our insecurity.'[45] What all my three writers seem to me to be saying is that we need a non-defensive form of memory if the world is to be a fairer, not to say safer, place.

I have one final anecdote that I take from Sara Roy's presentation at the event organized in November 2003 by the *London Review of Books* in tribute to Edward Said. I simply quote the opening lines of her piece which she kindly sent me:

Not too long ago, two reporters for the Israeli newspaper, *Yediot Ahronot*, were given the opportunity to purchase 100 olive trees. These trees, they discovered, were uprooted from Palestinian lands razed by Israel for the building of the new 'security' wall or separation barrier in the West Bank. Among these gnarled trees, some of which have found new homes in Israeli parks and private residences, was a 600-year old olive tree selling for $5,500 at an Israeli nursery.[46]

Some forms of displacement are simply a crime.

Response to Jacqueline Rose, 'Displacement in Zion'

Ali Abunimah

The century-long history of the modern conflict over
Palestine has reached a transitional moment. The political
actors and discursive agents have yet to apprehend and absorb
the new realities that this transition reveals.

In 1948, Zionists established Israel after the mass expulsion
of Palestinians from areas now delineated by the 1949 Rhodes
Armistice Line or 'Green Line'. Subsequently in June 1967,
Israel invaded and occupied East Jerusalem, the West Bank,
and Gaza Strip. The absence of any peace agreements—
compounded by the occupation—has created a situation
which can be described as both temporary and permanent.

Legally speaking, those Palestinians expelled in 1947–8 are
refugees or displaced persons and by definition are absent
from their homes only temporarily. Established international
law dictates that their right to return is undiminished by
time and is furthermore transmitted to all their direct descendants. The Fourth Geneva Convention, which governs
Israel's occupation of the West Bank and Gaza, assumes that
occupation is a temporary, short-term phenomenon.

However, life for Palestinians has not conformed to these
formal principles. Palestinians have been refugees, exiles, or
captives in their own land for almost six decades, and entire
lifetimes have been spent in this ostensibly temporary situation. UNRWA—the agency created in 1949 to care for the
Palestinian refugees—still persists and today provides services

to 4.1 million Palestinians, a number that grows every year. During its passing stay in the occupied territories, Israel has implanted 400,000 settlers. Legally, the settlements are, as the International Court of Justice recently reaffirmed, a blatant violation of Article 49 of the Fourth Geneva Convention which states that 'The Occupying Power shall not deport or transfer parts of its own civilian population into the territory it occupies.' This means that neither the settlers nor their descendants gain any legal rights or status as protected persons or beneficiaries of their illegal presence on the land. Yet reality does not always respect legality; many of the settlers were born in the settlements and know no other homes. Children born to the settlers are no more masters of their fate than children born to refugees.

The idea that these displacements—and the consequent violent conflicts and harsh suffering—is ephemeral has made life bearable for Palestinians and has given them the ability to remain steadfast in the face of ever-worsening conditions. The Palestinians' vision of their future, whether optimistic or pessimistic, has always comprised an end to their predicament.

We are at a point where it is now impossible to view these displacements as temporary. It becomes increasingly formidable to find hope in the future. This is not to say that we must accept the status quo as a fait accompli but that the dominant ideological framework is too narrow for considering the problems of Israel's creation. The end of the suffering and conflict will come—must come—but peace will appear in a different form from how we have imagined until now.

A human being cannot apprehend his life as anything but a journey from a lived and constantly reinterpreted past to an imagined and better future. Life becomes impossible once hope is lost that this future can ever be actualized. The present period of transition contains dangers because, for Palestinians, death can become preferable to life. At least this is what so many Palestinians who announce intentions to become 'martyrs' say: they have suffered so much and see no viable future, so death becomes preferable to life. If such a belief spreads through a community, anomie and alienation threaten the social order and all human relationships within a population. The threshold for this level of depredation is apparently quite high, because people have survived unimaginable horrors throughout history and have not lost hope.

For six decades, Palestinians have been in the paradoxical situation of receiving massive rhetorical and legal support for their cause while also experiencing continued alienation and dispossession from their rights and homes. The Palestinians' growing feeling of helplessness overcomes their essential human vision of a better future, and thus some of them resort to desperate tactics.

Jacqueline Rose explores several themes in her chapter that strike me as relevant in finding a way forward. She observes from the cases of the Croatian Catholic woman who in the space of months had transformed herself into a 'Jewish settler' in Gaza, railing against betrayal by Ariel Sharon, and a French schoolgirl appealing to her own pride as a Jew in the face of perceived discrimination in France, that there is a 'baggage of the mind', which people carry with them when they are 'on the move'.

Rose also introduces Freud's concept of displacement alongside the exposition of the term as it pertains to refugees and migrants. In the psychoanalytic idiom, as Rose explains, 'it signals the mobility—not to say agility—of mental life'. But the definition of displacement changes over time and comes to mean substitution: 'there is something you cannot bear to think about or remember, so you think about something else'.

Both of these ideas describe aspects of the current period of the conflict. The baggage that Israelis and Palestinians carry with them shapes their conceptions of the past, though it is notable that in the past two decades, Israeli views of history have begun to move closer to Palestinian conceptions. Thus it is now widely accepted in Israel that the rise of the 'Jewish state' is predicated upon the dispossession of another people. Efforts to reconcile the competing Israeli and Palestinian narratives about their pasts have been pervasive at all levels in these societies. Notwithstanding these accomplishments, our narratives about the future have stagnated and become a burden to us, which may be even larger than the past. I refer specifically to the apparent consensus that the solution to the Palestine conflict is the creation of a Palestinian state alongside Israel.

Elsewhere I have argued at length why I believe that the situation on the land, such as the complex overlapping of Israelis and Palestinians throughout historic Palestine has made such a partition impossible today—if it ever were possible. I have noted that there is increasing, though still marginal, discussion among Palestinians and Israelis about abandoning the quest for a two-state solution because of these facts on the ground. Instead a new political solution will include Israelis and Palestinians as full citizens in a single political entity.

Demonstrating that the premises of this debate are gaining credence despite official denial of this debate's legitimacy, the UK's Department for International Development co-authored with the Foreign Office a document leaked to the *Guardian*. It belies the increasingly common assurances from international officials that Israel must continue to exist as a 'Jewish state'. According to the *Guardian*, the document states, 'Without action soon, there is a real danger that facts on the ground (Israeli settlement expansion and construction of a separation barrier) may make a viable two-state solution almost impossible.' The assessment argues that 'the logical consequence of indefinite occupation by Israel' would be that a majority of Palestinians would drop support for a two-state solution, and 'instead back a single bi-national state from the Jordan to the Mediterranean. Palestinians would outnumber Jewish Israelis in such a state within the next decade.'[1]

Whether the point of no return has been reached for the two-state solution is a matter for legitimate disagreement, but what is indisputable is that the matter is urgent and the prospect of action commensurate with the challenge of building a Palestinian state is non-existent. Among Israelis, the professed fear of a Palestinian 'demographic time bomb' (projections that Palestinians will outnumber Jewish Israelis in Israel, the West Bank, and Gaza within a few years) animates their desperate desire for separation. This jingoistic paranoia fuels support for Israel's monstrous and illegal barrier being built in the West Bank. Israel has created a reality it now wishes to conceal behind a wall.

Perhaps we are witnessing an intense form of displacement, in the Freudian sense of substitution. As the two-state solution becomes obsolete, the discourse that promotes it on the international scene intensifies. US President George Bush loses no opportunity to trumpet his support for his 'Road Map for Middle East Peace'. Virtually every newspaper editorial in the English language has endorsed it. The EU, the UN, and Russia are along with the US the three corners of the 'Quartet', whose plan promised a Palestinian state by 2005 without ever providing the political will or pressure on Israel needed to advance the goals outlined in the plan.

Perhaps among professedly moderate Israelis, the displacement is most intense. Many left-wing Israelis associated with the peace movement performed a great service by helping debunk the myth of Camp David: that Palestinians rejected a 'generous offer' from ex-prime minister Ehud Barak and chose the path of violence instead. Unfortunately, a Camp David counter-myth has arisen in its place, which can be summarized like this: there is an agreement to be had, there is a Palestinian partner, and the parameters of the agreement are largely known if not self-evident, and all that needs to be done is to sit down and hammer it out. This belief has given rise to a number of other initiatives, such as the ersatz Geneva Accord and the Nusseibeh-Ayalon plan. Each of these plans obfuscates fundamental issues—particularly settlements and the fate of refugees—and ultimately resolves them at the expense of the Palestinians. These plans fail for the same reasons as Camp David but to different degrees.[2]

Kathleen Christison, in a critique of liberal pro-Israeli but anti-Sharon Jewish activists in the United States, offers one explanation for why interest in these so-called peace plans persists. Describing her encounters with 'Valerie', one such activist, Christison writes:

Like the conviction that Palestinians are out to destroy Israel, peace plans are another refuge, an escape, for Valerie and people like her. Peace initiatives provide a comfortable space from which they can promote an amorphous concept of 'peace,' declaring their dedication to 'balance' and giving all-out support by writing letters to politicians and newspapers, without having to face the grim realities of why peace plans are necessary in the first place, or why they always fail.

Promoting 'peace' allows them to escape the details of the actual realities on the ground. Valerie is an enthusiast for the People's Voice plan drawn up by Israeli Ami Ayalon and Palestinian Sari Nusseibeh, as she is for the Geneva Accord, but her enthusiasm allows her to escape the details that the authors of those plans know all too well and openly recognize.[3]

All this noise helps us avoid a rather different and more plausible conclusion: no agreement was reached at Camp David or at the talks afterwards, because there is no solution based on partition that can satisfy the minimal demands of both Israelis and Palestinians. It may be possible that a partition which satisfies a bare majority of Israelis will be opposed by a huge majority of Palestinians and vice versa. Every proposed solution has begun with a position where Palestinian refugees are marginalized, yet their plight and future lie at the heart of the conflict. Their removal from Palestine was the fundamental condition for establishing Israel.

Considering this situation means that we must talk about the thing we do not want to talk about. It means that everyone must move their mental baggage, which at the moment seems much too heavy. How difficult that is was brought home to me in an interview I did with the Israeli peace activist and campaigner Peretz Kidron on 8 July 2004 for Beirut's *Daily Star* newspaper:

ABUNIMAH: At some point it no longer makes sense to talk about partition because partition means drawing lines that are just so inhuman because they divide people or they are just too ridiculous, or they involve moving people in inhumane ways. And I even include the settlers in that. Once you start talking about moving forty or fifty thousand people from a single settlement then it's also inhuman, especially if they've been there for generations and the children and teenagers didn't ask to be born there.

KIDRON: All of this is enormously difficult and gets harder with every month and every year. There's only one thing more difficult in my view, and that is a one-state solution. I don't think that would work. I think that's a sure-fire recipe for disaster. . . . Because we're divided. We have two ethnic groups, two nations divided by years of conflict.

ABUNIMAH: But don't Palestinians live as Israeli citizens now in Haifa, in Jaffa?

KIDRON: But it's a very difficult coexistence.

ABUNIMAH: But it's a better coexistence than that between Israelis and Palestinians in the West Bank.

KIDRON: Well I don't think that it would create a better situation. On the contrary, I think it would create a Bosnia situation in which the slightest incident—look what happened in Kosovo a couple of months ago—a couple of kids were fighting, and there was a riot, and dozens of people were killed.

ABUNIMAH: So why doesn't that happen in Haifa now?

KIDRON: It doesn't happen in Haifa because for many years there hasn't been conflict between Jews and Arabs in Haifa. But between Jews and Arabs in the Occupied Territories there has been, there is, an ongoing conflict.

ABUNIMAH: You say that the cause of that is the occupation, so if you remove the conditions of occupation so that everyone in this area is now equal or is a citizen of the same polity, then the proximate cause of the violence is gone.

KIDRON: Then you have a new cause. You have mutual suspicion, mutual mistrust, mutual fear, where the slightest spark can ignite terrible violence.

ABUNIMAH: That's terribly pessimistic. . . . You've got in Israel now over one million citizens who are Palestinians. And among those one million—they're not distinct from the Palestinians in the

West Bank or Gaza. They're different by accident. . . . We're talking about the same people and the same conditions.

KIDRON: But we're not talking about the same numbers.

ABUNIMAH: But you've got a million plus Palestinians who live inside Israel in peace, despite the fact that they are second-class citizens, despite the fact that they have also had their land taken away from them. But they still live in peace. So you are offering a vision in which conflict is inherent and inevitable but which is actually belied by the experience of Israel.

KIDRON: It's not something in the genes—in the Jewish genes or the Arab genes. What I'm saying is that it is inherent in the political situation, precisely where there is a demographic balance between the ethnic groups then the suspicion and the fear might break down.

ABUNIMAH: But isn't that simply saying that one way or another you need to keep some kind of Jewish supremacy in order to maintain the peace?

KIDRON: I wouldn't use the term Jewish supremacy. I'd say a majority.

Kidron's view is absolutely typical of the consensus on the Israeli left against any kind of one-state or binational solution even though this consensus offers no viable alternatives based on separation, their explicit desire. What is interesting about Kidron's perspective is that he seems to be looking everywhere for evidence to counter the one thing all these liberal and leftist peace activists say they want: coexistence. He also proposes that the choice before us is between a necessarily disastrous multi-ethnic solution and one based on nation-states. Like many Israelis, he hankers after a 'normal' Israel that resembles perhaps a northern European social democracy, as if such countries, who cope with influxes of immigrants, are not also in crises about their identity and their definition of citizenship.

The reality, however, is that Israel and the territories it occupies already form a multi-ethnic state. Of course there are Israeli Jews and Palestinians, but among Israeli Jews there are many different and sometimes antagonistic groups: Ethiopians, the ruling elite European Jews, Jewish Arabs, Russian Jews, and Christians. Since Israel began preventing Palestinians from leaving their towns and villages in the early 1990s, hundreds of thousands of Thai, Romanian, Chinese, and other migrant workers have settled in the country.

The question then is not 'who shall live here?' but 'who shall have power?' In order to avoid sharing power, even the progressive peace activist is prepared to contemplate a massive reordering of the physical and human landscape, which would involve at the very least moving tens of thousands of Israeli settlers, and leaving millions of Palestinians in exile. Morally this is little different from what the creators of Israel did originally. It just aims to tinker with the results. Can this really be easier than a reordering of our mental landscapes such that all the human beings in Palestine/Israel become acceptable neighbours to each other, and so that the return of a Palestinian refugee is no more threatening than the arrival of a new Jewish immigrant?

Answering this question, and discussing it as widely as possible, while also continuing to organize against Israeli state oppression, is the intellectual and political work that we urgently need to do if we are ever to find a way out of the impasse.

Endnotes

r *Thomas More*: Passages attributed to Shakespeare', in The
prton Shakespeare, ed. Stephen Greenblatt, Walter Cohen, Jean
. Howard, and Katharine Eisaman Maus (New York and
,ondon: W. W. Norton, 1997), 2011–19, lines 1–24, 79–94, 130–
;2. The whole play was recently performed at The Swan theatre,
Stratford-upon-Avon, by the Royal Shakespeare Company. It is
one of a number of recent theatrical and filmic explorations of
issues relating to asylum and migration. Other notable examples
include Ariane Mnouchkine's play, *Le Dernier Caravanserail
(Odyssées)*, and Nicolas Clotz's film, *La Blessure* (2004).

Notes to Introduction

1. The *Sun*, 4 July 2003.
2. The Home Office report of the inspection of Campsfield
    House, carried out in 2002, reports that most detainees did
    not know why they were being detained (sect. 4.2, p. 15). For
    the report, see http://www.homeoffice.gov.uk/docs/
    campsfieldhouse.pdf, accessed 16 Sept. 2005.
3. For the full text, see http://www.unhchr.ch/html/menu3/b/
    o_c_ref.htm, accessed 16 Sept. 2005.
4. *Divided Cities: The Oxford Amnesty Lectures 2003*, edited by
    Richard Scholar (Oxford: Oxford University Press, 2005).
5. See e.g. Jacques Derrida, *Cosmopolites de tous les pays, encore un
    effort!* (Paris: Éditions Galilée, 1997), translated by Mark Dooley
    in *On Cosmopolitanism and Forgiveness* (London and New York:
    Routledge, 2001), 3–24.

Notes to Chapter 1

1. See my 'A Short Hundred Years of Long Weeks', *Times Higher Education Supplement*, 30 July 2004.

2. For good discussions of human rights, see David Beetham, ed. *Politics and Human Rights* (Oxford: Blackwell, 1995); L. J. Macfarlane, *The Theory and Practice of Human Rights* (London: Maurice Temple Smith, 1985); Stephen Shute and Susan Hurley, eds. *On Human Rights* (New York: Basic Books, 1993); Tim Dunne and Nicholas J. Wheeler, eds., *Human Rights in Global Politics* (Cambridge: Cambridge University Press, 1999); Jack Donnelly, *Universal Human Rights in Theory and Practice* (Ithaca: Cornwell University Press, 1989); and C. S. Nino, *The Ethics of Human Rights* (Oxford: Clarendon Press, 1991).

3. Although these two concepts belong to different philosophical traditions and differ in important respects, I use them interchangeably in this chapter. For a fuller discussion, see my *Rethinking Multiculturalism* (London: Palgrave, 2000), 126 ff.

4. If we did not value human capacities or think that human beings have an intrinsic worth, these capacities would not be the basis of rights. Every theory of human rights is grounded in a wider normative conception of human beings.

5. Alisdair MacIntyre, *After Virtue: A Study in Moral Theory* (London: Duckworth, 1990), 69.

6. Although modernity developed the concept of rights including human rights, the idea of what is due to human beings and which may not be denied to them is much older. In premodern times it took rationalist, religious, and other forms in the writings of the Stoics, the Christian theologians, and others. Its current secular individualist articulation is peculiar to modernity.

7. The condition of mentally disabled and subnormal people does not affect the validity of this argument. See my *Rethinking Multiculturalism*, 130 f.

8. For an excellent discussion and a critique of the recurrent

tendency to give a homogeneous and one-dimensional account of morality, see Charles Taylor, *Philosophy and the Human Sciences: Philosophical Papers* (Cambridge: Cambridge University Press, 1985), ii. ch. 9.

9. The Chinese do not much like the abstract and universalist vocabulary of human rights. They prefer to talk of 'due rights' (*yingyou quangli*) that is, those rights that members of a society ought to have in order to be whole persons or lead worthwhile lives as defined by its highest values. These are not universal but nationally specific human rights.

10. A. J. M. Milne criticizes the United Nations Declaration as a mixed bag, and substitutes his own austere list of six basic human rights. These strangely include the right to be dealt with honestly and to have one's distress relieved. See his 'The Idea of Human Rights: A Critical Inquiry', in F. E. Dowrick, ed., *Human Rights: Problems, Perspectives and Texts* (London: Saxon House, 1979), 33. There are good and bad reasons for multiplying the number of rights. Good reasons include responses to new historical experiences, claims of marginalized groups, new insights into the conditions of human development, the desire to be specific, etc. Bad reasons include political expediency, careless use of the term 'human rights', overinvestment in a regime of rights, etc.

11. John Rawls, 'The Law of Peoples', in Shute and Hurley, *On Human Rights*, 227 f.

12. These are not exaggerations. Individuals and groups giving evidence to the Select Committee on Human Rights of the British Parliament freely talk in these terms, as is evident in the Committee's various reports. This is also the standard language of pressure groups for children, the disabled, consumers, etc. Milan Kundera puts the point well. Human rights have become 'a kind of universal stance of everyone towards everything, a kind of energy that turns all human desires into right [. . .]; the desire for love a right to love, the desire for rest a right to rest,

the desire for friendship a right to friendship' (*Immortality* (London: Faber, 1991), 153).

13. In a vastly unequal world in which a quarter of the world's population lives in desperate conditions, Kant's argument implies that if the rich West really valued human rights, it should remove all restrictions on international movement of people. Kant did not have this in mind, but provides no coherent argument against it.

14. Much of the widespread criticism of the current Labour government's public sector reform in Britain has centred on these and related considerations, and even some members of the government now concede its validity.

15. The idea of human rights is an integral part of the liberal tradition, and has been viewed with suspicion by the socialists, especially those inspired by Marx. For the latter, it is individualist in its orientation, legitimizes the capitalist social relations because of the pride of place it gives to the right to property, and frustrates the egalitarian redistribution of resources.

16. Siân Miles, ed., *Simone Weil: An Anthology* (New York: Weidenfeld & Nicolson, 1986), 63.

Notes to Response to Chapter 1

1. I have consulted various German and English translations of Kant's work: 'Zum Ewigen Frieden. Ein philosophischer Entwurf [1795]', in *Immanuel Kants Werke*, ed. A. Buchenau, E. Cassirer, and B. Kellermann (Berlin: Bruno Cassirer, 1923); 'Perpetual Peace', in *On History*, trans. and ed. Lewis White Beck (Indianapolis and New York: Library of Liberal Arts, 1957); 'Perpetual Peace: A Philosophical Sketch', in *Kant: Political Writings*, trans. H. B. Nisbet, ed. Hans Reiss (Cambridge: Cambridge Texts in the History of Political Thought, 2nd and enlarged edn., 1994).

2. Kant, *Werke*, 434–46; Kant, *On History*, 99–108.

3. Kant, *Werke*, 443; Kant, *On History*, 320.
4. See http://www.unhchr.ch/udhr/lang/eng.htm, accessed 16 Sept. 2005.
5. Kant, *Werke*, 443.
6. See John Locke [1690], *Second Treatise of Civil Government*, ed. and with an introduction by C. B. McPherson (Indianapolis and Cambridge, Mass.: Hackett Publishing, 1980), 19.
7. Kant, *On History*, 107. See also Sankar Muthu, 'Enlightenment and Anti-Imperialism', *Social Research*, 66:4 (Winter 1999): 959–1007; 'Justice and Foreigners: Kant's Cosmopolitan Right', *Constellations*, 7:1 (March 2000); and *Enlightenment and Empire* (Princeton: Princeton University Press, NJ, 2003).
8. See Seyla Benhabib, *The Rights of Others: Aliens, Residents and Citizens (The John Seeley Memorial Lectures)* (Cambridge: Cambridge University Press, 2004), ch. 4.

Notes to Chapter 2

1. Steven Erlanger, 'In One Kosovo Woman, An Emblem of Suffering', *New York Times*, 12 May 1999, A13.

Notes to Chapter 3

I am indebted to Thomas Uthup and Muhammad Yusuf Tamim for research and bibliographical assistance.

1. On these tumultuous times, see Efraim Karsh and Inari Karsh, *Empires of the Sand: The Struggle for Mastery In the Middle East, 1789–1923* (Cambridge, Mass.: Harvard University Press, 1999), and also consult William Hare, *Struggle for the Holy Land: Arabs, Jews, and the Emergence of Israel* (Lanham, Md.: Madison Books, 1995).
2. For a succinct discussion of the events leading to the Balfour Declaration, see Walter Laqueur, *A History of Zionism* (New

York: MJF Books, 1997), 181–205; and for a longer treatment, see Leonard Stein, *The Balfour Declaration* (Jerusalem: Magnes Press, The Hebrew University, 1983).

3. A short history of the crusades may be found in Thomas F. Madden, *A Concise History of the Crusades* (Lanham, Md.; Rowman & Littlefield, 1999).

4. Biographies of this dashing figure include Malcolm Brown, *T. E. Lawrence* (New York: New York University Press, 2003); Jeremy Wilson, *Lawrence of Arabia: The Authorized Biography of T. E. Lawrence* (New York: Atheneum, 1989, 1990) and J. B. Villars, *T. E. Lawrence*, trans. Peter Dawney (New York: Duell, Sloan & Pierce, 1959).

5. Indeed, Lawrence was aware of the empty nature of these promises; see Hare, *Struggle for the Holy Land*, 131–2.

6. The League of Nations Covenant, particularly Article 20, provided what was ultimately a false hope to the Arabs that they would achieve independence; see Hare, *ibid.* 273–4.

7. See David Garnett, ed., *Letters of T. E. Lawrence* (London and Toronto: J. Cape, 1938), 514.

8. Villars, *T. E. Lawrence*, 291.

9. Cited in Garnett, *Letters of T. E. Lawrence*, 262–3.

10. T. E. Lawrence, *Seven Pillars of Wisdom* (London: Privately printed 1926; New York: Doubleday, 1935), 23–4.

11. In fact, Lawrence even refused the knighthood; see Wilson, *Lawrence of Arabia*, 577–8, for an account.

12. On the name change, see Garnett, *Letters of T. E. Lawrence*, 535.

13. Consult Hare, *Struggle for the Holy Land*, 231.

14. For the impact of Ataturk on Turkey's modernization path, see e.g. Ali Kazancigil and Ergun Özbudun, eds., *Atatürk, Founder of a Modern State* (London: Hurst & Co., 1997).

15. Studies of German colonialism in Africa include Richard A. Voeltz, *German Colonialism and the South West Africa Company, 1884–1914* (Athens, Ohio: Ohio University, Center for International Studies, 1988); and Prosser Gifford and Wm. Roger

Louis, eds., *Britain and Germany in Africa: Imperial Rivalry and Colonial Rule* (New Haven, Conn.: Yale University Press, 1967).

16. Critical discussions of the American empire may be found in Chalmers Johnson, *Blowback: The Costs and Consequences of American Empire* (New York: Henry Holt, 2001, 1st Owl Books edn.) and Michael Parenti, *Against Empire* (San Francisco, Calif.: City Lights Books, 1995).

17. September 11th has apparently shaken American commitment to civil rights, although several critiques have emerged; see e.g. Nat Hentoff, *The War on the Bill of Rights, and the Coming Resistance* (New York: Seven Stories Press, 2003); David Cole, *Enemy Aliens: Immigrants' Rights and American Freedoms in the War on Terrorism* (New York: New Press, 2003); David Cole and James X. Dempsey, *Terrorism & the Constitution: Sacrificing Civil Liberties in the Name of National Security* (New York: New Press, 2002), 2nd rev. edn. 2002; and Wendy Kaminer, *Free For All: Defending Liberty in America Today* (Boston: Beacon Press, 2002).

18. All quotations from the Qur'an, unless otherwise mentioned, are from the translation by Ahmed Ali, *Al-Qur'an: A Contemporary Translation* (Princeton, NJ: Princeton University Press, 1988).

19. Ibid.

20. Consult Adil Salahi, *Muhammad: Man and Prophet* (Shaftesbury, UK, and Boston, Mass.: Element, 1998), 575.

21. Ibid. 196–207.

22. Mark Mathabene has recommended the African experience for the Middle East in an op-ed piece, 'The Cycle of Revenge Can be Broken', *New York Times* (5 July 2002), 21.

23. For further reading on the Biafra war, consult Zdenek Cervenka, *The Nigerian War, 1967–70: History of The War, Selected Bibliography and Documents* (Frankfurt am Main: Bernard & Graef, 1971).

24. For an overview of the transition from white rule to black rule in Zimbabwe, see Anthony Parsons, 'From Southern Rhodesia

to Zimbabwe, 1965–1985', *International Affairs*, 9:4 (November 1988), 353–61; also see Victor De Waal, *The Politics of Reconciliation: Zimbabwe's First Decade* (London: Hurst; Cape Town: David Philip, 1981).

25. Reported in the *New York Times* (23 March 1999), 6.

26. Jomo Kenyatta, *Suffering Without Bitterness* (Nairobi: East African Publishing House; Chicago: Northwestern University Press, 1968).

27. The Saudi reserves are under great stress due to the increasing demand worldwide for energy; a detailed report may be found in the *New York Times* (24 February 2004), 1 and c2.

28. The members of OPEC are Algeria, Iraq, Iran, Libya, Kuwait, Indonesia, Nigeria, Saudi Arabia, Venezuela, Qatar, and the UAE; see the website www.opec.org (accessed 16 Sept. 2005) for reserves and other data.

29. For an elaboration on the *ujamaa* concept, see Donatus Kumba, 'Contribution To Rural Development: Ujamaa And Villagization', in Colin Legum and Geoffrey Mmari, eds., *Mwalimu: the Influence of Nyerere* (London: Britain-Tanzania Society in association with James Currey; Dar es Salaam: Mkuki Na Nyota; Trenton, NJ: Africa World Press, 1995), 32–45.

30. The burgeoning literature on the concept of reparations to Africa and African Americans includes, among others, Raymond A. Winbush, ed., *Should America Pay?: Slavery and the Raging Debate on Reparations* (New York: Amistad, 2003); John Torpey, ed., *Politics and the Past: On Repairing Historical Injustices* (Lanham, Md.: Rowman & Littlefield, 2003); Richard F. America, 'Reparations and Public Policy', in Thomas D. Boston, ed., *Leading Issues in Black Political Economy* (New Brunswick, NJ: Transaction Publishers, 2002), 305–14, and Randall Robinson, *The Debt: What America Owes to Blacks* (New York: Dutton, 2000). For an economic rationale for the payment of reparations, see Robert S. Browne, The Economic Basis for Reparations to Black America', *Review of Black Political*

Economy 21 (Winter 1993), 99–110. Also consult Clarence J. Mumford, *Race and Reparations: A Black Perspective for the Twenty-First Century* (Trenton, NJ: Africa World Press, 1996), and Ali A. Mazrui, 'Global Africa: From Abolitionists to Reparationists', *African Studies Review* 37:3 (December 1994), 1–18.

31. On the German reparations to Israel, see Nicholas Balabkins, *West German Reparations to Israel* (New Brunswick, NJ: Rutgers University Press, 1971).

32. Even some Western countries' leaders have called for this, as e.g. Hedemarie Wieczorek-Zeul, the German Minister for Economic Cooperation and Development who called for a permanent seat for Africa on the Security Council; see *Amsterdam News* (17 May 2001). For an overview of suggested measures for restructuring of the membership of the Security Council, see Bruce Russett, ed., *The Once and Future Security Council* (New York: St Martin's Press, 1997), 170–1 and also Karen A. Mingst and Margaret P. Karns, *The United Nations in the Post-Cold War Era* (Boulder, Colo.: Westview Press, 2000), 204.

33. For a discussion of racism in American Christianity, see e.g. Lewis T. Tait, Jr. and A. Christian van Gorder, *Three-Fifths Theology: Challenging Racism in American Christianity* (Trenton, NJ: Africa World Press, 2002).

34. An accessible and readable biography of this remarkable man may be found in H. A. L. Craig, *Bilal* (London and New York: Quartet Books, 1977).

35. Sura 49: 13, in Ali, *Al-Qur'an*.

36. These lines are taken from the last sermon of the Prophet Muhammad; for one rendering of the complete text, see http://www.-islamicity.com/mosque/Lastserm.htm, accessed 16 Sept. 2005.

37. For instance, women in Iraq were well-educated and capable of being leaders in the move towards a new regime, although the US-sponsored Coalition Provisional Authority and the Iraqi Governing Council have not made full use of this resource; see the op-ed piece by two members of the Iraqi Governing

Council, Raja Habib Khuzai and Songul Chapouk, 'Iraq's Hidden Treasure', *New York Times* (3 December 2003), 31.

38. On Ayesha's role and the precedents it offered Muslim women, see Denise A. Spellberg, 'Political Action and Public Example: Aisha and the Battle of the Camel', in Nikkie Keddie and Beth Baron, eds., *Women in Middle Eastern History: Shifting Boundaries in Sex and Gender* (New Haven, Conn.: Yale University Press, 1999), 45–57.

39. See Lisa C. Ikemoto, 'Lessons From the Titanic', in Julia E. Hanigsberg and Sara Ruddick, eds., *Mother Troubles: Rethinking Contemporary Maternal Dilemmas* (Boston: Beacon Press, 1999), 157.

40. The recent Palestinian female suicide bombers have acted voluntarily; for a detailed analysis of the suicide bombers' psychology, see Suzanne Goldberg, 'Special report: A mission to murder: inside the minds of the suicide bombers', *Guardian* (London) (11 June 2002), 4.

41. Consult Fadwa El Guindi, *Veil: Modesty, Privacy and Resistance* (Oxford and New York: Berg, 1999), 85.

42. Relatedly, see Ruth Barnes and Joanne B. Eicher, eds., *Dress and Gender: Making and Meaning in Cultural Contexts* (New York: Berg and St Martin's Press, 1992).

43. Consult Anthony L. Smith, 'Reluctant Partner: Indonesia', *Asian Affairs: An American Review* 30:2 (Summer 2003), 142–50.

44. In the process, of course, more Africans are apt to die than Middle Easterners or Westerners. As *The Economist* has noted: 'When terrorists murder Westerners in Africa, a much larger number of Africans usually die, too.' See 'Now for Africa', *Economist* (5 July 2003), 9.

45. Even in Iraq, for all of Saddam Hussein's abuses, his regime was relatively progressive on legislation relating to women. Women were not allowed to marry prior to the age of 18, and there was no favouritism towards men in inheritance, divorce, and child custody. See *Washington Post* (3 February 2004), 2.

46. Readers interested in this topic may consult e.g. Richard C. Foltz, Frederick M. Denny, and Azizan Baharuddin, eds., *Islam and Ecology: A Bestowed Trust* (Cambridge, Mass.: Center for the Study of World Religions, Harvard Divinity School, distributed by Harvard University Press, 2003); and for an earlier work, see Fazlun M. Khalid with Joanne O'Brien, eds., *Islam and Ecology* (New York, NY: Cassell, 1992).

47. Consult, relatedly, Michael Darkoh and Apollo Rwomire, eds., *Human Impact on Environment and Sustainable Development in Africa* (Aldershot, UK, and Burlington, Vt.: Ashgate, 2003) and also Valentine U. James, ed., *Environmental and Economic Dilemmas of Developing Countries: Africa in the Twenty-First Century* (Westport, Conn.: Praeger, 1994).

48. For one detailed analysis of the water issue in the Middle East, see Tony Allan, *The Middle East Water Question: Hydropolitics and the Global Economy* (London and New York: I. B. Tauris, 2002).

49. However, as population grows in the Middle East, demand for, and management of, water may be a pivotal factor in the stability and security of the region. Actual and potential conflicts over water in the Middle East are not just between the traditional antagonists—Israelis and Palestinians—but other states such as Iraq, Syria, Egypt, and so on; on these security threats, see Naji Abi-Aad and Michel Grenon, *Instability and Conflict in the Middle East: People, Petroleum, and Security Threats* (Houndmills: Macmillan; New York: St Martin's Press, 1997); and specifically, on the inequity in access to water between the Israelis and Palestinians, see the op-ed piece by Mark Zeitoun, 'Avoiding a Mideast Water War', *Washington Post* (4 February 2004), 23.

50. The economic impact of the petroleum bounty was not always positive; for a detailed country assessment, see Jahangir Amuzegar, *Managing the Oil Wealth: OPEC's Windfalls and Pitfalls* (London and New York: I. B. Tauris, 2001), 116–88.

51. Part of this is due to the sudden wealth changing many formerly ascetic people, as detailed by Saad E. Ibrahim, *The New*

Arab Social Order: A Study of the Social Impact of Oil Wealth (Boulder, Colo.: Westview; London: Croom Helm, 1982).

52. The Prophet Muhammad encouraged tree planting, conservation, and protection of flora and fauna; see S. H. Nasr, 'The Contemporary Islamic World, And The Environmental Crisis', in Foltz, Denny, and Baharuddin, eds., *Islam and Ecology*, 97–8.

53. For a discussion of African totems, consult Theo Sundermeier, *The Individual and Community in African Traditional Religions* (Hamburg: Lit; Piscataway, NJ: Transaction, 1998), 114–19.

54. Details on this affair may be found in Abdul-Rasheed Na'Allah, ed., *Ogoni's Agonies: Ken Saro-Wiwa and the Crisis in Nigeria* (Trenton, NJ: Africa World Press, 1998).

55. The incident received wide coverage in the *New York Times*; see the reports on 11 November 1995.

56. For an overview of the nexus between population, the environment, and economic development, consult e.g. Kerstin Lindahl-Kiesling and Hans Landberg, *Population, Economic Development, and the Environment* (Oxford and New York: Oxford University Press, 1994).

57. Alexander Pope, 'An Essay on Man' (1733–4) in *The Poems of Alexander Pope*, iii. no. 1 (London: Methuen; New Haven: Yale University Press, 1950), 51.

58. See World Bank, *World Development Indicators 2003* (Washington, DC: World Bank, 2003), 40.

59. Ibid. 114.

60. Consult Royal J. Schmidt, *Versailles and the Ruhr: Seedbed of World War I* (The Hague: Martinus Nijhoff, 1968).

61. These issues are explored in Ahron Bregman, *A History Of Israel* (Houndmills, New York: Palgrave Macmillan, 2003), 5–6, and Marvin Lowenthal, trans. and ed., *The Diaries of Theodor Herzl* (New York: Dial Press, 1956), 383; and for details on the Ugandan offer, see Michael Heymann, ed., *The Minutes of the Zionist General Council; the Uganda Controversy* (Jerusalem: Institute for Zionist Research by Israel Universities Press, 1970).

62. Of course, there were individual European leaders who took some actions and expressed sentiments that the Israeli government objected to; but the prevailing mood was one of mutual acceptance, and perhaps even forbearance. For one account of the complexities of Israel–Europe relations, consult Howard M. Sachar, *Israel and Europe: An Appraisal in History* (New York: Alfred Knopf, 1999).

63. In 2002, a petition was circulated in Europe urging a boycott of Israeli scientists by European institutions; see *Nature*, 417: 6884 (2 May 2002), 1.

64. Ian Buruma, 'How to Talk About Israel', *New York Times Sunday Magazine* (31 August 2003), 28.

65. The complex set of issues leading to conflict and competition among Christians, Jews, and Muslims is detailed in F. E. Peters, *The Monotheists: Jews, Christians, and Muslims in Conflict and Cooperation* (Princeton, NJ: Princeton University Press, 2003); and more specifically on Christians and Jews, see Marvin Perry and Frederick M. Schweitzer, eds., *Jewish–Christian Encounters Over the Centuries: Symbiosis, Prejudice, Holocaust, Dialogue* (New York: P. Lang, 1994).

66. This quotation is from a slightly different edition of T. E. Lawrence, *Seven Pillars of Wisdom* (first published 1926) (Garden City, NY: Doubleday, Doran & Co., 1935), 333.

67. Relatedly, consult e.g. Bernard Wasserstein, *Divided Jerusalem: The Struggle for the Holy City* (New Haven, Conn.: Yale University Press, 2001).

68. Although Americans are not always willing to admit that the United States is an imperial power; see Dimitri K. Simes, 'America's Imperial Dilemma', *Foreign Affairs* 82:6 (November–December 2003), 93.

69. See Kevin Baker, 'We're All in the Army Now: The G. O. P.'s Plan to Militarize Our Culture', *Harper's Magazine* 307:1841 (October 2003), 43.

70. Software is perhaps the most intensive area where Indian brains

are pressed into service for US companies. The outsourcing issue has attracted a lot of attention; see e.g. *Business Week* (11 March 2004), 84–95. It was also one of the major subjects in Secretary of State Colin Powell's March 2004 South Asia visit; indeed, a student questioner in India suggested that the US should outsource the counting of US presidential election results; see *Washington Post* (17 March 2004), 16.

71. Nigeria was one of the prominent examples of the 'Indirect Rule' policy; in this regard, see Olufemi Vaughan, *Nigerian Chiefs: Traditional Power in Modern Politics, 1890s–1990s* (Rochester, NY: University of Rochester Press, 2000), 22–43.

72. Events in Haiti in March 2004 also raise the possibility that President Aristide was forced from power as part of US-sponsored 'regime change' in the Caribbean; see 'the Truth About Haiti,' *New Statesman* 133: 4678 (8 March 2004), 6–8.

73. Although reformers in the kingdom of Saudi Arabia have been emboldened to press for political reforms, some of the bolder ones were jailed, days before Secretary of State Colin Powell's arrival in Riyadh. See *Washington Post* (17 March 2004), 17, and *New York Times*, Week in Review Section (21 March 2004), 3.

74. In this regard, see the interesting comments of Sheik Mohammed Hussein Fadlallah (former spiritual leader of Hezbollah and one of the first Muslim clerics to condemn the 9/11 bombing) on the challenges to democratic reform in the Arab world; these comments are reported in the op-ed column by David Ignatius, 'Real Arab Reform', *Washington Post* (12 March 2004), 23.

75. For instance, the Reverend Jerry Falwell called the Prophet Muhammad a 'terrorist' in an interview on the CBS News '60 Minutes' programme in October 2002; see the report in *New York Times* (4 October 2002), 17.

76. See Todd M. Endelmann, 'Benjamin Disraeli and the Myth of Sephardic Superiority', in Todd M. Endelman and Tony Kushner, eds., *Disraeli's Jewishness* (London and Portland, Oreg.:

Vallentine Mitchell, 2002), 34, and Bernard Glassman, *Benjamin Disraeli: The Fabricated Jew in Myth and Memory* (Lanham, Md.: University Press of America), 35–6.

77. Sura *Iqra* or *Alaq*/Sura 96: 1–8, Ali, *Al-Qur'an*, 543.

78. These issues are discussed more fully in Ali A. Mazrui and Alamin M. Mazrui, 'Islam and Civilization', in Majid Tehranian and David W. Chapell, eds., *Dialogue of Civilizations: A New Peace Agenda* (New York: L. B. Tauris 2002), 139–60.

79. For a comprehensive history of the Ottoman Empire, consult Donald Quatert, *The Ottoman Empire, 1700–1922* (Cambridge: Cambridge University Press, 2000).

80. A copy of this report may be found at the web-site of the United Nations Development Programme (UNDP) at http://www.rbas.undp.org/ahdr2.cfm?menu=9, accessed 16 Sept.2005.

81. For the text of Mahathir's comments, see the excerpts in the *New York Times* (21 October 2003), 13, and for a look at the comments in the full context, visit the http://www.oicsummit 2003.com/oicsummit/ website (accessed 16 Sept. 2005). Interestingly, when Paul Krugman, a columnist for the *New York Times* linked Mahathir's comments to Bush administration policies, he was the target of an outcry from conservatives; see the piece by Eric Alterman, 'The New Know-Nothingism', *Nation* 277: 16 (17 October 2003), 10.

82. See Samuel Huntington, *The Clash of Civilizations and the Remaking of World Order* (New York: Simon & Schuster, 1996).

83. A bibliography of Diop's work may be found in Christopher Gray, *Conceptions of History in the Works of Cheik Anta Diop and Theophile Obenga* (London: Karnak House, 1989), 109–13. Some major works that may be consulted include Cheik Anta Diop, *Civilization or Barbarism: An Authentic Anthropology* (Brooklyn, NY: Lawrence Hill Books, 1991), and *Pre-colonial Black Africa: A Comparative Study of the Political and Social Systems of Europe and Black Africa, From Antiquity to the Formation of Modern States* (Westport, Conn.: L. Hill, 1987).

84. These lines are from his poem, 'Journal of a Homecoming' ('Cahier d'un retour au pays natal'), trans. Mireille Rosello with Annie Pritchard (Highgreen, Northumb.: Bloodaxe Books, 1995), 116–17. For commentary, see Gregson Davis, *Aimé Césaire* (Cambridge: Cambridge University Press, 1997), 20–61.

85. J. P. Sartre, 'Introduction to African Poetry', in *Black Orpheus*, trans. S. W. Allen (Paris: Presence Africaine, 1963), 41–3.

86. For a bibliography on 'negritude', consult Colette V. Michael, *Negritude: An Annotated Bibliography* (West Cornwall, Conn.: Locust Hill Press, 1988). An English-language version of Senghor's thoughts on negritude may be found in his *The Foundations of 'Africainité' or 'Négritude' and 'Arabité'* (Paris: Présence Africaine, 1971). See also Ali A. Mazrui and JF Ade Ajayi et al., 'Trends in Philosophy and Science in Africa', *Africa Since 1935* in Ali A. Mazrui and C. Wondjii, eds., *UNESCO General History of Africa* (London: Heinemann Educational Books, 1993), viii. 633–77.

87. This African song of reaffirmation is paraphrased from programme 9 of Ali A. Mazrui's television series, *The Africans: A Triple Heritage* (BBC/PBS and Nigeria's Television Authority, 1986).

Notes to Response to Chapter 3

1. Mainstream political parties and opinion groups seem to expect equitable treatment and equal opportunities for asylum-seekers and immigrants but show no sign of actively supporting them.

2. The British National Party and other racist outfits, assisted by the tabloids and often with the tacit approval of the mainstream parties, have been encouraging Hindus, Sikhs, and Buddhists in Britain to believe that their animus is directed exclusively against Muslims. By problematizing Islam as a multi-dimensional threat, they aim to diminish cross-ethnic solidarity.

3. Niall Ferguson, the British historian now teaching at New York

University, has attempted to popularize British imperial history and clearly feels a profound nostalgia for it. His popular television series, *Empire*, argued that American ideologues should learn from the British experience. Ferguson's recent book *Colossus* remains sympathetic to the British Empire while showing some unease with US foreign relations. It also shows insufficient knowledge of recent American foreign policy issues, notably the Vietnam War. Ferguson tends to ignore the fact that societies resistant to Pax Americana also possess information technology and that this, combined with greater politicization, could offer formidable resistance to American unilateralism. It is childish to predict a repetition of history while ignoring the enormity of subsequent change, in particular the greater politicization of post-colonial societies. (See Niall Ferguson, *Colossus: The Rise and Fall of the American Empire*, New York, 2004. For an interesting review of this book by Leonard Garden, see *Times Higher Education Supplement*, 30 July 2004.) Fareed Zakaria, the well-known Indian-American journalist, is concerned that anti-Americanism would become rife if democracy were permitted in West Asia and thus advises that the US should work through 'liberal' or 'moderate' Muslim leadership, a category not exclusive of authoritarian governments. This trade-off between democracy and the liberalization of Muslim society is self-contradictory. It treats the Muslim world as a unitary populace with nothing better to do than hate the West. His prescriptive (essentially Neo-Orientalist) ideas are popular with those American legislators and policy-makers who prefer a 'go slow' policy to Neo-Con radicalism. (See Fareed Zakaria, *The Future of Freedom*, London, 2003.) Michael Ignatieff's preoccupation with reordering the post-Cold War world revolves around American intentions and pretensions. His patronizing panacea of 'benevolent' imperialism combined with a gradual push towards democratization recalls the views of his colonialist forefathers. (See Michael Ignatieff, *Empire Lite: Nation-building in Bosnia, Kosovo and Afghanistan* (London, 2003).) Tom Friedman similarly vacillates between the extremes of direct control and cooption of a local elite including Muslim religious leaders. (See Friedman: *Longitudes and Attitudes: Exploring the World Before and After September 11* (London, 2003).) Fukuyama has often worked closely with the Neo-Cons. His idealization of the North Atlantic political economy allowed him to see in it the end of all previous political polarities. However, he has since gained a more realistic view of world politics and drifted into other disciplines. To Arundhati Roy, Gore Vidal, Norman Mailer, and Noam Chomsky the US-led imperial project is already well established though they take it as largely subservient to specific interests.

4. Oliver Miles, 'Lewis Gun', a review of Bernard Lewis: *From Babel to Dragomans, Guardian*, 17 July 2004.

5. Some authors and diplomats have been warning that close collaboration with Israel combined with disregard for Muslim views and interests can only add to the current chaos. See Stefan Halper and Jonathan Clarke, *America Alone: The Neo-Conservatives and Global Order* (Cambridge: Cambridge University Press, 2004), 3–11. Diplomats from the US, UK, and Australia point out that these policies have already alienated the majority of the world's Muslim population.

6. These categories are avoided by serious scholars. The media—including the BBC—use them without hesitation. Thus 'Will' Cummins, in a series of Islamophobic articles in the *Sunday Telegraph*, rebuked the Anglican Church and the UK government for their accommodating attitude toward Muslims. Islam had, said Cummins, a 'black heart' and a 'black face' while 'all Muslims, like all dogs, share some common characteristics' and needed to be contained before they could 'get us'. He described Muslims as inherently anti-Christian and announced that the Muslim agenda in Europe went well beyond economic welfare: Muslims were aiming at the creation of an Islamicized

West and Islamo-Fascist newspapers like the *Guardian* were facilitating it. The author of these alarmist views was exposed by the *Guardian*: he is Harry Cummins, senior Press Officer at the British Council. He was subsequently suspended with full salary. See Will Cummins's serialized pieces in the *Sunday Telegraph*, 4, 11, 18, and 25 July 2004; see also the *Guardian*, 3 August 2004. Ian Buruma, a former *Guardian* columnist, sought evidence in the Islamophobic Bernard Lewis to buttress his own case against Muslims. See Ian Buruma, 'Driven by history and hate: Islam's holy warriors', *The Times*, 3 August 2004. The tabloids and certain broadsheets seem to be vying with one another in their Islamophobic articles.

7. 'The claims of western values are mocked by Iraq and the rise of Asia'. Martin Jacques, 'Our moral Waterloo', *Guardian*, 15 May 2004.

8. This 'Orientalization' of Islam is not merely an intellectual construct; it has a wider agenda. It is the feminization and infantilization of the Muslim peoples, rendering them 'pliant, sensuous, passive, awaiting penetration by the rational masculine west'. This facilitates the justification of military campaigns and other hostile policies. See Jonathan Raban, 'Emasculating Arabia', ibid., 13 May 2004.

9. As recent studies have shown, Israeli intelligence agencies orchestrated a smear campaign against Yasser Arafat even before the Barak-Arafat parleys at Camp David in 2000. President Clinton blamed Arafat for lacking statesmanlike qualities, but several new works have revealed a pervasive animus against the Palestinian leadership in the Clinton Administration. For Clinton's views, see Bill Clinton, *My Life* (London: Knopf, 2004), 943–5. The role of the Israeli intelligence agencies (led by Amos Gilad) in drumming up hatred against Arafat has been confirmed by Amos Malka and Robert Malley and is fully documented. See David Hirst, 'Don't blame Arafat', *Guardian*, 17 July 2004. Israeli agencies and lobbies in America played a

vital role in urging the Bush Administration to mount the invasion of Iraq. For details, see James Bamford, *A Pretext for War. 9/11, Iraq and the Abuse of American Intelligence Agencies* (New York: Doubleday, 2004). Seymour Hersch published a long piece outlining Israeli infiltration in Iraq and Iran to incite and train Kurds against Iraqi Arabs, Iran, and Syria. Some Israeli agents were even involved in interrogating Iraqi prisoners in the notorious Abu Ghraib Jail. See Seymour Hersch, 'Plan B', *New Yorker*, 28 June 2004.

10. Muslim communities do not have access to powerful policy-making institutions in the North Atlantic and Australasian regions, and Muslim voices are rarely heard in the media and the corridors of power. This leads to stereotyping of Muslims, combined with ignorance, arrogance, or indifference—and hostile policies on Muslim issues. The murder of Muslims by Western regimes or by the Israeli, Russian, and Indian governments consequently fails to evoke much sympathy; the victims are subtly portrayed as perpetrators.

11. Even the Congressional Commission that purported to investigate 9/11 did not take into account the larger political issues across the Muslim world where US policies have justifiably been seen as anti-Islam. It would have been helpful if the commission, led by Thomas Kean, had gone into the causes of Muslim alienation from US policies. See the National Commission on Terrorist Attacks upon the United States (chaired by Thomas H. Kean), *The 9/11 Commission Report* (Washington, DC and London, 2004).

12. 'US guards "filmed beatings" at terror camp', *Observer*, 16 May 2004. The Red Cross and Amnesty International had highlighted these issues to London and Washington but a wall of secrecy prevailed until Seymour Hersch's pieces in *The New Yorker*, similar photographs in the *Washington Post*, a special programme on the CBS's '60 Minutes', and illustrated reports on the NBC and ABC carried the shocking pictures and details

about the brutalization of internees. The former detainees, in their interviews, also offered first-hand information on their routine maltreatment, in contravention of the Geneva Conventions of 1949. Following admissions by President Bush and regrets by Donald Rumsfeld, Sir Jeremy Greenstock also apologized for overlooking the reports from the Red Cross and Amnesty International on the serious violations of the Geneva Conventions. Jeremy Greenstock was the British envoy to the UN during the build-up to invasion of Iraq and was working with the Paul Bremer-led Provisional Coalition Authority (PCA) in Baghdad. The confession and apology by the former British diplomat were made in an interview with Jon Snow on Channel Four on 19 May 2004.

13. Ahdaf Soueif, 'This torture started at the very top', *Guardian*, 5 May 2004.

14. Haifa Zangana, 'I, too, was tortured in Abu Ghraib', ibid. 11 May 2004.

15. Baruch Kimmerling, *Politicide: Ariel Sharon's War Against Palestinians* (London: Verso, 2003); Greg Philos and Mike Barry, *Bad News from Israel* (London: Pluto, 2004). Rana Kabbani argued that the Muslims are 'the new Jews of the world' during the Bosnian crisis in 1992 in some of her writings and speeches. She had earlier characterized Bosnians as 'the new Palestinians of Europe'.

Notes to Chapter 4

I have benefited greatly from comments by Jeremy Goldman, David Turton, and Chimène Bateman.

1. Bertholt Brecht, 'Emigrant's Lament', trans. Edith Rosevanne and repr. in A. Motion, *Here to Eternity: An Anthology of Poetry* (London, Faber & Faber: 2002).

2. David A. Martin, ed., *The New Asylum Seekers: Refugee Law in the 1980s* (Dordrecht: Martinus Nijoff, 1988,), 9.

3. The British tabloid newspaper, *The Sun*, announced on its front page of 4 July 2003 that asylum-seekers were responsible for stealing the Queen's swans and barbecuing them for food. Despite the fact that no evidence was ever given to prove its truth, in an environment of general tabloid hostility to refugees, the story was widely repeated across London.

4. 'Australian treatment of asylum-seekers "deeply troubling" says WCC', World Council of Churches, August 2001, at www.vic.uca.org.au/media/releases/TampaRefugees_WCC_mediarelease.pdf, accessed 16 Sept. 2005.

5. Catherine Dauvergne, 'Human Rights are for the Tricky Cases, Too', *Globe and Mail*, December 3. 2003, at http://www.law.ubc.ca/news/faculty/2003/dec/03dec03.html, accessed 16 Sept. 2005.

6. Randall Hansen and Desmond King, 'Illiberalism and the New Politics of Asylum', *The Political Quarterly*, 71:4 (2000), 396–403.

7. Ian Buchanan, 'August 26, 2001: Two or Three Things Australians Don't Seem to Want to Know About "Asylum Seekers" ', *Australian Humanities Review*, May 2003, at http://www.lib.latrobe.edu.au/AHR/archive/Issue-May–2003/buchanan2.html, accessed 16 Sept. 2005.

8. Gil Loescher, *Beyond Charity: International Cooperation and the Global Refugee Crisis* (New York: Oxford University Press, 1993); Matthew J. Gibney, *The Ethics and Politics of Asylum: Liberal Democracy and the Response to Refugees* (Cambridge: Cambridge University Press, 2004).

9. Aristide R. Zolberg, Astri Suhrke, and Sergio Aguayo, *Escape from Violence: Conflict and the Refugee Crisis in the Developing World* (New York: Oxford University Press, 1989).

10. Stephen Castles and Mark A. Miller, *The Age of Migration*, 3rd edn. (Basingstoke: Palgrave, 2003).

11. Guy Martin, 'International Solidarity and Co-operation in Assistance to African Refugees: Burden Sharing or Burden

Shifting', *International Journal of Refugee Law*, special issue (1998), 250–73.

12. Gerry Van Kessel, 'Global Migration and Asylum', *Forced Migration Review* 10 (2001), 10–13.

13. Matthew J. Gibney and Randall Hansen, 'Deportation and the Liberal State', *UNHCR New Issues in Refugee Research Working Paper* 77, February 2003.

14. Aristide R. Zolberg, 'Introduction: Beyond the Crisis', in Aristide R. Zolberg and Peter Benda, eds., *Global Migrants, Global Refugees: Problems and Solutions*, (New York: Berghahn, 2001).

15. Gibney, *The Ethics and Politics of Asylum*.

16. BBC News, 'UK rejects UN asylum claims', 1 June 2002 at http://news.bbc.co.uk/1/hi/uk_politics/2020716.stm, accessed 16 Sept. 2005.

17. Matthew J. Gibney and Randall Hansen, 'Asylum Policy in the West: Past Trends, Future Prospects', in George J. Borjas and Jeff Crisp, eds., *Poverty, Immigration and Asylum* (London: Palgrave, 2005), 86.

18. I borrow freely in this section from Gibney and Hansen, 'Asylum Policy in the West', ibid. I would like to thank Randall Hansen for permission to do this.

19. Areti Sianni, 'Interception Practices in Europe and their Implications', *Refuge*, 21:4 (2003), 25–34, at 26.

20. Ibid.

21. Elspeth Guild, 'The Borders of the European Union: Visas and Carriers Sanctions', *Tiddskriftet Politik*, 3:7 (2004), 34–43, at 36.

22. Sianni, 'Interception Practices', 27.

23. T. D. Jones, 'A Human Rights Tragedy: The Cuban and Haitian Refugee Crises Revisited', *Georgetown Immigration Law Journal*, 9:3 (1995), 479–523.

24. 'Sea change: Australia's new approach to asylum-seekers', US Committee for Refugees 2002, http://www.refugees.org/downloads/Australia.pdf, accessed 16 Sept. 2005.

25. R. I. Perusse, *Haitian Democracy Restored: 1991–1995* (Lonham, Md.: University Press of America, 1995).

26. Jessica Howard, 'To Deter and To Deny: Australia and the Interdiction of Asylum Seekers', *Refuge*, 21:4 (December 2003), 35–50.

27. *The Guardian*, 23 May 2002.

28. If this analogy seems extreme, it is important to remember that the use of the military base at Guantanamo Bay as a holding place for aliens in US custody began when asylum-seekers from Haiti and Cuba were sent there in the early 1990s. Criticisms of the territory as a lawless zone where foreigners lack the kinds of protections they would have on US soil were aired long before fighters from Afghanistan arrived in January 2001. See, for example, Jones, 'A Human Rights Tragedy'.

29. House of Lords, 23 January 2002.

30. Wolfgang Bosswick, 'Development of Asylum Policy in Germany', *Journal of Refugee Studies* 13:1 (2000), 43–60, at 51.

31. *The Guardian*, 9 October 2004, 18.

32. 'U.S.: Don't Turn Away Haitian Refugees', *Human Rights Watch* at http://www.hrw.org/english/docs/2004/02/26/usdom7674.htm, accessed 16 Sept. 2005.

33. H. Grotius, *De Jure Belli Ac Pacis Libri Tres*, Book II, trans. F.W. Kelsey (Washington, Carnegie Institute, 1925); John Rawls, *A Theory of Justice* (Oxford: Oxford University Press, 1971); Michael Walzer, *Spheres of Justice* (New York: Basic Books, 1983); Gibney, *The Ethics and Politics*.

34. Immanuel Kant, 'Perpetual Peace: A Philosophical Sketch', in *Kant: Political Writings*, trans. H. B. Nisbet, ed. Hans Reiss (Cambridge: Cambridge Texts in the History of Political Thought, 1991), Grotius, *De Jure Belli*; E. de Vattel, *The Law of Nations or the Principles of Natural Law*, trans. C. G. Fenwick (Washington, Carnegie Institute, 1916), iii.

35. This seems, for example, to be the implication of Kant's statement in 1795 that foreigners in need of 'resort' are 'entitled to

present themselves *in* the society of others by virtue of their right to communal possession of the earth's surface' (Kant, 'Perpetual Peace', 105–6; my emphasis). Kant did not address the question of the morality of measures that prevent needy individuals from *accessing* 'the society of others', though such a right seems to follow from his statement.

36. In using the concept of 'uniqueness' I wish merely to capture the fact that the relationship must be one that differentiates the state concerned from other states (in its paradigmatic form, the refugee is our responsibility because he or she is at *our* border).

37. Walzer, *Spheres of Justice*.

38. I do not have the space here to consider the important question of whether different degrees (or modes) of moral connection might give rise to different degrees of responsibility to address a refugee's plight (for example, whether in some circumstances states might be obliged to allow a refugee access to asylum on its territory, but in other cases required only to ensure that a refugee is not returned to face persecution).

39. Joseph H. Carens, 'Refugees and the Limits of Obligation', *Public Affairs Quarterly*, 6:1 (1992), 31–44, at 39.

40. The Government spokesman in the House of Lords, Lord Falconer, explained that 'reducing abuse of the asylum system [. . .] is not just about legislation. We are [he said] making progress in moving border controls to the Continent, in extending the use of biometrics on visas and ports, and in agreements with other countries to return failed asylum-seekers' (House of Lords, 15 March 2004).

41. Liza Schuster, *The Use and Abuse of Political Asylum in Britain and Germany* (London: Frank Cass, 2003); 'News: Press Myths', Refugee Council (United Kingdom) July 2004, http://www.refugeecouncil.org.uk/news/myths/myth001.htm, accessed 16 Sept. 2005.

42. 'News: Press Myths'.

43. UNHCR, *The State of the World's Refugees* (Oxford: Oxford University Press, 2000), 325.

44. Clair Brolan, 'An Analysis of the Human Smuggling Trade and the Protocol Against the Smuggling of Migrants by Land, Air and Sea (2000) from a Refugee Protection Perspective', *International Journal of Refugee Law*, 14. 4 (2003), pp. 561–596; John Morrison and Beth Crosland, 'The Trafficking and Smuggling of Refugees: the End Game in European Asylum Policy?', *UNHCR Working Paper* 39 (April 2001). The 1951 Refugee Convention requires (art. 31) that states not 'impose penalties, on account of their illegal entry or presence, on refugees', as long as they come directly from a country where their life or freedom is threatened and present themselves to the authorities giving good cause for their illegal presence. Arguably, many recent practices implemented by government (including mandatory detention in Australia and the US) are in contravention of this article.

45. For a discussion of the idea of the 'double effect', see John Finnis, 'The Rights and Wrongs of Abortion', in R. W. Dworkin, *The Philosophy of Law* (Oxford: Oxford University Press, 1977), pp. 141–5.

46. 'Interdiction and Refugee Protection: Proceedings of an International Workshop', Canadian Council for Refugees, May 29, 2003 (Ottawa, Canada) A9.

47. Gregor Noll, Negotiating *Asylum: The EU Acquis, Extraterritorial Protection and the Common Market of Deflection* (The Hague: Martinus Nijoff, 2000), p. 181.

48. Dallal Stevens, *UK Asylum Law and Policy: Historical and Contemporary Perspectives* (London: Sweet and Maxwell, 2004), p. 92–3.

49. 'UNHCR Calls For Government Re-Think On Zimbabwe Visas', UNHCR Public Information at http://www.unhcr. org.uk/press/press_releases2003/pr20Jan03.htm, accessed 16 Sept. 2005.

50. This point is, I think, reinforced by the way the British government now publicly sets targets for the reduction of numbers of asylum-seekers. If the number of refugees needing protection is determined by world events (wars, human rights violations), how can any state know in advance the number of asylum-seekers it will need (or be required by law) to accept? See *The Guardian*, 10 February 2003.

51. Oliver Letwin, quoted in *The Guardian*, 27 December 2002.

52. Manfred Kanther, quoted in 'Germany's Lead on European Immigration', *Immigration Laws*, Number 15 (August 2004) at http://www.migrationint.com.au/news/kuwait/ aug_1994–15mn.asp, accessed 16 Sept. 2005.

53. I am, of course, assuming here that refugees constitute a 'burden' for the states that receive them. This assumption is not meant to deny the important economic, social, and cultural contributions that refugees can make to their host countries.

54. Stephen Castles and Sean Loughna, 'Trends in Asylum Migration to Industrialized Countries: 1990–2001', *UN University/Wider, Discussion Paper*, 2003/31.

55. Gibney, *The Ethics and Politics*.

56. In practice, however, Australia has complained bitterly about what it considers 'secondary movers' and used them as part of its justification for restrictive asylum measures. See 'Australian Refugee Policy is "nor for Export" ', *Human Rights Watch*, 26 September 2002 at http://www.hrw.org/press/2002/09/australia0926.htm, accessed 16 Sept. 2005.

57. Guy, 'International Solidarity'.

58. One reason might be that they force those seeking asylum into using more dangerous routes to bypass control measures to enter the West.

59. I elaborate on this issue in my *The Ethics and Politics of Asylum*, 243–9. There I argue that the principle of humanitarianism requires Western states to work towards creating domestic and international environments where the amount

of protection available to refugees at 'low cost' will be maximized.

60. It is undeniable that offshore processing raises difficult legal and ethical problems: are the countries proposed really safe and secure sites for asylum-seekers? What will happen to those who make unsuccessful asylum claims? Under what conditions will those applying for asylum be kept? But the benefits of allowing many refugees to seek asylum in the West without having to travel intercontinentally provide strong reasons to look for ways around these difficulties, if at all possible. For a discussion of some of these questions, see Gil Loescher, et al., 'Responding to the Asylum and Access Challenge', ECRE & USCR (2003), online at http://www.ecre.org/publications/gmfreport.pdf, accessed 16 Sept. 2005.

61. I have (shamelessly) stolen this excellent simile from Guild, 'The Borders of the European Union', 41.

62. Gil Loescher, *Beyond Charity: International Cooperation and the Global Refugee Crisis* (New York: Oxford University Press, 1993); B. S. Chimni, 'The Geopolitics of Refugee Studies: A View from the South', *Journal of Refugee Studies* 11:4 (1998), 350–74.

63. Matthew J. Gibney, 'The State of Asylum: Democratization, Judicialization and the Evolution of Refugee Policy', in S. Kneebone (ed.), *The Refugees Convention 50 Years On: Globalisation and International Law* (Aldershot: Ashgate, 2003).

64. David Turton, 'Forced Displacement and the Nation State, in Jenny Robinson, *Development and Displacement* (Oxford: Oxford University Press, 2002); Zygmunt Bauman, 'Europe of Strangers', *Transnational Communities*, Working Paper, 1998, Department of Social and Cultural Anthropology, University of Oxford. Online at: http://www.transcomm.ox.ac.uk/working%20papers/bauman.pdf, accessed 16 Sept. 2005.

65. Gibney, 'The State of Asylum'.

Notes to Response to Chapter 4

1. Michael Walzer, *Spheres of Justice* (New York. Basic Books, 1983).
2. Jeremy Waldron, 'Security and Liberty: The Image of Balance', *Journal of Political Philosophy*, 11:2 (2003), 191–210.
3. Walzer, *Spheres of Justice*, 50.
4. This clause, which is s. 33 (1), is however qualified by s. 33 (2) as follows: 'The benefit of the present provision may not, however, be claimed by a refugee whom there are reasonable grounds for regarding as a danger to the security of the country in which he is, or who, having been convicted by a final judgment of a particularly serious crime, constitutes a danger to the community of that country.'
5. Matthew J. Gibney, *The Ethics and Politics of Asylum: Liberal Democracy and the Response to Refugees* (Cambridge: Cambridge University Press, 2004), 229.
6. Indeed, non-arrival measures arguably also breach Article 16 of the Convention, which guarantees refugees 'free access to the courts of law on the territory of all Contracting States'—not, notice, only on the territory of some state where he or she has managed to arrive.
7. Christopher Kutz, *Complicity: Ethics and Law for a Collective Age* (Cambridge: Cambridge University Press, 2000), 89–96.
8. Neil Ascherson, 'Reflections on International Space', *London Review of Books*, 23:10 (24 May 2000), 7–11.

Notes to Chapter 5

1. For the fullest treatment of my concept of the global city, see the updated second edition of my *The Global City: New York, London, Tokyo* (2001).
2. See Hague Convention. 1954. Available online at http://icomos. org/hague/hague.convention.html, accessed 16 Sept. 2005.

3. Michael R. Marrus, *The Unwanted: European Refugees in the Twentieth Century* (New York: Oxford University Press, 1985).

4. Kim Rubenstein and Daniel Adler, 'International Citizenship: The Future of Nationality in a Globalized World', *Indiana Journal of Global Legal Studies* 7:2 (2000), 519–48.

5. Peter Spiro, 'Dual Nationality and the Meaning of Citizenship', *Emory Law Review* 46:4 (1997), 1412–85; Rubenstein and Adler, 'International Citizenship'.

6. Saskia Sassen, *Losing Control?: Sovereignty in an Age of Globalization* (New York: Columbia University Press, 1996), ch. 2.

7. Bryan Turner, 'Cosmopolitan virtue: loyalty and the city', in Engin Isin, ed., *Democracy, Citizenship and the Global City*, (New York: Routledge, 2000).

8. See e.g. Frank Munger, *Laboring Under the Line* (New York: Russell Sage Foundation, 2001).

9. Laurence Roulleau-Berger, ed., *Youth and Work in the Postindustrial Cities of North America and Europe* (Leiden: Brill, 2002).

10. T. H. Marshall, 'Citizenship and Social Class', in *Class, Citizenship, and Social Development* (Chicago: University of Chicago Press, 1977 [1950]).

11. Peter Saunders, 'Citizenship in a Liberal Society', in Bryan Turner, ed., *Citizenship and Social Theory* (London: Sage, 1993).

12. Saskia Sassen, *Guests and Aliens* (New York: New Press, 1999); Karen Knop, *Diversity and Self-Determination in International Law* (Cambridge: Cambridge University Press, 2002).

13. John Shotter, 'Psychology and Citizenship: Identity and Belonging', in Turner, ed., *Citizenship and Social Theory*; Aihwa Ong, *Flexible Citizenship: The Cultural Logics of Transnationality* (Durham: Duke University Press, 1999), chs. 1 and 4.

14. See Aihwa Ong, 'Strategic Sisterhood or Sisters in Solidarity?: Questions of Communitarianism and Citizenship in Asia', *Indiana Journal of Global Legal Studies* 4:1 (1996), 107–35; Linda Bosniak, 'Universal Citizenship and the Problem of Alienage', *Northwestern University Law Review* 94:3 (2000), 963–84.

15. Max Weber, *The City* (New York: Free Press, 1958).

16. See e.g. Kenneth Karst, 'Citizenship, Law, and the American Nation', *Indiana Journal of Global Legal Studies* 7:2 (2000), 595–601.

17. Iris Marion Young, *Justice and the Politics of Difference* (Princeton: Princeton University Press, 1990); Charles Taylor, 'The Politics of Recognition', Charles Taylor and Amy Gutmann, eds., *Multiculturalism: Examining the Politics of Recognition* (Princeton: Princeton University Press, 1992).

18. Michael Walzer, *Spheres of Justice* (New York: Basic Books, 1985); Linda Bosniak, ' "Nativism" The Concept: Some Reflections', in Juan Perea, ed., *Immigrants Out!: The New Nativism and the Anti-Immigrant Impulse in the United States*, (New York: New York University Press, 1996).

19. Kenneth Karst, 'The Coming Crisis of Work in Constitutional Perspective', *Cornell Law Review* 82:3 (1997), 523–71. In Karst's interpretation of US law, aliens are 'constitutionally entitled to most of the guarantees of equal citizenship, and the Supreme Court has accepted this idea to a modest degree' (Karst, 'Citizenship, Law and the American Nation', 599); see also ibid. n. 20 where he cites cases). Karst also notes that the Supreme Court has not carried this development nearly as far as he might wish.

20. Marshall, 'Citizenship and Social Class'; Joel Handler, *The Poverty of Welfare Reform* (New Haven: Yale University Press, 1995).

21. Seyla Benhabib, Judith Butler, Drucilla Cornell, and Nancy Fraser, *Feminist Contentions: A Philosophical Exchange* (New York: Routledge, 1995); Kimberlé Crenshaw, Neil Gotanda, Gary Peller, and Kendall Thomas, *Critical Race Theory: The Key Writings that Formed the Movement* (New York: New Press, 1996); Richard Delgado and Jean Stefancic, eds., *Critical Race Theory: The Cutting Edge* (Philadelphia: Temple University Press, 1999); Seyla Benhabib, *Democratic Equality and Cultural Diversity: Political Identities in the Global Era* (Princeton: Princeton University Press, 2002).

22. Karst, 'The Coming Crisis'.

23. Sassen, *Losing Control?*, Ch. 2; Saskia Sassen, *Territory, Authority and Rights: From Medieval to Global Assemblages* (Princeton: Princeton University Press, 2006).

24. Peter Schuck and Roger Smith, *Citizenship Without Consent: Illegal Aliens in the American Polity* (New Haven: Yale University Press, 1985).

25. NACARA is The 1997 Nicaraguan Adjustment and Central American Relief Act. It created an amnesty for 300,000 Salvadorans and Guatemalans to apply for suspension of deportation. This is an immigration remedy that had been eliminated by the Illegal Immigration Reform and Immigrant Responsibility Act in 1996 (see Susan B. Coutin, 'Denationalization, Inclusion, and Exclusion: Negotiating the Boundaries of Belonging', *Indiana Journal of Global Legal Studies* 7:2 (2000), 585–94).

26. Yasemin Nuhoólu Soysal, *Limits of Citizenship: Migrants and Postnational Membership in Europe* (Chicago: University of Chicago Press, 1994); Coutin, 'Denationalization, Inclusion and Exclusion'.

27. Sarah Mahler, *American Dreaming: Immigrant Life on the Margins* (Princeton: Princeton University Press, 1996).

28. Coutin, 'Denationalization, Inclusion and Exclusion'; Mahler, *American Dreaming*.

29. Linda Basch, Nina Glick Schiller, and Christine Blanc-Szanton, *Nations Unbound: Transnational Projects, Postcolonial Predicaments, and Deterritorialized Nation-States* (Langhorne, Pa.: Gordon & Breach, 1995); Héctor Cordero-Guzmán, Robert C. Smith, and Ramón Grosfoguel, *Migration, Transnationalization, and Race in a Changing New York* (Philadelphia: Temple University Press, 2001).

30. Robin Leblanc, *Bicycle Citizens: The Political World of the Japanese Housewife* (Berkeley: University of California Press, 1999).

31. See e.g. Norma Chinchilla and Nora Hamilton, *Seeking*

Community in the Global City: Salvadorans and Guatemalans in Los Angeles (Philadelphia: Temple University Press, 2001).

32. Pierrette Hondagneu-Sotelo, *Gendered Transitions: Mexican Experiences of Immigration* (Berkeley: University of California Press, 1994).

33. For the limits of this process see e.g. Rhacel Salazar Parreñas, *Servants of Globalization: Women, Migration and Domestic Work* (Stanford: Stanford University Press, 2001).

34. Bosniak, 'Universal Citizenship'.

35. See e.g. Gertrude Himmelfarb, *One Nation, Two Cultures: A Searching Examination of American Society in the Aftermath of Our Cultural Revolution* (New York: Vintage Books, 2001). For Karst, 'In the US today, citizenship is inextricable from a complex legal framework that includes a widely accepted body of substantive law, strong law-making institutions, and law-enforcing institutions capable of performing their task' ('Citizenship, Law and The American Nation', 600). Not recognizing the centrality of the law is, for Karst, a big mistake. Post-national citizenship lacks an institutional framework that can protect the substantive values of citizenship. Karst does acknowledge the possibility of rabid nationalism and the exclusion of aliens when legal status is made central.

36. See e.g. Soysal, *Limits of Citizenship*; David Jacobson, Rights Across Borders: Immigration and the Decline of Citizenship (Baltimore: Johns Hopkins Press, 1996); Torres, 'Transnational Political and Cultural Identities: Crossing Theoretical Borders', in Frank Bonilla, Edwin Mélendez, Rebecca Morales, and Maria de los Ángeles Torres, eds., *Borderless Borders* (Philadelphia: Temple University Press, 1998); Rodolfo D. Torres, Jonathan Xavier Inda, and Louis F. Miron, *Race, Identity, and Citizenship* (Oxford: Blackwell, 1999).

37. 'Feminism and Globalization: The Impact of The Global Economy on Women and Feminist Theory', *Indiana Journal of Global Legal Studies* (Special Issue) 4:1 (1996).

38. Bosniak uses 'denationalized' interchangeably with 'post-national' ('Universal Citizenship'). I do not.

39. For example, *Territory, Authority and Rights*.

40. Jacobson, *Rights across Borders*.

41. In this regard, I have emphasized as significant (*Losing Control?*, ch. 2) the introduction in the new constitutions of South Africa, Brazil, Argentina, and the Central European countries, of a provision that qualifies what had been an unqualified right of the sovereign—if democratically elected—to be the exclusive representative of her or his people in international fora.

42. Sassen, *Losing Control?*, ch. 2.

43. See the concept of the global city in Sassen, *The Global City*, and also Sassen, 'Spatialities and Temporalities of the Global: Elements for a Theorization', *Public Culture* 12:1 (2000), 215–32.

44. Ira Katznelson, *Marxism and the City* (Oxford: Clarendon Press, 1992).

45. Engin Isin, 'Introduction', to id., ed., 'Democracy, Citizenship and the City' (New York: Routledge, 2000); John Allen, Doreen Massey, and Michael Pryke, eds., *Unsettling Cities* (London: Routledge, 1999); Gary Bridge and Sophie Watson eds., *A Companion to the City* (Oxford: Blackwell, 2000).

46. Isin, *Democracy, Citizenship and the Global City*, 7.

47. Henri Lefebvre, *The Production of Space* (Cambridge: Blackwell, 1991); *Writing on Cities* (Cambridge: Blackwell, 1995).

48. Only in Russia—where the walled city did not evolve as a centre of urban immunities and liberties—does the meaning of citizen diverge from concepts of civil society and cities, and belong to the state, not the city (Weber, *The City*).

49. Sassen, *The Global City*.

Notes to Response to Chapter 5

1. For overviews (on the particularly interesting European scene), see Randall Hansen and Patrick Weil, eds., *Toward a European*

Nationality (Basingstoke: Palgrave Macmillan, 2001); also Christian Joppke, 'Citizenship Between De- and Re-Ethnicization', *Archives européennes de sociologie* 44:3 (2003), 429–58.

2. This literature has both started and peaked with Rogers Brubaker's *Citizenship and Nationhood in France and Germany* (Cambridge, Mass.: Harvard University Press, 1992).

3. For instance, Alexander Makarov, *Allgemeine Lehren des Staatsangehörigkeitsrechts* (Stuttgart: Kohlhammer, 1947), and more recently Gérard-René de Groot, *Staatsangehörigkeitsrecht im Wandel* (Cologne: Heymanns Verlag, 1989).

Notes to Response to Chapter 6

1. Achille Mbembe, *On the Postcolony*, trans. A. M. Berrett et al. (Berkeley: University of California Press, 2001), 29.

2. T. S. Eliot, 'The Waste Land', *The Complete Poems and Plays* (London: Faber, 1969), 74.

3. From Phillips's 1982 play, *Where there is darkness*, quoted in Bénédicte Ledent, *Caryl Phillips* (Manchester: Manchester University Press, 2002), 106.

4. Caryl Phillips, 'Crossing the River': Interview with Maya Jaggi, *Wasafiri* 20 (Autumn 1995), 28.

5. Caryl Phillips, *A New World Order* (London: Vintage, 2002), 5.

6. Quoted in Caryl Phillips, *The Atlantic Sound* (London: Faber, 2000), 173.

7. Ibid. 178.

8. Ledent, *Caryl Phillips*, 106.

9. Caryl Phillips, *A Distant Shore* (London: Secker & Warburg, 2003), 1.

10. Jonathan Heawood, 'Distance Learning', *Observer Review* (23 March 2003), 17.

11. Caryl Phillips, *Higher Ground* (London: Faber, 1989), 97.

Notes to Chapter 7

1. On the transnational work of Wilberforce and the British anti-slavery movement, see generally Betty Henry Fladeland, *Men and Brothers: Anglo-American Anti-Slavery Cooperation* (Urbana: University of Illinois, 1972).
2. See generally Ethan A. Nadelmann, *Global Prohibition Regimes: The Evolution of Norms in International Society*, 44 Intl. Org. 479, 491–8 (1990) (reviewing this history). For the classic account, see David Brion Davis, *Slavery and Human Progress* (1984).
3. Philip D. Curtin, *The Atlantic Slave Trade* (Madison: University of Wisconsin, 1969), 268.
4. Michael Craton, *Sinews of Empire: A Short History of British Slavery* (New York: Anohor Press, 1974), 289, 378 n. 8.
5. *U.S. Trafficking Victims Protection Act* of 2000, 22 USC sect. 7101.
6. President Addresses UN General Assembly, New York, September 23, 2003, available at http://www.state.gov~/p/io/rls/rm/2003/24321.htm, accessed 16 Sept. 2005.
7. Superintendent Michael Hoskins, 'Trafficking in Women for Sexual Exploitation: Assessment of the Current Threat Within Central London', *Metropolitan Police Service*, June 1996.
8. *European Race Audit Bulletin*, 25 (25 November 1997) Institute of Race Relations, London.
9. For elaboration of this argument, see Harold Hongju Koh, 'Why Do Nations Obey International Law?', 106 Yale LJ 2599 (1997); Harold Hongju Koh, 'How Is International Human Rights Law Enforced?', 74 Ind. LJ 1397 (1999); Harold Hongju Koh, 'The 1998 Frankel Lecture: Bringing International Law Home', 35 Hous.L. Rev. 623 (1998); Harold Hongju Koh, 'Transnational Legal Process', 75 Neb. L. Rev. 181 (1993), Harold Hongju Koh, 'The "Haiti Paradigm" in United States Human Rights Policy', 103 Yale LJ 2391–2 (1994), Harold Hongju Koh, 'Transnational Public Law Litigation', 100 Yale LJ 2347, 2358–75 (1991).
10. For discussions of how such transnational networks are formed

and influence human rights policy, see e.g. Margaret Keck and Kathryn Sikkink, *Activists Beyond Borders: Advocacy Networks in International Politics* (1998); Annelise Riles, *The Network Inside Out* (2000); Jackie Smith, Charles Chatfield, and Ron Pagnucco, eds., *Transnational Social Movements and Global Politics: Solidarity Beyond the State* (1997).

11. Koh, 'Bringing International Law Home', 625.

12. See generally Glen Petrie, *A Singular Iniquity: The Campaigns of Josephine Butler* (New York: Viking Press, 1971); Paul McHugh, *Prostitution and Victorian Social Reform* (London: Croom Helm, 1980).

13. The 1921 Convention for the Suppression of Traffic in Women and Children called for the prosecution of persons who trafficked in children and women (irrespective of the woman's 'consent'), as well as licensing of employment agencies and the protection of women and children who immigrate or emigrate. In the 1933 Convention for the Suppression of the Traffic in Women of Full Age, which was concluded in Geneva in October 1933 and amended by a protocol signed at Lake Success, New York, in Novembeer 1947, the parties agreed that '[w]hoever, in order to gratify the passions of another person, has procured, enticed, or led away even with her consent, a woman or girl of full age for immoral purposes to be carried away in another country, shall be punished, notwithstanding that the various acts constituting the offence may have been committed in different countries.' See http://untreaty.un.org/English/CTC/CTC_04.asp, accessed 5 Oct. 2005.

14. Subsequently, the General Assembly, the Economic and Social Council, the Commission on Human Rights and the Commission on the Status of Women all passed resolutions on trafficking, including: General Assembly resolution 50/167 of 22 December 1995; Commission on Human Rights resolution 1995/25 of 3 March 1995; Commission on the Status of Women resolutions 39/6 of 29 March 1995 and 40/4 of

22 March 1996; Commission on Human Rights resolution 1996/24 of 19 April 1996; Commission on Human Rights resolution 1997/19 of 11 April 1997, adopted without vote; Economic and Social Council resolution 1998/20 of 28 July 1998; Commission on Human Rights resolutions 1998/30 of 17 April 1998 and 1999/40 of 26 April 1999.

15. See generally http://hrw.org/doc/?t=women_trafficking &document_limit=20,20, accessed 16 Sept. 2005.

16. See generally http://www.catwinternational.org, accessed 16 Sept. 2005.

17. The *New York Times*, for example, has recently run a series of stories by columnist Nicholas Kristof and a cover story in the *New York Times Magazine* on the subject of trafficking. See Peter Landesman, 'Sex Slaves on Main Street', *New York Times Magazine*, 25 January 2004, at 30. A recent Google search reveals some 268,000 entries mentioning 'trafficking, women and children'.

18. See Report of the Special Rapporteur on violence against women, its causes and consequences, Ms Radhika Coomaraswamy, on trafficking in women, women's migration, and violence against women, submitted in accordance with Commission on Human Rights resolution 1997/44, E/CN.4/2000/68 (29 Feb. 2000), available at http://www.ohhchr.org/english/issues/women/rapporteur/, accessed 5 Oct. 2005.

19. A General Assembly resolution in December 1998 established the Ad Hoc Committee on the Elaboration of a Convention against Transnational Organized Crime (Ad Hoc Committee) with a mandate to draft the convention and the trafficking protocol by the end of 2000. In February 2000, the Office of the United Nations High Commissioner for Human Rights (UNHCHR), the Office of the United Nations High Commissioner for Refugees (UNHCR), the United Nations Children's Fund (UNICEF), and the International Organization for Migration (IOM), submitted a joint statement to the Ad Hoc

Committee recommending the following definition of trafficking, which has become widely used: 'the recruitment, transportation, transfer or harboring or receipt of any person for any
purpose or in any form, including the recruitment, transportation, transfer or harboring or receipt of any person by the threat
or use of force or by abduction, fraud, deception, coercion or
abuse of power for the purposes of slavery, forced labor (including bonded labor or debt bondage) and servitude'.

20. UN Doc. A/RES/55/25 (2000). For an up-to-date list of signatories, see *http://www.unodc.org/unodc/en/crime_cicp_signatures.
html*, accessed 16 Sept. 2005.

21. Michael Specter, 'Traffickers New Cargo: Naïve Slavic Women
Contraband Women', *New York Times*, 18 January 1998, at
A1.

Notes to Response to Chapter 7

1. See http://www.freetheslaves.net/home.php, accessed 16 Sept.
2005.

2. Kevin Bales, *Disposable People: New Slavery in the Global Economy*
(Berkeley: University of California Press, 1999).

3. See 'What is Modern Slavery,' Anti-Slavery International at:
http://www.antislavery.org/homepage/antislavery/modern.
htm, accessed 16 Sept. 2005.

4. *Hidden Slaves: Forced Labor in the United States*, A report by
Free the Slaves and the Human Rights Center, University of
California, Berkeley, September 2004 at: http://www.
freetheslaves.net/home.php.

5. See Ko-lin Chin, 'The Social Organization of Chinese Human
Smuggling', and Peter Kwong, 'Impact of Chinese Human
Smuggling on the American Labor Market', in David Kyle and
Rey Koslowski, eds., *Global Human Smuggling: Comparative
Perspectives* (Baltimore, Md.: Johns Hopkins University Press,
2001).

6. See the testimony of Nicolas M. Gess, Michael S. Teitlebaum, and Steven Galster before the US House Committee on Resources, 106th Congress, Thursday, 16 September 1999, http://www.freetheslaves.net, accessed 5 Oct. 2005.

7. Scott McPherson, 'Human Smuggling is Morally Good', Commentary, Future of Freedom Foundation, 19 December 2003.

8. Kevin Bales, 'Understanding the Demand behind Human Trafficking', manuscript posted at: http://www.freetheslaves.net/resources/whitepapers/, accessed 5 Oct. 2005.

9. See interviews with the trafficked workers and their lawyer in the Public Broadcasting Service documentary 'Dying to Leave', http://www.pbs.org/wnet/wideangle/shows/dying/index.html, accessed 16 Sept. 2005.

10. Wayne A. Cornelius, 'Controlling "Unwanted" Immigration: Lessons from the United States, 1993–2004', *Stanford Journal of Law and Policy*, forthcoming Spring 2005.

11. See Audrey Singer and Douglas S. Massey, 'The Social Process of Undocumented Border Crossing Among Mexican Migrants', *International Migration Review*, 32:3 (Autumn 1998), 561–92; Peter Andreas, 'The Transformation of Migrant Smuggling Across the U.S.–Mexican Border', and David Spener, 'Smuggling Migrants through South Texas: Challenges Posed by Operation Rio Grande', in David Kyle and Rey Koslowski, eds., *Global Human Smuggling in Comparative Perspectives* (Baltimore, Md.: Johns Hopkins University Press).

Notes to Chapter 8

1. Chris McGreal, 'Gaza's settlers dig in their heels', *Guardian*, 4 February 2004.

2. David Grossman, 'Two Years of Intifada', *Death as a Way of Life—Dispatches from Jerusalem* (New York: Farrar, Straus, & Giroux, 2003), 177.

3. Vada Schiffer speaking at the second meeting of the Jewish Forum for Justice and Human Rights, London, 9 February 2004.

4. In the week of this lecture, I read in *Ha'aretz* a feature on the settlers of Gush Katif in Gaza, which includes the following comment from Laurence Baziz, a former Parisian who has lived in the settlement for eighteen years: 'They [the settlers] are very attracted by the soul, the ideological theme [. . .] There is a rise of Islamic influence in France. The French themselves don't like outsiders; there are a great many French people who feel the takeover of Islam. I illuminate that point.' *Ha'aretz*, 20 February 2004.

5. Sigmund Freud, 'The Neuro-Psychoses of Defence', 1894 *The Standard Edition of the Complete Psychological Works* (London: Hogarth, 1953–74), iii.

6. Freud, 'Screen Memories', 1899, *Standard Edition*, iii.

7. Tom Segev discusses the extent to which later Arab attacks were seen as pogroms in *One Palestine Complete—Jews and Arabs under the British Mandate* (London: Abacus, 2000), 137–8, 180–1, 324–5.

8. According to Daud Abdullah of the Palestinian Return Centre, 2 per cent of Israelis live on refugee land, 62 per cent of all refugees came from rural areas in mandate Palestine, most of which villages are still vacant; over 75 per cent of Israelis live in 15 per cent of Israel's areas; letter to *Guardian*, 9 January 2004.

9. Chaim Weizmann, 'Awaiting the Shaw Report', Paper 116, *Letters and Papers* (London: Oxford University Press), i. 591.

10. Yeshayahu Leibowitz, 'Right, Law and Reality', 1976, in Eliezer Goldman, ed., *Judaism, Human Values and the Jewish State* (Cambridge, Mass.: Harvard University Press, 1992), 230–1.

11. Bhikhu Parekh, 'Love is . . . desirable but it's by no means a right', *Times Higher Educational Supplement*, 6 February 2004.

12. Hannah Arendt, 'Zionism Reconsidered', 1944; 'The Jewish

State Fifty Years After—Where Have Herzl's Politics Led?',
1946, in Ron Feldman, ed., *The Jew as Pariah* (New York: Grove
Press, 1978), 156, 172, 141.

13. Dorothy Thompson, *Refugees—Anarchy or Organisation* (New
York: Random House, 1938), 45.

14. Ernest Jones, *Sigmund Freud—Life and Work*, iii. *The Last Phase
1919–1939* (London: Hogarth, 1980), 254.

15. Thompson, *Refugees*, 5.

16. Ibid. 3.

17. Ibid. 6.

18. Ibid. 107.

19. Ibid. 78.

20. Theodor Herzl, *The Jewish State*, 1896; 2nd edn. (London:
Central Office of the Zionist Organisation, 1934), 29.

21. Thompson, *Refugees*, 102–3.

22. Herzl, *Jewish State*, 70.

23. Thompson, *Refugees* 78–9.

24. *Freudiana: From the Collections of the Jewish National and Uni-
versity Library*, Jerusalem, 1973, cited by Yosef Hayim
Yerushalmi, *Freud's Moses—Judaism Terminable and Interminable*
(New Haven: Yale University Press, 1991), 13.

25. Weizmann, 'Zionism Needs a Living Context', 1914, in Arthur
Hertzberg, *The Zionist Idea*, (Philadelphia and Jerusalem: Jewish
Publication Society, 1977), 575.

26. Rajeh Shehadeh, *The Third Way—A Journal of Life in the West
Bank* (London: Quartet, 1982), 87–9.

27. Weizmann, 'Awaiting the Shaw Report,', 598; id., *Zionist Policy,
an Address* (London: British Zionist Federation, 1919), 10.

28. David Ben-Gurion, *Israel—A Personal History* (London: New
English Library, 1972), 72.

29. Sara Roy, 'Save Your Outrage for the End', *Index on Censorship*
32:3 (2003), 206.

30. Grossman, 'The Holocaust Carrier Pigeon', *Death as a Way of
Life*, 13.

31. Grossman, *See: under Love* (New York: Farrar, Strauss, & Giroux, 1989), 13.

32. Ibid. 197.

33. Ibid. 380.

34. Smilansky was responding to Itzhak Epstein who had argued the year before in *HaShiloah* that the Jewish nation must not be built without respect for morality and justice, the essential foundations of Zionism, cited Georges Bensoussan, *Une histoire intellectuelle et politique du Sionisme 1860–1940* (Paris: Fayard, 2002), 190, 552.

35. Benjamin Netanyahu, *A Place Among the Nations—Israel and the World* (London: Bantam, 1993), 392.

36. Ronit Chacham, *Breaking Ranks—Refusing to Serve in the West Bank and Gaza* (New York: Other Press, 2003), 16.

37. Carl Sherer, letter, *The Guardian*, 28 August 2003.

38. Grossman, *See: under Love*, 67.

39. Sara Roy, 'Save Your Outrage', 208–9. For a further discussion of Roy's writing in this context see Marc Ellis, *Israel and Palestine Out of the Ashes—the Search for Jewish Identity in the Twenty-First Century* (London: Pluto, 2002).

40. Chris McGreal, 'I can't imagine anyone who considers himself a human can do this', *The Guardian*, 28 July 2003.

41. Jacques Lacan, 'The Function and Field of Speech and Language in Psychoanalysis', *Écrits* (London: Tavistock, 1953), 86.

42. W. G. Sebald, *Austerlitz* (London: Hamish Hamilton, 2001), 359–60.

43. Sebald, *Austerlitz*, 19–20.

44. Ibid. 21.

45. Ibid. 16–17.

46. Sara Roy, 'The Legacy of Edward Said', Symposium organised by the *London Review of Books*, Brunei Gallery, School of Oriental and African Studies, London University, 28 November 2003.

Notes to Response to Chapter 8

1. Patrick Wintour, 'Alarm at US drift over Middle East: UK report reveals fears for future of Palestinians', *The Guardian*, 21 July 2004.
2. See Ali Abunimah, 'Palestinian Rights in the Document Shredder: The Nusseibeh-Ayalon Agreement', The Electronic Intifada, 7 September 2002, http://electronicintifada.net/cgi-bin/artman/exec/view.cgi/4/651, accessed 16 Sept. 2005; and Ali Abunimah, 'A disastrous dead end: the Geneva Accord', *The Daily Star* (Beirut), 28 October 2003.
3. Kathleen Christison, 'Offending Valerie: Dealing with Jewish self-absorption', *CounterPunch*, 7–8 February 2004.

Index

Lightning Source UK Ltd.
Milton Keynes UK
176554UK00008B/2/P